Maimonides's Yahweh

Maimonides's Yahweh

Rabbinic Judaism's Attempt to Answer
the Incarnational Question

AMY KAREN DOWNEY

Foreword by Leo Percer

WIPF & STOCK · Eugene, Oregon

MAIMONIDES'S YAHWEH
Rabbinic Judaism's Attempt to Answer the Incarnational Question

Copyright © 2019 Amy Karen Downey. All rights reserved. Except for brief quotations in critical publications or reviews, no part of this book may be reproduced in any manner without prior written permission from the publisher. Write: Permissions, Wipf and Stock Publishers, 199 W. 8th Ave., Suite 3, Eugene, OR 97401.

Wipf & Stock
An Imprint of Wipf and Stock Publishers
199 W. 8th Ave., Suite 3
Eugene, OR 97401

www.wipfandstock.com

PAPERBACK ISBN: 978-1-5326-7337-5
HARDCOVER ISBN: 978-1-5326-7338-2
EBOOK ISBN: 978-1-5326-7339-9

Manufactured in the U.S.A.   MARCH 12, 2019

Scripture quotations taken from the New American Standard Bible® (NASB), Copyright © 1960, 1962, 1963, 1968, 1971, 1972, 1973, 1975, 1977, 1995 by The Lockman Foundation Used by permission. www.Lockman.org

To Barbara Ellen Downey, who was told as a child that girls did not need to go to college but can now say, "My daughter, the doctor."

and to the 97% who keep me awake at night and keep me going during the day—Romans 1:16.

Contents

Foreword by Leo Percer | ix
Preface | xi
Acknowledgements | xiii

1   Establishing the Premise of Maimonides's Yahweh | 1

2   A Brief Examination of Jewish-Christian History (AD 70 to 1290) and Its Impact on Maimonides | 10

3   Moses Maimonides the Man (1135/38–1204) | 50

4   Maimonides the Theologian and His Writings | 64

5   Maimonides and His Reaction to Controversy and Christianity | 97

6   Maimonides's Impact on Modern Judaism | 127

7   Modern Judaism's Understanding of Specific Christian Doctrines in Light of Maimonides and His Yahweh | 150

8   Development of an Apologetic Approach for Evangelism among the Jewish People in Light of Maimonides's Yahweh | 160

Bibliography | 193

Foreword

THE LIFE OF MOSHE ben Maimon (Maimonides) remains a mystery to many within evangelical Christianity, and yet he is often celebrated as a kind of "Second Moses" within some branches of contemporary Judaism. In many ways, Maimonides is deserving of the title, as his understanding of the nature of God is often used in rabbinic Judaism to create a rationale for rejecting the messianic claims of Jesus as understood by Christians. His attempt to create an apologetic against Christianity focused on the issue of the incarnation and helped to fashion a Judaism that (from a Christian viewpoint) creates hostility to Christian readings of the Hebrew Scripture. Indeed, this work argues that Maimonides's view may even overlook or obscure some of the truth claims found in the Hebrew Scripture. As a result, a response to Maimonides from an evangelical Christian perspective is needed to provide Christians with information to respond to the claims from this enigmatic man. In this work, Dr. Amy Downey offers a critical overview and response to Maimonides and his theological and apologetic thoughts.

I have known Downey for several years, primarily as one of my students in the PhD in Theology and Apologetics program at Liberty University. As both the director and an instructor in that program, I had the honor of becoming familiar with Amy and her work. When I first met Downey, we quickly discovered that we shared a love for the Jewish backgrounds of Christianity and for the Jewish people. In her doctoral work, Downey focused her studies in developing theological and apologetic materials that would be helpful to Christians for starting a dialogue with their Jewish friends with the intent of helping them understand the claims of Christianity regarding the messianic status of Jesus of Nazareth. Many of her written assignments and presentations reflected her desire to share the good news of Jesus with the people through whom he was born and among whom he lived. The culmination of this research was her dissertation on Moshe ben Maimon which is republished here for a wider audience.

As a member of the committee that worked with Amy on this project, I remember reading some of the first materials she produced, and I saw an idea developing that needed to be published and made available to Christians on a wider scale. The book you hold in your hand is the result of a great deal of research and discussion. In the end, Downey completed her research, defended her dissertation, and continued her ministry to the Jewish people. She kindly offered me the honor to introduce her work to you. In this volume, Downey offers you her response to Maimonides in an apologetic and theological format. She states her intention clearly, she defines her approach well, she offers a cogent overview of the issues considered, and she supports her conclusions with solid research and passionate conviction. I am honored to recommend this work to you, and I hope as you read it you will find that the claims of Christianity regarding Jesus can be defended in the arena of ideas. I also think you will find yourself better equipped to deal with questions or criticisms that may arise in discussions regarding the views about Jesus from both a Jewish and a Christian perspective. I know the journey upon which you are about to embark, and I am sure that you will find the material here interesting, thought provoking, and helpful.

Leo Percer

Preface

I TALK ABOUT MY travels to Cordoba, Spain, throughout this book; however, I do not know if I can express adequately how much that trip to the Andalusian region changed my worldview. Walking in a Jewish Quarter that is empty of Jewish inhabitants—unless they were tourists like myself—caused me truly to fathom how the Spanish Inquisition and Expulsions emptied a country of a rich heritage and culture. Walking into a semi-restored synagogue—that perhaps even Maimonides prayed in—that was turned into a hospital for patients stricken with rabies after the Expulsions broke something within me as the Spanish people who remained saw a place of worship as truly nothing more than a place to discard the "discardable people." As a historian, this trip to Spain and in essence traveling back to the time of Maimonides changed me and still does to this day.

One can see how the rabbi in question was distrustful of anyone who wore the label Catholic and/or Christian. One can see how his worldview leaned more towards trusting, as many Jewish people in his day did, the religion of Islam because it portrayed itself as more monotheistic than the iconographic-laden churches he would have seen. One can also see how Rambam (another name for Maimonides) would have wanted Judaism to be restored to the religious, political, and economic prominence that he believed it was due, and this I believe is the crux behind much of why he wrote what he wrote.

The pages beyond this preface will seek to examine not only the history of Maimonides's time but also the personal history of the man himself. The pages will examine how the theology of the rabbi transformed and, I will argue, misinformed Judaism for the last 800 years out of an attempt to circumvent any desire of his people to be interested in, attracted to, or desire a relationship with Messiah Jesus. Finally, this work will seek to begin the developmental stages of a true apologetic and Christian model of Jewish evangelism that has not been established or tested since the first followers of Jesus in Acts 2. Incidentally, those first followers were Jewish and perhaps they knew something that we should again model today . . .

Acknowledgements

IF YOU ASK MY friends and family, they will tell you that this section could easily become entirely too long. I am known for being verbose and a little emotional. However, I do want to express my love to my sister (Janice) and my niece (Kate) who exhibit what it means to be women of strength. Our immediate family has been reduced to a small cadre of women and my niece's husband John, as my daddy and brother-in-law (Tony) are now in heaven; but I know they are with us in spirit. As far as my mom is concerned: you are a rock upon which we all lean and you personify the Proverbs 31 woman. You are my hero and the strongest woman I know.

I also want to thank all my doctoral professors at Liberty University, especially Ed Smither and Ken Cleaver who allowed and encouraged me to explore some of the darker corners of church history. It is also a credit to the program dean, Leo Percer, who encourages his PhD faculty to challenge the students beyond the confines of our comfort zones and to push us to think outside the box.

The past and current board members of Tzedakah Ministries are a blessing beyond all measure to me. As the president of this ministry of Jewish evangelism, I am thankful that I have you to push me forward when I am too cautious, to have my back when needed, and to comfort me when I am down. This additional note of appreciation might sound odd when read by some people; however, I could not have completed much of what I did during my doctoral work without Whataburger #944 in Waxahachie, Texas. I spent many hours in their booths and drank inordinate amounts of Diet Dr. Pepper doing research and writing page after page until the wee hours of the morning. Thank you, John Jones and all the Whataburger employees for your encouragement along the way.

In every life there are teachers who change one's life. I was blessed by many, but I would not be here without four in particular. Virginia Dailey allowed a precocious first-grader to go forward at her own pace and never held me back even though it would have been easier for her. Ketta Casey stimulated me in the sixth grade to go beyond just reading the *Diary of Anne Frank* and encouraged an awkward nerd to pursue more when social pressures were pushing me back. Melba Britton (of blessed memory), as a high school choir teacher, believed in me as more than a second soprano and stood up for me when I could not stand up for myself. C. Barnwell Anderson made it cool to love history in college and he is still the most brilliant American history professor I have ever met. He never allowed childhood polio to slow him down and is still an inspiration today.

In a previous book, *Paul's Conundrum*, I dedicated the work to three men who changed my theological world—Jack Henry Downey, James Leo Garrett Jr., and Calvin Miller. Nothing has changed in this regard, as my father showed me the love of God every day and lived it as a pastor until his passing in 2000. It has been said of James Leo Garrett that he has forgotten more theology than the rest of us will ever learn . . . I believe this to be true and at more than ninety years old he is still teaching me. Calvin Miller was taken from the world too soon but his artistry and love of God's creativity still moves me. I was blessed to call him friend and mentor.

Jack Bass, Vera Schlamm, William and Rosalie Schiff, Josef Hausner, and Agnes Hoffman are heroes whose names should never be forgotten. They survived the worst atrocity of the twentieth century or perhaps any century, and never learned to hate those who massacred their families and sought to murder their humanity. I am blessed to say they were and are my friends. You are forever in my heart and I will never let the world forget what happened.

I

Establishing the Premise of Maimonides's Yahweh

ACCORDING TO STATISTICS FROM the Joshua Project regarding the unreached spiritual condition of the Jewish people, 96.8 percent of the estimated 14.7 million Jewish people in the world today are separated from a personal relationship with Jesus the Jewish Messiah.[1] On many levels, this should be perceived as implausible when one realizes that the Christian faith is predicated on the Old Testament (aka Hebrew Scriptures or Tanakh) and that Jesus himself was Jewish. However, the overwhelming majority of the Jewish people today do not accept the Messiahship of Jesus nor acknowledge the possibility of such Christian concepts as the Trinity and/or the incarnational deity of Jesus.[2]

Therefore, a place to begin the study of why modern rabbinic Judaism, which this book will argue is clearly different than the Judaism of the Old Testament, would reject the identity of Messiah Jesus, must include the evaluation of early Jewish theologians and scholars who were the most vocal in rejecting Jesus's divinity and deity. *Maimonides's Yahweh*, therefore, will examine the life, thought, and legacy of one of the most predominant Jewish scholars and rabbinical forces in Judaism—Moses Maimonides

---

1. Joshua Project, "Jews." https://joshuaproject.net/ accessed 24 October 2018; however, the statistics are fluid. Please note that there is an ongoing debate within the circles of Jewish evangelism and missiologists as to whether this number itself is optimistic; however, and because there is no concrete number, I will allow this number to stand even though I believe it is optimistic.

2. Halpern, *Choose Life*, 25–33, 36–37; Levine, *You Take Jesus, I'll Take God*, 69–70, 77–81; and Eckstein, *What Christians Should Know about Jews and Judaism*, 259–68.

(1135–1204).[3] I will also argue that while the official separation from Judaism's biblical moorings began much earlier than Maimonides, it reached its greatest fruition in the life and teachings of the twelfth-century scholar, whose teachings continue to influence and quite literally block the gospel message from the Jewish people in this present twenty-first century.

Why will this book make this argument? Simple. In many of Moses Maimonides's teachings and writings, one finds it difficult to find any association to the identity, accessibility, and possibility of a personal relationship with God. In essence, Rambam (as he was also known) believed that God could only be known by what was unknown about the Deity.[4] Marilyn McCord Adams describes Maimonides's and other similar views as one that believes that "God does not literally *feel* mercy (etymologically, *misericordia* meaning 'have a miserable heart') or anger, but only produces effects of the sort that merciful or angry human rulers would produce."[5] This concept of knowing God by what is unknowable—I will argue—will ultimately create not only a disconnect between the Jewish connection to Christianity but also the Jewish people's connection to God.

For there is a disconnect between Christianity and rabbinic Judaism in relationship to the identity of Jesus due to what will be described in this book as Maimonides's "un-God concept." This disconnect, which I will seek to both identify and rectify, needs to be evaluated in order to bring the truth of Messiah Jesus and the second member of the Godhead, to the people for whom He first came (Matt 10:1–28, esp. v. 6; 23:13–37; Rom 1:16). Therefore, and in the closing chapter of the book, I will also seek to develop an apologetic method which will counteract the theological error of Maimonides and diminish the arguments against the Messiahship and Deity of Jesus. An error which is found not only in his monumental work, *The Guide for the Perplexed*, in which he writes—"Know that the negative attributes of God are the true attributes: they do not include any incorrect notions or any deficiency whatever in reference to God, while positive attributes imply polytheism, and are inadequate as we have already shown . . . Then I shall show that we cannot describe the Creator by means except by negative attributes"[6] but also throughout the rest of his writings. As an example, Moshe Halbertal writes that Maimonides displayed what could almost be

---

3. Arbel, *Maimonides*, 12, 176; Robinson, *Essential Judaism*, 415–21; and Telushkin, *Jewish Literacy*, 175–77.

4. Buijs, "Negative Theology of Maimonides and Aquinas," 728–29.

5. Adams, *Horrendous Evils and the Goodness of God*, 169. It should be noted that Adams compiles her quotation through the words of Anselm, Aquinas, and Maimonides.

6. Maimonides, *Guide for the Perplexed*, 148.

Establishing the Premise of Maimonides's Yahweh 3

described as an "Almohad-ish"[7] fervor towards debunking any possibility of a vision of God that included anthropomorphic concepts, incidentally concepts that most of Christendom also rejects. Halbertal writes that Rambam saw that "God's wisdom, as revealed in nature, was to be seen as the highest expression of His revelation—a position very much at odds with the conventional view that God's presence in the world was expressed primarily through the extraordinary and the miraculous."[8]

BRIEF HISTORICAL OVERVIEW OF THE JEWISH-CHRISTIAN WORLD

However, and in order to understand the analytical and theological mind of Maimonides, especially in his relationship to his understanding of God in the negative, it is necessary to provide a brief historical overview of the world in which Maimonides found himself living in on a daily basis. In the second chapter, a full but brief historical overview will be provided; however, it was deemed sufficient for this chapter to provide an overview of Christian-Jewish relations in the years following Jesus and the disciples up to and including the years of this Jewish sage.[9]

It is impossible to give anything but a cursory survey of Christianity's anti-Semitic history. This ambivalent atmosphere began with one of the earliest church fathers in a post-apostolic world—Justin Martyr (c. 100–165). Questions abound as to the validity of an actual debate occurring between a Jewish traveler Trypho and Justin Martyr. The one constant that is agreed upon, however, is the fact that this dialogue laid the foundation for the doctrine of replacement theology.[10]

Replacement theology, also known as supersessionism, is the belief that the church had replaced Israel as God's chosen people, as evidenced by the destruction of the temple, and began to fester within the minds of

---

7. The term "Almohad" was the term for the Muslims who invaded Spain and harbored no possibility of any faith but Islam in the Iberian Peninsula. Perhaps not the best term to be utilized but "Crusader" bears unfortunate connotations for the Jewish people as well.

8. Halbertal, *Maimonides*, 2.

9. The primary vehicle for this overview will be an edited excerpt from my own presentation at the International Society of Christian Apologetics meeting in April 2010. The entire presentation paper is available at http://www.isca-apologetics.org/papers/isca-2010/apologetic-response-how-share-gospel-messiah-jesus-light-holocaust..

10. Justin Martyr, "Dialogue with Trypho," 92–99; Gager, *Origins of Anti-Semitism*, 228.

church leaders.[11] This belief, albeit first voiced in the late first or early second century Epistle of Barnabas,[12] found its expression in the allegorical theology of Origen (c. 182–251);[13] a voice which was to influence many theologians and councils after his passing.

The Council of Nicaea (325), known primarily for responding to the controversy related to Arian teachings, also set the official and possibly final stage for the division of the church from its Jewishness.[14] The council determined it was necessary to separate the calendar date for remembering the resurrection of Jesus from the sacrificial redemption story of Passover, Feast of Unleavened Bread, and Feast of First Fruits because of their Jewish connections.[15] Emperor Constantine's letter at the conclusion of the council provides evidence of this desire for partition when the emperor supposedly wrote according to early church historian Eusebius of Caesarea:

> And first of all, it appeared an unworthy thing that in the celebration of this most holy feast we should follow the practice of the Jews, who have impiously defiled their hands with enormous sin, and are, therefore, deservedly afflicted with blindness of soul. For we have it in our power, if we abandon their custom, to prolong the due observance of this ordinance to future ages, by a truer order, which we have preserved from the very day of the passion until the present time. Let us then have nothing in common with the detestable Jewish crowd; for we have received from our Saviour a different way. A course at once legitimate and honorable lies open to our most holy religion. Beloved brethren,

---

11. Frend, "Some North African Turning Points in Christian Apologetics," 2; Dunn, "Tertullian and Rebekah," 127–28; and Simon, *Verus Israel*, 65, 66, 69.

12. Downey, *Paul's Conundrum*, 111; Kinzer, *Postmissionary Messianic Judaism*, 189–91; Wilson, *Related Strangers*, 126–27, 139; and Hann, "Supersessionism, Engraftment, and Jewish-Christian Dialogue," 331–32.

13. Carroll, *Constantine's Sword*, 167; and Hellig, *Holocaust and Antisemitism*, 208–9.

14. I will seek to argue in this research that the Council of Nicaea was the third stage of separation with the first stage being the destruction of the Temple in AD 70 and the second stage being the failed Bar Kokhba rebellion in AD 135. These three stages also gave rise to the concept of Judaism that was more Rabbinical than biblical in perspective. Rabbinical Judaism can be simply defined as the Judaism developed after the losses of the first two stages in which modifications were forced to be made because of the inability to offer sacrifices in the Temple at Jerusalem (definition is mine alone but was compiled from a variety of sources which could be argued as common knowledge). However, a simplistic definition is available online at http://judaism.about.com/od/abcsofjudaism/g/mishnah.htm. A fuller definition is offered by Jacob Neusner online at http://www.brill.com/rabbinic-judaism-0.

15. Melnick, *They Have Conspired Against You*, 23–25.

Establishing the Premise of Maimonides's Yahweh

> let us with one consent adopt this course, and withdraw ourselves from all participation in their baseness... 3254 [The idea seems to be (as explained by Valesius) that if they joined the Jews in celebrating this feast they would seem to consent to their crime in crucifying the Lord.—*Bag.*] He carried out his reprobation of the Jews in his actions in discriminating laws at least, and perhaps in actual persecution. For how should they be capable of forming a sound judgment, who, since their parricidal guilt in slaying their Lord, have been subject to the direction, not of reason, but of ungoverned passion, and are swayed by every impulse of the mad spirit that is in them?[16]

This separation perhaps created the final nail in the coffin between the church and its roots of Judaism. This separation continues to this day as both sides of the spectrum do not seem to realize how the two faith systems are intertwined over the identity of Jesus and the possibility of the incarnation.

However, it was Augustine (354–430) who built from the replacement of Justin Martyr, Barnabas, and the Nicene Council an allegorical comparison of the church and the Jewish people to Abel and Cain.[17] This allegory of the Jews as Cain manifested into the "Wandering Jews" who were destined to remain on earth to serve as emblems of what happens to those who reject Jesus. Augustine encouraged not pity nor sympathy but rather a cautionary tale of the dangers of rejecting Jesus.[18] Augustine advocated perhaps what could be described as a "fate worse than death" in Book XII of *The City of God*:

> For whoever destroys them in this way shall suffer sevenfold vengeance, that is, shall bring upon himself the sevenfold penalty under which the Jews lie for the crucifixion of Christ. So to the end of the seven days of time, the continued preservation of the Jews will be a proof to believing Christians of the subjection merited by those who, in the pride of their kingdom, put the Lord to death.[19]

The writings, sermons, and advocacy of the church fathers paved the way for the next 1,500 years of Christian history. The inglorious Crusades, which

---

16. Eusebius, *Life of Constantine*, 3:17.

17. Hellig, *Holocaust and Antisemitism*, 207–9.

18. Carmichael, *Satanizing of the Jews*, 36. Carmichael explains this wandering punishment as—"That was why they survived—to be eternal witnesses precisely to their own guilt, as well to the truth of the prophecies embedded in their own Scriptures, now properly understood only by the Church, and to be witnesses too to the very Triumph of the Church."

19. Augustine, "Reply to Faustus, the Manichean," 28–32 (quotation from page 31).

were ultimately neither holy nor triumphant, began when Pope Urban II called Europe to arms in 1095.[20] Perhaps it could be argued that more persecution was done to the Jewish people than actual victories achieved in the battles against the Muslims. Jewish citizens of France and Germany were forced to either convert or die.[21] These faulty evangelism tactics only resulted in false converts (i.e., *marranos*[22]) or Jewish martyrs who died for their faith which resulted in eternal separation from the God of their fathers. "The Chronicle of Solomon bar Simson" recalls this futile eternal martyrdom:

> Twenty-two people were slain there and the majority were forcibly converted because of our many sins and great guilt. The forced converts remained there until the day of indignation passed, and afterwards they returned to the Lord with all their heart; may God accept their penitence and forgive the sins of His people . . . It is now fitting to recount the praises of those who were forcibly converted. They risked their lives even in matters pertaining to food and drink. They slaughtered the animals they ate in accordance with Jewish ritual, extracted the forbidden fat, and inspected the mean in accordance with Rabbinic law. They did not drink prohibited wine and rarely attended church, and whenever they did go, it was under great coercion and fear, and they went with aggrieved spirits.[23]

The Crusades of the eleventh and twelfth centuries opened the door for more horrors to follow for the Jewish people.[24] The Inquisition, which was focused on uncovering the false converts of the Crusader period, brought about growing suspicions about the Jewish people. These "urban legends" of blood libel and host desecration today are seen as the naïve beliefs of illiterate Middle Age citizens; however, to the Jewish people they often meant torture and death.[25]

---

20. Carroll, *Constantine's Sword*, 238–39; and Hellig, *Holocaust and Antisemitism*, 211.

21. Berger, "Mission to the Jews," 577; Carroll, *Constantine's* Sword, 246–48, 260–63; Hellig, *Holocaust and Antisemitism*, 211–14; Melnick, *They Have Conspired Against You*, 30–31; and Carmichael, *Satanizing of the Jews*, 57–63.

22. The term *marranos* (as well as *anusim*) is a loaded and often considered a pejorative term today in the twenty-first century; however, it was the correct and accurate historical term at the time. It should be acknowledged that one can freely alternate the wording *conversos* as well.

23. "Chronicle of Solomon bar Simson," 67, 68.

24. Rubenstein, *Armies of Heaven*, 5–7, 49–53.

25. Prager and Telushkin, *Why the Jews*, 97–103; Carroll, *Constantine's Sword*, 268–77. Prager and Telushkin bring out the fact that the accusation of host desecration led

Maimonides existed in a world that included almost daily threats against the Jewish people from the people who called themselves Christian. He also existed in a world, which will be explored in more detail, in which the Muslim people for periods of time were more open to Jewish people than the followers of the Jewish Messiah.[26] It would be safe to assume, therefore, that the skewed and skewered message of Jesus would be one that would necessitate a Jewish scholar to create a rebuttal argument.

WHY IS THIS BOOK NECESSARY AND NEEDED?

There is a missing component, as I have discovered in 19 years of Jewish missions, that connects the dots for most Jewish people who are seeking to understand the identity of the Jewish man that the Christian church recognizes as both Messiah and God. For example, when asked what are the biggest obstacles to Jewish evangelism in the twenty-first century, I always have two answers: the Holocaust and the Trinity. If there was a means to respond to one of the barriers to Jesus through this book, then work could begin in earnest on the other issues of concern.

Additionally, the obstacle of Moses Maimonides is an ever-present reality as well. His philosophy is lurking behind the issues of the Holocaust and the Trinity. His influence is there and will not leave. Therefore, this book will seek to answer the following eight issues throughout its pages:

1. What is the historical perception of the Jewish people that has created the disconnect noted in the research problem which indicates the probability that Maimonides established a Jewish or Hebraic-centric negative theology premise to offset the incarnational argument of Christianity?

---

to the Fourth Lateran Council (1215) which ordered the wearing of a yellow badge of all Jews so that they could be identified and perhaps even targeted. See Mork, "Christ's Passion on Stage."

An anonymous letter (See "Narrative of the Old Persecutions," 102) from the Jewish people of France provides a glimpse of this barbarity in the name of Christ with this warning:

> When the errant ones and burghers heard this, they cried out. They all assembled, anyone of capable of drawing and bearing a sword, big and small, and declared: Behold, the time has come to avenge him who was nailed to the wood, whom their forefathers slew. Now, let no remnant or vestige of them be allowed to escape, not even a babe or suckling in the cradle.

26. Menocal, *Ornament of the World*.

2. What about Maimonides's past encounter with Christians necessitated his creation of the "un-God" concept?

3. Why would such a concept as Maimonides's be attractive to a rabbinic Jewish audience?

4. What has Judaism lost by creating this separation between God and his people?

5. Has Maimonides created in essence a deistic Judaism by his response to an incarnational theology?

6. How has the Christian's general misunderstanding of what is meant by the term "incarnational theology" impacted the necessity of Jewish evangelism?

7. What can be done within the Christian faith to reunite the Jewish people with their God—which would thereby bring them to Jesus as well?

For there is a disconnect present which limits or inhibits effective and widespread Jewish evangelism. In my view, this disconnect revolves primarily around rabbinic Judaism which was established in a post-temple environment. The two primary voices which have appeared to transcend time and criticism are Moses Maimonides and Shlomo Yitzchaki (aka Rashi). Both live within the same general time parameters and both are considered as the voices of modern or rabbinic Judaism for many Jewish people.

Therefore, and as mentioned in the opening pages, at least 96.8 percent of the Jewish people living in the world today are separated from a personal relationship with Messiah Jesus. The history of the Christian church has played the greatest role in their spiritually lost condition. However, I would argue the doctrine and teachings of rabbinic Judaism, influenced heavily by the teachings of Moses Maimonides, has also played a role in their separation from the Jewish Messiah and the Godhead. For even Halbertal has the honesty to recognize that in many ways "Maimonides belonged to the rare and unique species of religious reformers—even, one may say, of religious founders."[27] Joel L. Kraemer believes that Rambam in his own writings saw himself "as a Moses *redivivus*"[28] perhaps because even today Maimonides

---

27. Halbertal, *Maimonides*, 4. Halbertal (11) quotes from Maimonides's "Introduction" to the *Mishneh Torah* an example of what some might consider the Spanish rabbi's hubris and belief in his absolute understanding of Judaism:

> Hence, I have entitled this work *Mishneh Torah* (Repetition of the Law), for the reason that a person who first reads the Written Law and then this compilation, will know from it the *whole of the Oral Law, without having occasion to consult any other book between them* (emphasis added).

28. Kraemer, *Maimonides*, 51, 165, 166, 237, 471–72. Kraemer bases this proposition

can be known by the term the "Great Eagle."²⁹ Therefore, it is the belief of this writer that this book will provide a new instrument in the evangelistic tool bag that will seek to not only provoke the Jewish people to jealousy (Rom 11:11) but also will bring them to Jesus the Jewish and gentile Messiah.

(expanded upon in his fn. 44 for p. 51) on three sections of *The Guide of the Perplexed* (I:71; II:2 and III:31) which if read do allow for a consideration that Rambam expected his views to be received as fiat.

> But the truth is undoubtedly as we have said, that every one of the six hundred and thirteen precepts serves to inculcate some truth, to remove some erroneous opinion, to establish proper relations in society, to diminish evil, to train in good manners or to warn against bad habits. All this depends on three things: opinions, morals, and social conduct. We do not count words, because precepts, whether positive or negative, if they relate to speech, belong to those precepts which regulate our social conduct, or to those which spread truth, or to those which teach morals. Thus these three principles suffice for assigning a reason for every one of the Divine commandments. (III:31)

29. Kraemer, *Maimonides*, 209. See also 367, where Kraemer again quoting directly from Maimonides from *The Guide of the Perplexed*'s introduction writes that Rambam saw "himself in the first person as the man of destiny to carry out the task":

> Lastly, when I have a difficult subject before me—when I find the road narrow, and can see no other way of teaching a well-established truth except by pleasing one intelligent man and displeasing ten thousand fools—I prefer to address myself to the one man, and to take no notice whatever of the condemnation of the multitude; I prefer to extricate that intelligent man from his embarrassment and show him the cause of his perplexity, so that he may *attain perfection* and be at peace (emphasis added).

2

A Brief Examination of Jewish-Christian History (AD 70 to 1290) and Its Impact on Maimonides

SEEKING TO EXAMINE THE history of the Christian church and its relationship with its Jewish relatives resembles the legendary battle between the Hatfields and McCoys of American Appalachian folklore. What began as an inter-doctrinal squabble between followers of the new Jewish sect known as "The Way" and the establishment directed from the temple leadership of the Sadducees and the Sanhedrin directed by the Pharisees became something that has created division, confusion, hatred, and, sadly, death for almost two millennia. This chapter will seek to briefly examine this separation and its causes for the time period both preceding the time of Moses Maimonides and the immediate time frame following his death. For it was in this time frame that one begins to see the beginning days of expulsion for the Jewish people from first England and then other areas of Europe. It was also in this time that we see established a seemingly impenetrable dividing wall between the faith of Jesus the Jewish Messiah and the Jewish people. Therefore, this is the wall that must be torn down if the twenty-first century church is to return the gospel to the brothers and sisters of Messiah Jesus (Rom 11:11).

RAMIFICATIONS OF THE DESTRUCTION OF THE TEMPLE (AD 70)

In Matt 24:1–2, one can read what I view as the only overt prophetic statement of Jesus. For while the Olivet Discourse in Matthew and the other Synoptic Gospels deliver the essence of Jesus's declaration concerning what will happen in the "end times," the future destruction of the temple is a clear promise that had immediate results in the lives of the disciples—"Jesus came out from the temple and was going away when His disciples came up to point out the temple buildings to Him. And He said to them, '"Do you not see all these things? Truly I say to you, not one stone here will be left upon another, which will not be torn down."'[1] Approximately forty years later, the fulfillment of this prophecy was realized as the future Emperor Titus destroyed Jerusalem with only the outer wall that separated the temple itself from the community (today known as the Kotel, or the Wailing Wall) remaining erect. However, there were ramifications to the destruction of the Second Temple in AD 70 that would ultimately lead to the separation of Jewish Christianity and traditional Judaism.

Theodore Stylianopoulos writes, "the New Testament marks the beginning of Christianity, when the Christian church was born from the matrix of Judaism, and testifies both to the close connections between the two communities of faith as well to the decisive factors which separate them."[2] While on the surface, the statement exhibits a certain connectivity between Judaism and followers of the Christian faith, there is on the other hand an immediate contradistinction which assumes that there was always a separation between the two religious views. Stylianopoulos's argument however is overstated. For while James Parkes misses the overall point as well, he does come closer to the truth when he wrote that "the Jewish communities of apostolic and sub-apostolic times provided the bases from which the apostolic message was preached; and that without them the church would have had a much more difficult task of interpretation and explanation to the Hellenistic and Asiatic worlds."[3] The actual truth is that until AD 70 and even after, the messianic sect which followed Jesus of Nazareth were considered as much Jewish in ethnicity and religion as the Essenes in Qumran and the Pharisees in Jerusalem. This is because the followers of "The Way" taught from, believed in, and practiced the same practices of Jewish Scriptures as

---

1. Unless otherwise noted, all Scripture references are from the NASB.
2. Stylianopoulos, "New Testament Issues in Jewish-Christian Relations," 586.
3. Parkes, "Jewish Background of the Incarnation," 36.

anyone else. It was only in the annals of history that this began to change in both the perception of Judaism and Christianity.

Jews of the Sanhedrin—Development of Rabbinic/Modern Judaism

Just exactly who were the non-Christian Jewish people at the time of the destruction of the Second Temple, from the development of rabbinic (i.e., modern) Judaism to the disappearance of the other religious groups that existed at the time of the great tragedy? Yes, the differences between Jewish believers in Jesus and the Sanhedrin non-believers were sharpest in contrast and views, including accusations of blasphemy and non-monotheistic views.[4] However, this could be because these two groups were the only ones to survive the Great Revolt of AD 66–70 which led to the destruction of the Second Temple.[5]

The germination of rabbinic Judaism began in the days of the Sanhedrin. For while there is a question as to the formation and formulation of the Sanhedrin in both the times prior to Jesus and during his days, even Lester Grabbe, who seeks to question the gospel account of the power of body and even the naming of the body, acknowledges the existence of such an entity.[6] Howard Clark Kee affirms the existence of the Sanhedrin and examines the power of the body from both the writings of the Talmud and the historian Josephus, albeit acknowledging that there could have been more than one group which called itself Sanhedrin in pre-AD 70 times—the Great Sanhedrin with seventy-one members and the Small Sanhedrin with twenty-three members.[7] There is a traditional view for the Sanhedrin that is archaeologically supported by the tombs of "Elders of the Great Sanhedrin" even if absolute historical evidence is impossible to affirm.[8] Coincidentally, Kee would argue that the existence of the Sanhedrin was such an integral part of

---

4. Hurtado, "Pre-70 CE Jewish Opposition to Christ Devotion," 33–34.

5. Jervell, "Mighty Minority," 15–37. Jervell's article, it should be acknowledged, attempts to slander Paul as anti-Jewish in his theology; however, he does an adequate job of illustrating the continuing Jewish-Christian presence within the church up to at least the year AD 100.

6. Grabbe, "Sanhedrin, Sanhedriyyot, or Mere Invention?," 1–19. Grabbe provides a historical overview from the Persian period to the time of Agrippa. Interestingly, Joshua Efron goes further than Grabbe and discounts the existence of the organizational body as a ruling body, except perhaps in some lesser religious decisions of no consequence thereby seeking to negate the power of the Sanhedrin to play a role in the death of Jesus. Efron, "Sanhedrin as an Ideal and as Reality," 44–49, esp. 45, 46, and 49.

7. Kee, "Central Authority in Second-Temple Judaism," 51, 55, 57, 59, 61.

8. Kloner and Zissu, "'Caves of Simeon the Just' and 'The Minor Sanhedrin,'" 134–35.

Judaism that it played a role in the formative days of rabbinic Judaism; and, hence, why one of the tractates was named *Sanhedrin*. Kee wrote, "The aim, however, was to regain orientation of the religious community in an age in which the past was gone and a new era was emerging, so that the goal was to build up a trustworthy mode of shared existence."[9]

This is why the idea of "regaining orientation" is a concept that Jacob Neusner examined as he recognized that a Judaism which would not include Jesus was in a crisis mode after the destruction of the Second Temple.[10] As the fires still burned throughout Jerusalem in AD 70, it was rabbis such as Johannan ben Zakkai that lived out the concept of a new orientation in which a new rabbinic Judaism would be born due to the fact that in their minds the old biblical Judaism was no longer possible because the sacrificial system had been forever abolished.[11] Ephraim Urbach takes this idea of new orientation one step further and begins to argue that rabbinic Judaism began to isolate itself and become a "self-enclosed movement."[12] Therefore, I conclude that ultimately biblical Judaism for or in rabbinic Judaism was abolished along with the Essenes and other religious groups, and the isolation of rabbinic thought would consequently allow for the question of whether one could be Jewish and also believe in Jesus.

Disappearance of the Essenes and Other Religious Groups

Despite Jacob Neusner's analytical genius, he was incorrect in writing that the temple's destruction only impacted the religious Jews in Judah proper.[13] For even though the Essenes had abandoned worship in Jerusalem long before AD 70,[14] the destruction of Jerusalem spelled the end of Sadducean control of the temple complex; the Essenes lost their own spiritual stronghold and were in a large sense forced to find refuge with the secular Jews of their time residing at Masada.[15] Ultimately, and as William Stegner

---

9. Kee, "Central Authority in Second-Temple Judaism," 57.

10. Neusner, "Judaism in a Time of Crisis," 313.

11. Sigal, "Aspects of the Fall of Jerusalem," 162–63; Tomson, "Wars against Rome," 7–8, 11; and Neusner, "Judaism in a Time of Crisis," 321, 324–25.

12. Urbach, "Self-Isolation or Self Affirmation in Judaism," 269.

13. Neusner, "Judaism in a Time of Crisis," 314.

14. Neusner, "Judaism in a Time of Crisis," 317. See also Fraade, "Ascetical Aspects of Ancient Judaism," 267. Fraade goes into more detail as to why the Essenes left Jerusalem for worship in the wilderness.

15. Stegner, "Breaking Away," 8 and Tomson, "Wars against Rome," 4. Emanuel Tov argues that while he does not believe that the Masada Qumranian texts were written while they sojourned with the rebels, he does believe that they lived with them long

points out by the end of the war and the destruction of Masada,[16] there were only two groups strong enough to vie for control of Jewish religious thought—Pharisaical (rabbinical) Judaism and Jewish Christianity.[17]

Jews of the Sect Known as The Way (Acts 9:1–2)

In the first two verses of Acts 9, we find an interesting location and expression as it refers to the early followers of Jesus: "Now Saul, still breathing threats and murder against the disciples of the Lord, went to the high priest, and asked for letters from him to the synagogues at Damascus, so that if he found any belonging to the Way, both men and women, he might bring them bound to Jerusalem." The followers of Jesus were going to be found in the synagogues of Damascus, in contradistinction to the argument made by David Flusser,[18] as they were Jewish and had taken on the identity of Jesus's description of himself in John 14:6, "The Way."[19]

Therefore, there should be no question that the earliest followers of Jesus were Jewish. It can be seen that they continued to follow and observe Jewish festivals, albeit with a fulfillment perspective.[20] And across the theological spectrum, the acknowledgement of this fact is affirmed. From the Jewish perspective, Jacob Neusner describes a believer as a "Christian [who] was another kind of Jew and saw himself as such."[21] Bruce Malina even attempted to provide a definition for first-century Christian Judaism that would be permissible in a Second Temple milieu.[22] From the Christian perspective, we find the dichotomy of Schuyler Brown who sought to find

---

enough that it could have been written. Tov, "Qumran Origin for the Masada Non-Biblical Texts?," 62.

16. The focus of the book does not necessitate a full historical breakdown of the Masada martyrdom; therefore, the following source will provide the only information that is required at this point. Netzer, "Last Days and Hours at Masada."

17. Stegner, "Breaking Away," 8. See also Guttmann, "Foundations of Rabbinic Judaism," 454. Guttmann describes Pharisaical Judaism as a "living force" and as unofficially "the true interpreters of Judaism."

18. Flusser, "Jewish-Christian Schism (Part I)," 41.

19. Hann, "Judaism and Jewish Christianity in Antioch," 341, 343.

20. Ben Ezra, "'Christians' Observing 'Jewish' Festivals of Autumn," 53–73 and Buchanan, "Worship, Feasts and Ceremonies," 279–97. It should be noted that Buchanan attempts to show the deviations and similarities between the practices as well as noting how the church fathers saw these practices as somewhat deviant from normative church views.

21. Neusner, "Judaism in a Time of Crisis," 319.

22. Malina, "Jewish Christianity or Christian Judaism," 49–56.

the balance between the "ecumenical" Paul who allowed the gentiles into the fold with the "restrictive" leaders in Jerusalem who sought to maintain fidelity to the Jewish past.[23] We also find the definitional struggle of James D. G. Dunn who argued that Paul was a Jewish believer but wondered just what kind of Jewish believer?[24] Ultimately, it should be recognized that Jewish believers of the first centuries were not just simply members of the heretical Ebionite sect;[25] but, were Jewish believers seeking to find their place as both Christians and Jewish in a Second Temple and non-temple world. For as L. W. Barnard notes, "Jewish-Christianity in the diaspora was not eclipsed by the fall of Jerusalem in A.D. 70," for while they might have been moved to such places as Pella, the existence and persistence of recognized Jewish believers in Jesus continued within Judaism at least until the disaster known as the Bar Kokhba Rebellion.[26]

RAMIFICATIONS OF THE BAR KOKHBA REBELLION (AD 135)

Even before the disaster known as the Bar Kokhba Rebellion, there is value in considering whether there was a continuing Jewish-Christian presence in Palestine following the destruction of the Second Temple in Jerusalem. David Sim and Jacob Jervell not only argue against such a presence but also argue that the Jewish-Christian emphasis had been a complete failure.[27] This approach is negated on both a pragmatic level by Eric Meyers and an esoteric concern by Theodore Stylianopoulos;[28] however, the most obvious answer as to whether and how the message of the Jewish Jesus impacted the Jewish community can be seen by their response both before and after

---

23. Brown, "Matthean Community and the Gentile Mission," 193–94, 207, 212–13. See also Stegner, "Breaking Away," 7.

24. Dunn, "Who Did Paul Think He Was?," 175, 179.

25. Skarsaune, "Ebionites," 423, 439, 445–46 and Hann, "Undivided Way," 235, 237. Hann falls prey to the stereotypical approach while Skarsaune in his chapter does not.

26. Barnard, "Early Roman Church, Judaism, and Jewish-Christianity," 371–72, 374, 375, 377–78; Bourgel, "Jewish-Christians' Move from Jerusalem," 107–9, 111, 121, 122, 124, 127, 129, 130–32, 134, 136; and Scott, "Effects of the Fall of Jerusalem," 149–57.

27. Sim, "How Many Jews Became Christians in the First Century?," 426 and Jervell, "Mighty Minority," 13. Sim in his article creates this convoluted mathematical algorithm that estimates that the number of Jewish believers in Jesus never exceeded one thousand; however, this necessitates his denunciation of the biblical accounts in Acts and his lack of understanding that the converts at the Day of Pentecost would themselves have been Jewish as they were there for the Jewish festival of Sukkot.

28. Meyers, "Early Judaism and Christianity in the Light of Archaeology," 69, and Stylianopoulos, "New Testament Issues in Jewish-Christian Relations," 587–89.

the Bar Kokhba Rebellion. Megan Hale Williams and Burton L. Visotzky, writing for Jewish academic journals, express the continual confusion even into the twentieth and twenty-first century as to what should be done with Jewish believers in Jesus, much in the same way as the rabbinic scholars did in the early centuries of the Common Era.[29]

Therefore, it is the penultimate catastrophe of the Bar Kokhba Rebellion that in many ways created one of the true fissures between traditional Judaism and a Judaism that believed and affirmed Jesus as Messiah.[30] This divorce which caused the rabbis to consider the once Jewish-dominated sect as nothing more than "notzerim" (Nazarenes) also opened the door for the official foundation of rabbinic Judaism.[31] Therefore, it is of some value to briefly examine the theological significance of a rebellion that was short-lived and short-sighted.[32]

In many ways, after the destruction of Jerusalem in AD 70, traditional Jews wavered on the brink of despondence until Rabbi Akiva announced the arrival of "the Messiah"—Simeon Bar-Kokhba.[33] While there has been recent scholarly debate as to whether Rabbi Akiva indeed made the proclamation of Bar Kokhba's messiahship, there is no doubt that such a man existed and he ruled as a "despot of record in the Jewish homeland."[34] There is also little doubt that Bar Kokhba led a "Messianic-type" rebellion in the mode of the Maccabees against Rome that resulted in utter destruction and the expulsion of all Jews (believers in Jesus or not) from the now-named

---

29. Williams, "No More Clever Titles," 40, 45, and Visotzky, "Prolegomenon to the Study of Jewish-Christianities," 47–48. Both Williams and Visotzky struggle with what to do with Jewish believers; while Williams refers to the mountain of sources that validate the struggle, Visotzky simply writes, "They just don't fit very neatly; they never did. Ever since it became clear that the law-free mission to the gentiles would create a church and not a synagogue, Jewish-Christianity has been an uncomfortable reality with which to deal" (47).

30. Tomson, "Wars against Rome," 22–23. Tomson includes the Eusebius citation (*Hist. eccl.* 4.8.4) which notes that Bar-Kokhba sought out punishment for the Jewish Christians who would not deny Jesus as Messiah.

31. Schiffman, "How Jewish Christians Became Christians." See also Stowers, "Text as Interpretation," 17.

32. The historical significance of Bar Kokhba will only be considered in a cursory fashion due to two factors. The first is space consideration and the second is that it is not significant to the overall theme of this book.

33. Telushkin, *Jewish Literacy*, 144–46.

34. Novenson, "Why Does R. Akiba Acclaim Bar Kokhba as Messiah?," 551–72 (esp. 568). Novenson is the one who seeks to cast doubt on Rabbi Akiva's acclamation; but, there is evidence for both positions and one must discern for themselves what they believe.

Aelia Capitolina (i.e., Jerusalem).[35] This short-lived messianic dream also resulted in the deaths of more than half a million Jewish lives.[36] However, it was not until Bar Kokhba that Jewish-Christians had their faith and ethnicity put to the test literally and figuratively. Up until this time, Jewish believers in Jesus, according to Yehudah Liebes, were not only included in the synagogue but allowed to be prayer leaders to the point that they even modified the *Et Zemah* blessing to reflect their faith and ethnicity.[37] However, when Bar Kokhba required allegiance even to the point of messianic recognition or possible death, the Jewish-Christians were required to follow their faith even at the perceived expense of their own people.[38] And it was this choice that many surmise was one of the "final coffin nails" between the Jewish church and the Jewish synagogue.[39]

Before one answers this section's question fully, one must consider whether the foundation for such a reaction was already in the preparatory stages. Was there antipathy building toward Jewish believers in Jesus among the Jewish leadership before Bar Kokhba, even though they were generally accepted in the synagogue? Stegner would argue such a paradigm was taking place as Jewish-Christians were breaking boundaries that "leaders of formative Judaism" were so desperately trying to maintain.[40] While perhaps a leading voice for doubt on the subject, Steven T. Katz allows for the possibility of such opposition because of the need "to find a new equilibrium in the face of the disaster of 70."[41]

Two leading rabbis of the immediate post-Second Temple period were Yohannan ben Zakkai and Gamaliel II. According to Neusner, Zakkai the Pharisee did not see the destruction of the temple as an end to Judaism and the possibility of atoning sacrifice and of the purity laws, and saw that the synagogue model could serve as an alternative approach to the sacrificial system.[42] Therefore, along with Gamaliel II and the other surviving Pharisees who escaped to Yavneh, Judaism would require a facelift that would not only supersede the sacrificial system but also consider the announcement of

---

35. Schiffman, "At the Crossroads," 155.
36. Telushkin, *Jewish Literacy*, 146.
37. Liebes, "Who Makes the Horn of Jesus to Flourish," 56–58.
38. Davies, "Early Christian Attitudes toward Judaism and the Jews," 74; Riddle, "So-Called Jewish Christians," 29; and Schiffman, "At the Crossroads," 155.
39. Riddle, "So-Called Jewish Christians," 29–30. Riddle leaves himself some room for error; however, he does propose that the edict against the *malshinim of* Gamaliel II's Eighteen Benedictions are primarily at Jewish Christians.
40. Stegner, "Breaking Away," 7.
41. Katz, "Issues in the Separation," 44.
42. Neusner, "Judaism in a Time of Crisis," 324–25.

the ultimate sacrifice of Jesus of Nazareth as heretical.[43] Consequently, and under the primary leadership of Gamaliel, the *Birkat Ha-Minim* (benediction against heretics) was revised with many believing the purpose was to separate and castigate Jewish believers in Jesus from traditional Judaism.[44] Therefore, the stage was established for a post-Bar Kokhba response to Jewish believers in Jesus who were considered by many to be traitors to the Jewish cause and to the Jewish people for not joining in the fight for liberation from Rome.[45]

As stated previously by Ephraim Urbach, Judaism in a post-Second Temple period found itself becoming more isolated and a "self-enclosed entity" from the world. Any desire for missionary work toward the world had disappeared in an effort to reconstitute itself in a post-sacrificial and post-temple world.[46] This hermetical reality became even truer after the debacle known as the Bar Kokhba Rebellion. The need to determine the loyalty of its membership reached a critical mass and the Jewish traitors known also as Christians could no longer be welcome in the fold. Both Peter Tomson and Asher Finkel acknowledge this separation beginning in the post-AD 135 period while Steven Katz seeks to push the dating to the beginning of the third century.[47] However, regardless of the exact dating of the separation of Jewish-Christians from non-believing Jews, the failure of Simon Bar Kokhba created a critical mass between the two.

Aside from the *Birkat Ha-Minim*, Ben Zion Bokser notes the inclusion of "sectarian writings" along with the Hebrew Scriptures to denounce Christian teachings and a translational replacement for the Septuagint by Aquila of Pontus.[48] Gideon Bohak also notes that in addition to the invoca-

---

43. Tomson, "Wars against Rome," 7–8. I have included some editorial license in developing Tomson's argument; however, I believe the essence of what Tomson wrote is not violated by my interpretation.

44. Kimelman, "*Birkat Ha-Minim*," 226–28; Mayo, "Role of the Birkath Haminim," 326, 327; Finkel, "Yavneh's Liturgy and Early Christianity," 232–33; Hirschberg, "Once Again—The Minim," 308; Stemberger, "Rabbinic Reactions to Christianization," 143–44; Liebes, "Who Makes the Horn of Jesus to Flourish," 63–65; Brown, "Matthean Community and the Gentile Mission," 215; and Davies, "Early Christian Attitudes Toward the Jews," 75. Stemberger also notes that some will use rabbinic texts to justify the "book burning" of scrolls owned by Jewish-Christians; this could also have occurred because of Gamaliel's benediction revision (144).

45. Stemberger, "Rabbinic Reactions to Christianization," 147; Tomson, "Wars against Rome," 18; and Neusner, "Judaism in a Time of Crisis," 325.

46. Urbach, "Self-Isolation or Self-Affirmation in Judaism," 269.

47. Tomson, "Wars against Rome," 22–23; Finkel, "Yavneh's Liturgy and Early Christianity," 242; and Katz, "Issues in the Separation," 46, 66.

48. Bokser, "Religious Polemics in Biblical and Talmudic Exegesis," 707–8.

tion against the *minim*, the rabbis were not necessarily opposed to magical incantations being cast against the Jewish believers in Jesus.[49] Philip Mayo, albeit citing Justin Martyr's *Dialogue with Trypho*, refers to the eight anti-Christian prayers that were uttered daily in the synagogue.[50] The antipathy following the Bar Kokhba Rebellion between Christians (including Jewish believers) and Jews was strong and would only grow stronger with the passing years. The *Birkat Ha-Minim* was only the beginning of the growing division between Judaism and its sect known as Christianity.

Codification of the Mishnah by Judah the Prince (Impact on Jewish Believers)

Rabbinic Judaism was created out of a desire to preserve the very existence of the Jewish people. An existence that was threatened by political catastrophes and a group of Jewish sectarians known as Christians who were beginning to make the claim in their gentile adherents that they were the true descendants of the "covenant promises."[51] Therefore, an alternative concept to what was lost when the Second Temple was destroyed was deemed necessary.[52] Following the defeat of Bar Kokhba in AD 135, the surviving rabbis not only saw concept as necessary but also imperative and thereby sought to reorganize the heart of Judaism in the city of Yavneh.[53]

The leading Jewish figure of this period in a post-Bar Kokhba world was Judah HaNasi, also known as Judah the Prince (c. AD 138–220).[54] He directed the codifying of the Jewish Oral Law, which resulted in the formation

---

49. Bohak, "Magical Means for Handling *Minim*," 267–68.

50. Mayo, "Role of the Birkath Haminim," 329. Mayo is referring to Justin Martyr's *Dialogue with Trypho* 137.2 for his source material. Mayo does acknowledge that Justin has an intrinsic bias but also puts forth the argument that bias or not, Justin's position is based on historical precedent.

51. Yuval, "Christianity in Talmud and Midrash," 56; Novak, "End of the Law," 35; Bokser, "Religious Polemics in Biblical and Talmudic Exegesis," 706; and Davies, "Early Christian Attitudes Toward the Jews," 73. Yuval specifically notes that the Talmud/Mishnah sought to be somewhat covert and obtuse in their accusations but it was primarily because the rabbis did not wish to give more press than necessary to this sectarian group of Jewish renegades.

52. Robinson, *Essential Judaism*, 310–12. Daniel's practice of praying three times towards Jerusalem in Daniel 6 has often been understood as an example of prayer replacing the sacrificial times when sacrifice is not possible.

53. Robinson, *Essential Judaism*, 322–23, 337–39. See also Cohen, "Significance of Yavneh," 27–53. However, one would disagree with Cohen's comment that Jewish believers were immediately "excommunicated" as Yavneh convened.

54. Robinson, *Essential Judaism*, 341.

of the Mishnah and Babylonian/Palestinian Talmuds, which many believe to have originated from the time of Mount Sinai.[55] In many ways, this action saved the practice of one type of Judaism but at the expense of the Jewish Old Testament or Hebrew Scriptures, even though there was originally opposition to Judah's effort at codification.[56] Rabbi Joseph Telushkin writes this about the Torah—". . . the Torah alone, even with its 613 commandments, is an insufficient guide to Jewish life."[57] Therefore, in today's Judaism you will find knowledge of Scripture but the default interpretation lies not with it but with what the Talmud says about the biblical passage. Ultimately, and because of his later writings, Maimonides has become as important as Moses in synagogues of the twenty-first century.[58]

As it relates to Jewish believers in Jesus, the Mishnah/Talmud and other extra-biblical sources from the days of Yavneh and Rabbi Judah forward create a dichotomy of responses and approaches. Constant revisions and adaptations of liturgical prayers because of Jewish-Christians are noted by Binyamin Katzoff and Harris Hirschberg.[59] A constant intertextual and intervarsity debate as to the terminology related to the usage of *minim* is found throughout the talmudic structure, specifically as to whether a *min* worships a plurality of deities or simply teaches that God has rejected Israel (both issues which reflect patristic Christian teachings).[60] And, ultimately, how one should define the person of Messiah as it could not be Jesus of Nazareth,[61] an individual that was written negatively about both in code and overtly in the Talmud/Mishnah.[62] This will come back to haunt both

55. Telushkin, *Jewish Literacy*, 149–53; Robinson, *Essential Judaism*, 323; and Scharfstein, *Torah and Commentary*, 533.

56. Halivni, "Reception Accorded to Rabbi Judah's Mishnah," 204–5, 208. Halivni would also argue against the position of Telushkin, Robinson, and Scharfstein in fn. 91 and merely allow that Judah was the anthologizer of the Mishnah (212).

57. Telushkin, *Jewish Literacy*, 148.

58. This statement is based upon personal experience of working in the field of Jewish missions for almost twenty years. Further insight into this concept can be found in the writings of Chaim Potok, specifically in his book, *In the Beginning*. Additionally, this is the point I will be making and the apologetic argument that I will be seeking to rebut and refute throughout this work.

59. Katzoff, "'God of our Fathers,'" 303–22 and Hirschberg, "Once Again—The Minim," 306–7.

60. Hayes, "Displaced Self-Perceptions," 261. The specific information noted here comes from Hayes's own footnotes 30 and 31.

61. Jacobi, "'In Its Time I Will Hasten It,'" 115, 117 and Neusner, "History Invented," 196, 202.

62. Much has been written about the rabbinical polemical rhetoric concerning the person of Jesus of Nazareth. Therefore, only a selection of resources will be provided in this footnote. Gero, "Stern Master and His Wayward Disciple," 287–311; Schwartz and

the rabbis and the Jewish people in the patristic period, for it will not only be used against them but also be used to justify the persecution that will be inflicted upon them, often in the name of Jesus himself.

RISE OF THE PATRISTICS AND CONSIDERATION OF THE JEWISH PEOPLE (AD 170 TO C. 500)

Joel Carmichael, who is probably approaching the question with a somewhat preconceived bias, helps to answer the question of how Jewish people in early church history, in the time of Maimonides in the Middle Ages, and today perceive our Christian past:

> The Church Fathers (Origen, Tertullian, Chrysostom), have abandoned the expectation of the Kingdom of God, welded Paul's ideas together and interpreted them as a part of a new philosophy, in which the Church, eternal and universal, the reflection of God on earth, was confronted by the enemies of God, the children of Satan, the Jews, whose paramount function was to epitomize the struggle of the Devil forces against God.[63]

Interestingly, and seemingly to justify Carmichael's claim, there is no verse in Scripture that should be considered as innocuous as Gal 6:16. However, I doubt that the Apostle Paul could have anticipated the debate and consternation that the following words would cause in the Church Age: "And those who will walk by this rule, peace and mercy be upon them, and upon the Israel of God." However, the question of who has the right to the designation of "Israel of God" was debated with vigor in the Church Age, and even is still being debated today among both the replacement theologians and those who avidly support the continuation of Israel as the people of God.

However, as it relates to the patristic period, Paul's epistle to the Galatian church creates a whole dynamic as to whether Paul was creating an

---

Tomson, "When Rabbi Eliezer Was Arrested," 145–81; O'Neill, "Mocking of Bar Kokhba and of Jesus," 39–41; Miller, "Minim of Sepphoris Reconsidered," 377–80; Parker, "Early Christianity as a Religion of Healing," 145; Levey, "Best Kept Secret of the Rabbinic Tradition," 452–69; Yuval, "Christianity in Talmud and Midrash," 63; Stemberger, "Rabbinic Reactions to the Christianization," 150, 151, 159; and Mayo, "Role of the Birkath Haminim," 339. Levey's article is quite interesting as it reveals one of the leading lights of rabbinic tradition who more than likely became a Jewish believer in Jesus—Simeon Ben Zoma. Rabbi Ben Zoma is worthy of further investigation.

63. Carmichael, *Satanizing of the Jews*, 31.

anti-Judaizing apologetic for Galatia or not,[64] one that allows for a supersessionistic interpretation. While Petra Heldt will argue that early patristic writers of the second and third centuries were more concerned about a proper understanding of the place of the *Nomos* in a Christian life, she will acknowledge that later church fathers examined the passage differently.[65] For example, Augustine's interpretation of Sarah and Hagar in Gen 4:21–31, which includes both a literal and heavenly place for the city of Jerusalem, places Sarah in the role of the church and Hagar in the role of the Jewish people.[66] This interpretation I counter creates a complete biological switch from the Genesis account of the story as it places the child of Sarah in the role of the lesser and Hagar's descendants in the role of the greater place of God's economy or chosen-ness.

Therefore, the prevailing patristic understanding of Gal 6:16 and the "Israel of God" reflects Augustine's concept of Gen 4:21–31. John Chrysostom in "Homily on Galatians 6.16" stated, "But those who oppose it, even if they have been born of Israel and carried Israel's name with them, have fallen away from Israel and from that name and family."[67] Cyprian wrote in *Three Books of Testimonies Against the Jews*, "According to what had been foretold in advance, the Jews had departed from God . . . Instead, the Christians have succeeded to their place, preserving well of the Lord by faith."[68] And the *Apostolic Constitutions*, compiled in c. 390, writes in relation to the idea of the phrase "Israel of God" the following statement: "To you, the converted Gentiles, is opened the gate of life. You were formerly not loved, but now you are beloved—a people ordained for the possession of God."[69] Therefore, as will be illustrated by the six selected patristic theologians, the idea of replacement and growing repugnance towards the Jewish people was present in the patristic age. This is a repugnance that will affect both the church and the scattered Jewish nation as they interact, interrelate, and consider each other, even to this day.

---

64. Verseput, "Paul's Gentile Mission," 37–38, 44–57. Verseput spends the majority of his article examining the Gal 2 passage.

65. Heldt, "Constructing Christian Communal Identity," 30–31, 35, 37–39.

66. Helleman, "'Abraham Had Two Sons,'" 37–39, 41, 51, 58. Helleman, while not justifying Augustine's response, does illustrate as well how the man took the analogy further to justify the church's attitude toward both the Jewish people and the Donatists—"to advise Donatists to return to the Catholic Church as the one universal and true Christian church" (63).

67. Edwards, *Galatians, Ephesians, Philippians*, 103.

68. Bercot, *Dictionary of Early Christian Beliefs*, 365. Both the Cyprian and the *Apostolic* quotation are from this source.

69. Bercot, *Dictionary of Early Christian Beliefs*, 365.

Justin Martyr

Often when a Christian hears the name Justin Martyr, they think of a man who suffered for his faith in Jesus. Christendom in general thinks of a man who left behind a legacy and a volume of work to be studied and admired. However, to hear the name of Justin Martyr with the ears of a Jewish person is to hear something negative and repugnant. Judaism thinks of a man who left behind a legacy and a polemical model that would be repeated and followed throughout the centuries.

Justin is known primarily as an apologist for the Christian faith. His best-known work is his supposed engagement with the Jewish Trypho in which he attempts to prove the Messiahship of Jesus. He is known as well for his argument in support of the miraculous and the virginal conception.[70] His defense of Christian miracles occurs predominantly in his *Dialogue with Trypho*, a subject which James Kelhoffer divides into five sections:

1. the power of Jesus to perform "exorcisms" as proof of his power;
2. the miracles of Jesus's disciples come via his Messiahship;
3. the belief that Jesus as Messiah is a miracle;
4. the miracles of Jesus which confirm the Dan 7 prophecy; and
5. the exorcisms done by the apostles to prove the truth of Jesus.[71]

Jules Lebreton sees Justin's apologetical approach focusing on two primary areas—the supremacy of Christian morality in a pagan world, which is the primary focus of the *First Apology*, and the proof texts of the prophecy passages from the Hebrew Scriptures.[72] This sense of moral supremacy, as well as on a lesser level prophecy, can be seen in his argument from chapter 12 in which he writes, "And more than all other men are we your helpers and allies in promoting peace, seeing that we hold this view, that it is alike impossible for the wicked, the covetous, the conspirator, and for the virtuous to escape the notice of God, and that each man goes to everlasting punishment or salvation according to the value of his actions."[73]

Bryan Litfin ultimately makes the best argument for why Justin Martyr was successful as perhaps the first true Christian apologist: "he tailored his

---

70. Garrett, *Systematic Theology*, 346–47, 588.
71. Kelhoffer, "Apostle Paul and Justin Martyr," 176–180. See also, Justin Martyr, *Dialogue with Trypho*, 30, 31, 35, 39, 76, 85.
72. Lebreton, "St. Justin. Martyr."
73. Justin Martyr, *First Apology*, 12.

message to his audience."[74] This is a concise response to a good question because while there are some that want to find egalitarianism in Justin, the focus of Justin's apologetics was to present the Messiah, regardless of whether it was done through analyzing miracles or engaging in a supposed conversation with a Jewish man.[75] One could argue that nothing else truly mattered to Justin.

Additionally, Peter Richardson and others after him have presented the case that Justin Martyr is the first Christian scholar to make the argument that the church has replaced Israel as the chosen ones.[76] R. Kendall Soulen is bluntly succinct when he writes, "But Justin insists that God's history with the Jews never possessed any saving significance in its own right. God's commerce with the Jews served either to restrain the particular wickedness of the Jewish people or to prefigure Christ."[77]

Matthew Bates in an article he wrote for the *Journal of Theological Studies* details exactly how Justin utilized the Scriptures of the Tanakh to take the prophecies of Isaiah "hermeneutically" and creatively discover a way to eliminate the Jewish people from the promises of Zion.[78] In fact, Bates sees that Justin Martyr considered not the church but Jesus himself as the true Israel.[79]

However, Bates has to balance his position by acknowledging that Justin viewed the words of the Tanakh to not belonging to the Jewish people but to the Christian church, and this is the point in which Bates contradicts his earlier argument by stating that Justin saw the church as Israel of God.[80] We can find evidence of Justin's bipolar argument in chapter 29 of the *Dialogue* when he writes the following:

> For these words have neither been prepared by me, nor embellished by the art of man; but David sung them, Isaiah preached them, Zechariah proclaimed them, and Moses wrote them. Are you acquainted with them, Trypho? They are contained in your Scriptures, or rather not yours, but ours. For we believe them;

---

74. Litfin, *Getting to Know the Church Fathers*, 62.

75. Bates, "Gender Ontology and Women in Ministry," 6.

76. Richardson, *Israel in the Apostolic Church*, 9–12; Soulen, *God of Israel and Christian Theology*, 35; and Gager, *Origins of Anti-Semitism*, 228–29.

77. Soulen, *God of Israel and Christian Theology*, 38.

78. Bates, "Justin Martyr's Logocentric Hermeneutical Transformation," 540, 549–50.

79. Bates, "Justin Martyr's Logocentric Hermeneutical Transformation," 540, 549–50.

80. Bates, "Justin Martyr's Logocentric Hermeneutical Transformation," 548, 553.

but you, though you read them, do not catch the spirit that is in them.[81]

However, and regardless of Justin's intention and views of Israel, the truth holds that he was one of the beginning voices of replacement theology that would become not merely a whisper but a shout from Tertullian, an allegorical view from Origen, a reprimand from Augustine, a false pity from Jerome, and outright disdain from John Chrysostom. Justin began a movement that continues to this day and for that we should remember both his positive attributes as well as his negative positions.

The significance that the *Dialogue with Trypho* plays in developing the Jewish-Christian relationship cannot be underestimated both positively and negatively. For what Justin more than likely meant as an evangelistic tract became a work that developed a theology of replacement and antipathy towards the physical descendants of Jesus and the apostles. This work of Justin, and the ones that followed,[82] has impacted and hindered any true evangelistic effort towards the people of Israel and still does today.

We do know according to Johannes Quasten that it "is the oldest Christian apology against the Jews that is extant" even if parts of it have been lost for perpetuity.[83] William Varner gives the reader a date of approximately AD 150 which is probably in the right time frame.[84] Quasten notes that the *Dialogue* must have been written after the *First Apology* because of a reference to it in the conversation with Trypho. One also can know that Antonius Pius, the emperor of the apology, reigned from AD 138 to 161.[85] Therefore, if *First Apology* was written first, we can ascertain a date of post-AD 135 because of a reference to the Bar Kokhba Rebellion in its pages.[86] Therefore, an estimated date of AD 150 represents a dark time in Jewish history as all hope for a warrior messiah ended with the deaths of untold thousands of Jewish men, women, and children.[87]

Therefore, the argument that Justin was offering an evangelistic balm to the Jewish people could on the peripheral surface be made; however, the

---

81. Justin Martyr, *Dialogue with Trypho*, 29.

82. Varner, "In the Wake of Trypho," 219, 221, 224–27. Varner argues that these anti-Jewish dialogues often work together and feed off of each other as well.

83. Quasten, *Patrology*, 202. Sadly the dialogue between Jason and Papiscus does not exist in extant form and cannot be examined for relevance and dating at this time.

84. Varner, "In the Wake of Trypho," 220.

85. Quasten, *Patrology*, 199, 202.

86. Justin Martyr, *First Apology*, 31. See also, Werline, "Transformation of Pauline Arguments," 81.

87. Wendel, "Interpreting the Descent of the Spirit," 95.

time of a predominant Jewish influence in the church was already on the wane[88] and one wonders if this was a balm or gloating moment? Quasten inadvertently offers the opportunity for the same question when he considers that while the audience was different than the leaders of Rome, Justin still focuses on verses which eliminates or replaces the Jewish people from God's covenant relationship.[89] This rationale for the purpose can be found in the words of Justin himself when he wrote:

> I do not process to have a mere verbal controversy with you, as I have not attempted to establish proof about Christ from the passages of Scripture which are not admitted by you? Which I quoted from the words of Jeremiah the prophet, and Esdras, and David; but from those which are even now admitted by you, which had your teachers comprehended, be well assured they would have deleted them, as they did those about the death of Isaiah, whom you sawed asunder with a wooden saw.[90]

Between all the visceral comments and attacks found within the words of the *Dialogue*, there remains only one question to answer—was Trypho real or an allegory? Eusebius votes in the affirmative and infers two arguments that will become a part of the urban legend folklore about the Jewish people:

1. the existence of a world plot instigated by the Jewish people to denigrate Jesus and
2. an accusation that states that the Jewish people have modified the Hebrew Scriptures to eliminate any reference to Jesus.[91]

Johannes Quasten and Marcel Simon, while not perpetuating the Eusebius plot allegation, do believe and affirm that Trypho was real, and in the case of Quasten was identified as "Rabbi Tarphon" from "the Mishnah."[92] William Varner, F. E. Talmage, and David Nirenberg vote in the negative.[93] Timothy J. Horner evaluates dozen of opinions and comes across with no true opinion.[94] Jon Nilson avoids the topic of Trypho's identity and instead argues that the audience was the focus of Justin's writing as he was trying to reach a

---

88. Werline, "Transformation of Pauline Arguments," 88–89.

89. Quasten, *Patrology*, 203. See also Wendel, "Interpreting the Descent of the Spirit," 95.

90. Justin Martyr, *Dialogue with Trypho*, 120.

91. Eusebius, *Ecclesiastical History*, 4:18.

92. Simon, *Verus Israel*, 12–13 and Quasten, *Patrology*, 202–203.

93. Varner, "In the Wake of Trypho," 222; Talmage, "Stumbling Block," 89–91; and Nirenberg, *Anti-Judaism*, 100.

94. Horner, *Listening to Trypho*, 15–32.

"non-Christian Gentile audience" who viewed positively both Judaism and Christianity but were "unable to adequately distinguish the one from the other."[95] However, the ultimate problem is not the identity of Trypho, but that the germination of Christian hatred, the accusations of deicide by the Roman Catholic Church, which were not renounced until Vatican II,[96] and Luther's venomous *On The Jews and Their Lies*,[97] had to begin somewhere and the argument can be made that it began in earnest with Justin.

Tertullian

The only exposure many have to Tertullian is centered on one statement: "The blood of the martyrs is the seed of the church." However, the actual statement was, "The oftener we are mown down by you, the more in number we grow; the blood of Christians is seed."[98] It is perhaps not as catchy, but I believe it is more emotively honest and should be an expression which defines this fallible yet fascinating Latin father.

There is great debate about how much, if any at all, contact that Tertullian and the Jewish community of Carthage actually had. Sabrina Inowlocki brings to the table the very real question of whether Tertullian knew any of the people he saw as the enemy.[99] Stéphanie Binder argues that Tertullian's *De Idoloatria* shows enough similarities to the Mishnah's Avodah Zarah that minimum general acquaintanceship must be allowed.[100] Geoffrey Dunn in *Tertullian's Aduersos Iudaeos* presents the gamut of academic scholarship in an attempt to answer the question but ultimately leaves the reader with these words: "Thus, Tertullian could declare a parting of the ways between Christian and Judaism on the theological level, yet still be engaged with Jews on a social basis."[101]

It should be acknowledged that the Latin father viewed the synagogue (presumably the one at Carthage included) with hostility as he perceived Judaism to be an antagonist against Christianity.[102] However, Robert MacLennan argues that the hostility towards the Jews of Carthage was

95. Nilson, "To Whom Is Justin's *Dialogue with Trypho* Addressed?," 39.
96. Carroll, *Constantine's Sword*, 35, 551–55.
97. Nirenberg, *Anti-Judaism*, 246–68.
98. Tertullian, *Apology*, ch. L.
99. Inowlocki, "Tertullian's Law of Paradise," 104.
100. Binder, "Jewish-Christian Contacts," 197–219. See also Ford, "Was Montanism a Jewish-Christian Heresy?," 155.
101. Dunn, *Tertullian's Aduersus Iudaeos*, 15–27.
102. Decret, *Early Christianity in North Africa*, 21.

really an attack on Marcionism in disguise.[103] This argument by MacLennan seems to be a stretch, as so many of Tertullian's works indicate an anti-Jewish bias[104] and they could not have been all about Marcion. In addition, Binder argues that Tertullian would have referenced Carthaginian rabbis as a tool in his battle against the threat of Marcionism,[105] a threat which was greater than his perception of Judaism, as Marcionites denied the truth of the Old Testament.[106]

However, and regardless of Tertullian's own personal antipathy towards the Jewish people, this did not stop him from incorporating Jewish symbols, both positive and negative, into his theological works. In a positive strain, Tertullian viewed the Passover season "as the most appropriate time" for catechumens to be baptized into the church,[107] perhaps due to the relationship of the resurrection to the Jewish holiday. In a mixed perception, Tertullian advocates a biblical understanding of a spiritualized circumcision (i.e., baptism) but rejects the physical act of Jewish circumcision (*bris*) with these words, "For, as the carnal circumcision, which was temporary, was inwrought for 'a sign" in a contumacious people, so the spiritual has been given for salvation to an obedient people; . . ."[108]

Therefore, the argument should be made that it is an early form of Tertullian's basic supersessionistic perspective that almost forces him to admit the Jewish people into the discussion of Jesus, but only to serve as a model of those who do not understand the identity of Jesus as Messiah and God because of their willful stubbornness.[109] Eric Osborn would argue such a Tertullian position when he considers that the Latin father saw "three stages in the development of the Christian Gospel" which, while including Judaism stopped at Moses, but did interestingly enough allow for the continued inclusion of "Greek philosophy."[110] Ultimately, therefore, for Tertullian, he would advocate that the Jewish people had "transgressed" God's law and the "whole race has denied natural virtue".[111] This antipathy towards the

103. MacLennan, "Four Christian Writers on Jews and Judaism," 200–201.

104. Dunn, *Tertullian*, 48.

105. Binder, "Jewish-Christian Contacts," 220.

106. Dunn, *Tertullian*, 49–51.

107. Tait, "Fire, Water, and a Risen Savior." See also Tertullian, *On Baptism*, chapter 19.

108. Leyerle, "Blood is Seed," 26–48, esp. 31, 41, and Tertullian, *Answer to the Jews*, chapter 3. A note of clarification as the word "contumacious" is defined as "stubbornly disobedient" and "rebellious" (Merriam-Webster Online).

109. Dunn, *Tertullian*, 49–51.

110. Osborn, *Tertullian*, 45.

111. Tertullian's complete quotation was "For neither does *grace* exist, except after

descendants of Jesus by virtue of DNA will find a loud voice in the *Adversus Judaeos* of Tertullian and those who followed him in church history.

If one were to place Tertullian in today's religious spectrum, it would be safe to surmise that in tone and tenor he would have fit in well with the style of the early twentieth-century preacher Billy Sunday. Paul Davies describes Tertullian's approach as being one who "with characteristic vigor took up the cudgels with all opponents of the faith, and the Jews did not escape."[112] The term "irascible" comes to mind when one considers Tertullian relationship's with the Jewish people and it should not be reduced as Stéphanie Binder or A. Lukyn Williams attempted to do by calling it an apologetic approach to evangelism.[113] The word "antipathy" is the polite word that should be utilized when it relates to Tertullian's basic feelings toward the Jewish people. Clark Williamson, despite his liberal and dual covenantal attitudes, states it correctly when he pens that "[T]he conflict between Judaism and Tertullian's Christ is strong, bitter, and profound."[114] It is bitter because Tertullian's supersessionistic tendencies cause him to reflect on the "superiority" of Christianity over the "ethnocentric" and displaced Judaism of his century.[115]

To describe Tertullian's approach in the most basic of ways would be as a baseball team who wins the World Series on the opponent's home field. Tertullian believed that Judaism was not only wrong but also evil, whether it was his view of them from the pages of Scripture or of a Carthaginian Jew who passed him on the street.[116] He believed that they were responsible solely for the death of Christ (deicide) and this can be illustrated from his own *Apology*: "Judea, whose God you Romans once honoured with victims, and its temple with gifts, and its people with treaties; and which would have never been beneath your scepter *but for that last and crowning offence*

---

offense; nor *peace*, except after war. Now, both the people (of Israel) by their transgression of His laws, and the whole race of mankind by their neglect of natural duty, had both sinned and rebelled against the Creator" (Tertullian, *Against Marcion*, book 5, chapter 5). See also Osborn, *Tertullian*, 114.

112. Davies, "Early Christian Attitudes toward Judaism and the Jews," 79.

113. Binder, "Jewish-Christian Contacts," 222–223 and Williams, *Adversus Judaeos*, 43.

114. Williamson, "Anti-Judaism in Process Christologies."

115. Williamson, "Anti-Judaism in Process Christologies."

116. Dunn, *Tertullian*, 51.

against God, in rejecting and crucifying Christ (–en)."[117] Such an attitude then made Jewish evangelism nearly impossible.[118]

Origen

Origen belongs in a patristic classification all to himself. He was a biblical allegorist. He was considered by many to be a heretic due to contradictory teachings regarding Jesus's divinity that would lead to charges of being a subordinationist and his official condemnation in 553.[119] He also influenced others in his allegorical approach to the Old Testament and, it can be argued, continues to impact how the Jewish people are viewed as the people of God even today. Interestingly enough, it could also be argued that Origen and Maimonides viewed the understanding of Scripture in a similar manner, albeit from a different perspective regarding the nature and person of Jesus of Nazareth.

Origen (c. 185–251/54) in many ways is the most famous of the Catechetical School of Alexandria exegetes. His legacy of being the son of the martyr Leonidas did not lead him away from faith in Jesus but more directly towards it until he encountered his own martyr's death in c. 251.[120] This desire towards a deeper faith with God and a salvific relationship with the Messiah Jesus of the gospel directly impacts his understanding of hermeneutics, regardless of the allegorical gymnastics he was forced to undertake.[121] Karlfried Froehlich describes Origen's understanding of exegesis in this manner: "Biblical hermeneutics [for Origen] presents the method for *anagōgē*, the ascent of the soul, which is at the heart of his soteriology."[122] This idea of "the ascent of the soul" fits naturally into what Christopher Hall saw as Origen's three-level understanding of the Bible.[123] He wanted people to go beyond the basic to the advanced level so they would achieve perfection and thereby receiving the "higher spiritual truths."[124] Ironically,

---

117. Tertullian, *Apology*, chapter 26. See also Tertullian, *Answer to the Jews*, chapter 8, when he wrote the following: "Accordingly, *all the synagogue of Israel did slay Him*, saying to Pilate, when he was desirous to dismiss him, 'His blood be upon us, and upon our children; . . .'"

118. Davies, "Early Christian Attitudes towards Jews and Judaism," 79.

119. Litfin, *Getting to Know the Church Fathers*, 157–58.

120. Kannengiesser, *Handbook of Patristic Exegesis*, 536, 539.

121. Amirav, "Christian Appropriation of the Jewish Scriptures," 42.

122. Froehlich, *Biblical Interpretation in the Early Church*, 18.

123. Hall, *Reading Scripture*, 144.

124. Stefaniw, "Reading Revelation," 233. See also Hall, *Reading Scripture*, 144.

this will become a Maimonidean hermeneutical argument in his approach to scriptural interpretation and one that will become commonplace in Jewish understanding today.

However, and regardless of the future kinship synergy that Origen and Maimonides might display in regards to hermeneutical strategy, Origen's own antipathy towards the Jewish people is prevalent. He was opposed to Jewish believers in Jesus maintaining any historical connection to their heritage, including the fasts.[125] Additionally, his hermeneutical approach to Hebrew Scriptures was so allegorical in interpretation that it stimulated the Jewish rabbis of his time and locale to fight Origen's attempt to find Jesus and the church in the Song of Songs.[126] Finally, this allegorical interpretation of Scripture allows for supersessionism to reign supreme as it relates to whether it is the "church" or the Jewish people that are the "chosen people" of God: "Those who are fully and truly sons of Abraham are sons of his actions (spiritually understood) and of the knowledge that was made manifest to him."[127] Origen took this allegory to the point that Deeana Klepper believed he saw the Jews as "Hagar thirsting in the desert . . . unable to drink the water of Scripture that was right in front of them."[128]

Augustine

The life of this Latin father and leading light of church history has so many nuances and twists that it could take away from the point of his influence and impact on Jewish-Christian relations for two millennia to focus on his life story. However, it would be remiss to not briefly note how his sojourn into Manichaeism and the impact of Ambrose played upon his perception of the physical descendants of Messiah Jesus.

What the Manichaean religion offered to a young Augustine were answers to questions that he felt he could not find in the Christianity of his day.[129] Specifically, Manichaeism looked at the world through a prism of darkness and light, evil and goodness, Satan and God. However, this religion did not look at these entities as separate concepts but as two sides of the same coin.

---

125. Demura, "Origen and the Exegetical Tradition," 66–70.

126. Kannengiesser, *Handbook of Patristic Exegesis*, 542, 551.

127. Bercot, *Dictionary of Early Christian Beliefs*, 565. The quotation is from Origen's *Commentary on the Gospel of John*.

128. Klepper, "Historicizing Allegory," 316.

129. O'Meara, *Young Augustine,* 47 and van Oort, "Manichaean Christians in Augustine's Life and Work," 507. See also Fredriksen, *Augustine and the Jews*, 108–12.

History reports of Augustine's gradual withdrawal from the cult of the Manichees—not because of a sudden realization of its error but because of a gradual understanding that while Manichaeism offered surface answers to life's questions, it did not answer the eternal ones.[130] However, until he encountered Ambrose,[131] the truth of the Christian faith was not his alternative to the errors of the Manichees, he subsisted with a sense of spiritual resignation.[132]

After his conversion, Augustine became an ardent critic of the religion he had once devoted a great deal of his young adult life to follow. However, it would be nothing more than short-sighted to not assume that Manichaeism influenced him in regards to Judaism and the Jewish people. The questions therefore become "to what extent?" and "positively or negatively?"

In the beginning days of Augustine's spiritual search, we find him struggling with the passages of the Old Testament which Maria Boulding states "repelled him."[133] This seeming repugnance at the "immoral" Old Testament fit in quite nicely with the Manichaean approach to the Hebrew Scriptures.[134] It appears that Manichaeism suffered from an almost bipolar existence which vacillated between self-hatred and thinly veiled absorption. Manichaeism rejected much of the New Testament because of what it saw as Jewish self-interest in the pages,[135] while rejecting the Old Testament because of the fulfillment of the New Testament.[136] However, Manichaeism also included Jewish apocalyptic sensibility in its teachings as well.[137]

Therefore, a position could be made that Ambrose's allegorical interpretation of Hebrew Scriptures was Augustine's antidote to Manichaeism. Ambrose's influence and leading of Augustine towards a real profession of

---

130. O'Meara, *Young Augustine*, 87–106.

131. Fredriksen, *Augustine and the Jews*, 122–25. See also Augustine, *Confessions*, 6.4.6–5.7.

132. Augustine, *Confessions*, 5.10.18.

133. Boulding, "Introduction," 16.

134. O'Meara, *Young Augustine*, 52, 53; Brown, *Augustine of Hippo*, 38–39; and Gruenwald, "Manichaeism and Judaism," 30.

135. O'Meara, *Young Augustine*, 54.

136. Hebblethwaite, "St. Augustine's Interpretation of Matthew 5, 17," 511, and Ferrari, "Isaiah and the Early Augustine," 742. The bipolar nature of Manichaean thought I propose is answered by the question that John Reeves of Winthrop College attempts to answer as to whether Mani was at one time attracted to and/or involved in the Jewish-Christian sect known as the Elchasai. There is no definitive answer to the question but it is an intriguing thought, as well as perhaps answering some of Augustine's antipathy. See Reeves, "'Elchasite' Sanhedrin of the Cologne Mani Codex," 68–91.

137. Gruenwald, "Manichaeism and Judaism," 34–36, 41–45.

faith in Jesus certainly places Ambrose's teaching, both good and bad, in the highest of esteem for Augustine.[138]

Consequently, and because of Ambrose's influence, Augustine developed and refined his eventual "Jewish Witness" to a theology that will hold sway for more than a millennia and is still prevalent in some circles today. For regardless of how well-intentioned Augustine wanted to be with this theology of the spiritual and familial outcome of the Jewish people, we can see its outcome in that "the gospel has been interpreted in the context of human religiosity more or less foreign to the theological idiom of the Bible.... [T]he gospel has been contextualized one-sidedly in the realm of the personal and private."[139]

For example, the story of Cain and Abel has long fascinated the readers of Scripture. However, for Augustine the story of Cain and Abel told a different story, a story which allegorized the Jewish people into the role of Cain and the church as the sympathetic and innocent Abel.[140]

> As Cain's sacrifice of the fruit of the ground is rejected, while Abel's sacrifice of his sheep and the fat thereof is accepted, so the faith of the New Testament praising God in the harmless service of grace is preferred to the earthly observances of the Old Testament. For though the Jews were right in practicing these things, they were guilty of unbelief in not distinguishing the time of the New Testament when Christ came, from the time of the Old Testament.[141]

We can also find that Augustine perhaps utilizes the Cain and Abel story as a precursor to his ultimate concept of "Jewish Witness." For in his reply to Faustus, the reader can see the germination of the idea that the Jewish people are present with a mark of Cain that protects them from destruction but enables the "children of Abel" to be able to identify them.

> It is a most notable fact, that all the nations subjugated by Rome adopted the heathenish ceremonies of the Roman worship; while the Jewish nation, whether under Pagan or Christian monarchs, has never lost the sign of their law, by which they are distinguished from all other nations and peoples. No emperor or monarch who finds under his government the people with this mark kills them, that is, makes them cease to be Jews, and

138. Carroll, *Constantine's Sword*, 200–201.
139. Soulen, *God of Israel and Christian Theology*, 17.
140. Brown, *Augustine of Hippo*, 320, and Benjamin, "Augustine on Cain and Abel," 130–33. See also Fredriksen, "Augustine and Israel," 126–27.
141. Augustine, "Reply to Faustus, the Manichean," 29.

as Jews to be separate in their observances, and unlike the rest of the world. Only when a Jew comes over to Christ, he is no longer Cain, nor goes out from the presence of God, nor dwells in the land of Nod, which is said to mean commotion.[142]

Paula Fredriksen in *Augustine and the Jews* affirms this position when she summarizes Augustine's concept of Cain symbolizing the Jewish people, "Without the visibility of their ancestral practices to identify them, Jews could not be of service to the church."[143] Ultimately, and in a different piece on the ministry and theology of the church father, Fredriksen places Augustine's point as being that the Jewish rejection of Jesus was not a simple case of "deicide" but instead "an elaborate ecclesial metaphor."[144]

However, and compared to other patristics and their relationship to the Jewish people of their times, Augustine comes across as an enlightened and quasi-evangelistic theologian. From chapter 10 of his *Adversus Judaeos* we see these closing thoughts:

> Dearly beloved, whether these divine testimonies with joy or with indignation, nevertheless, when we can, let us proclaim them with great love for the Jews. Let us not proudly glory against the broken branches; let us rather reflect by whose grace it is, and by much mercy on what root, we have been grafted. Then, not savoring of pride, but with a deep sense of humility, not insulting with presumption, but rejoicing with trembling, let us say: "Come ye and let us walk in the light of the Lord," because His "name is great among the Gentiles."[145]

On the surface, one should find little to argue with Augustine in this point. However, the point is that by reducing biblical Judaism and the Old Testament to a mere "opening act" for Jesus,[146] we have created a hermeneutical Jewish straw man that can serve both as a metaphorical punching bag for rejecting Jesus and a people group to be most pitied. Therefore, the question must be asked: was not Augustine's call for never-ending and difficult perse-

---

142. Augustine, "Reply to Faustus, the Manichean," 31.

143. Fredriksen, *Augustine and the Jews*, 319 (see also 271–73).

144. Fredriksen, "Excaecati Occulta Justitia Dei," 315. Fredriksen praises Augustine's usage and approach to utilizing Cain as a metaphor and notes that unlike other church fathers, Augustine did not turn this into anti-Jewish hatred.

145. Augustine, "In Answer to the Jews," 10.15. Interestingly enough, Augustine's "evangelistic" admonition for the Jewish people and the pagans of the Roman empire, while not as compassionate as noted above, continues in other sermons. Augustine, "Sermon 56," 92.

146. Williamson, "'Adversus Judaeos' Tradition in Christian Theology," 291.

verance throughout time a greater punishment than a quick, even painful, death? For in *The City of God*, it is found:

> Therefore God has shown the Church in her enemies the Jews the grace of His compassion, since, as saith the apostle, 'their offence is the salvation of the Gentiles.' And therefore He has not slain them, that is, He has not let the knowledge that they are Jews be lost in them, although they have been conquered by the Romans, lest they should forget the law of God, and their testimony should be of no avail in this matter of which we treat. But it was not enough that he should say, "Slay them not, lest they should at last forget Thy law," unless he had also added, "Disperse them;" because if they had only been in their own land with that testimony of the Scriptures, and not every where, certainly the Church which is everywhere could not have had them as witnesses among all nations to the prophecies which were sent before concerning Christ.[147]

Jeremy Cohen describes "this compliment" of the "Jewish Witness" in Augustine's eyes as being "recipients of divine blessing as well."[148] Cohen also notes that Augustine argued that the persistence of the Jewish survival and scattering is unique proof of the church's replacement and new title of "True Israel."[149] Augustine was in fact more merciful in his regards for their continued survival. He was also more, and perhaps this word is too strong, sadistic by condemning them to a lifetime of suffering and never-ending eternal damnation.

Jerome

Jerome exemplifies the term ambiguity throughout his life but never more than as it relates to his early days in Stridon, Dalmatia, when he was born to nominally observant Christian parents with dates ranging anywhere from 331 to 347.[150] After coming to faith, he attempted unsuccessfully to live the life of an ascetic;[151] however, he found his fulfillment as a monastic

---

147. Augustine, *City of God* 18:46.
148. Cohen, *Living Letters of the Law*, 32, 39. Adam Kirsch in the online e-zine, *Tablet*, writes a response to this concept, "With defenders like these, the Jewish reader might feel, who needs attackers" (Kirsch, "True Confessions").
149. Cohen, *Living Letters of the Law*, 33.
150. Rebenich, *Jerome*, 4–5 and Kelly, *Jerome*, 1–3, 337–39.
151. Kelly, *Jerome*, 47.

clergy who devoted himself to writing and translating commentaries and the Word of God.

In 392, he published *Lives of Famous Men,* an encylopedia which is remarkable for his daring at the time to include Jewish men.[152] However, it was not this controversy but his decision to include rabbinic sources, commentaries, and advice into his writings of commentaries and translation of Scripture that created the most drama.[153] He was in many ways not only a rebel but also an immensely difficult man who demanded loyalty but wavered in his loyalty toward others if the situation proved itself too difficult.[154] Jerome died c. AD 420, leaving behind a mixed legacy and the Vulgate, which truly changed the Christian world.[155]

Jerome was one of the few Christian theologians of his time who was unafraid to approach Jewish rabbis for assistance in understanding the Hebrew Scriptures (i.e., the Old Testament).[156] It was as Michael Graves describes a part of his "method of interpretation" that was necessary "to uncover the meaning of the text *ad litteram* or *iuxta historiam*."[157] Jerome procured the services of rabbis to teach him the language of the Hebrew Scriptures.[158]

His Hebraic ability, due in large part to his rabbinical teachers, rose to the point that he was able to write what Stefan Rebenich considered a quite remarkable work entitled *Hebrew Questions.*[159] However, this acclaim from some did not come without the recriminations of others, especially as it relates to the Vulgate. Most scholars, including Augustine, were content with the continued utilization of the Septuagint (the old Latin Bible) and

---

152. Rebenich, *Jerome,* 42 and Kelly, *Jerome,* 65.

153. Lössl, "Shift in Patristic Exegesis," 163–64.

154. Kelly, *Jerome,* 51, 243–58.

155. Kelly, *Jerome,* 331 and Rebenich, *Jerome,* 59.

156. Kelly, *Jerome,* 84. Kelly recounts the time when Jerome abandoned the opportunity to answer questions from Pope Damasus "to transcribe" works in Hebrew from a nearby synagogue.

157. Graves, "'Judaizing' Christian Interpretations of the Prophets," 144–46. Graves utilizes for this point an article by A. Vaccari that is unfortunately in Italian and not accessed by me. See also Simon, *Verus Israel,* 154, 185 and Rebenich, "Jerome," 57–58.

158. Kitchin, "Literary Influence of St. Jerome," 168–69; Kelly, *Jerome,* 134; and Simon, *Verus Israel,* 185. Kitchin interestingly enough creates a spotlight on the amount of money that Jerome had to pay for the lessons and the fact that the rabbis would only come at night. In today's world, most would consider that unnecessary information and with a tinge of anti-Jewish bias. However, Kitchin wrote in a different time and the pre-Holocaust world of 1921.

159. Rebenich, *Jerome,* 93.

believed any translation which involved Hebrew was inviting theological problems.[160]

The accusations of "Judaizer" were lobbed at Jerome throughout the biblical translation process. Jerome responded in two unique ways:

1. taking on an almost self-defensive stance by accusing others of Judaizing themselves[161] or

2. arguing with the bishop of Hippo, who defended as a privilege the right of Jewish Christians to continue the practice of their Hebrew heritage.[162]

A third approach was one that typifies Jerome's personality—he went on the attack.[163]

The work on the Vulgate began around AD 390[164] after he became convinced that the Hebrew version of the Tanakh was more accurate than the Greek Septuagint. He notes in his own preface to the *Vulgate* that the Greek translators amended some passages so as not to draw the ire and eye of Ptolemy that would allow for the presence of Christophanies in the Hebrew Scriptures.[165] There is more than just cause to disagree with Jerome's defense mechanism or to note if correct that the translators must have overlooked other possible Christophanic moments. However, Jerome did have a viable reason for the translation: one must always go back to the original text in order to discern the original meaning.

Joel Itzkowitz has asked a probative question as it relates to the core of Jerome's heart and theological mind—"how can the Jews, the people to whom God first spoke, the keepers of the Hebrew Bible, be cut off from the new dispensation, while at the same time still be of surpassing interest to him?[166] Itzkowitz asks another fundamental question regarding the life of Jerome—why or did Jerome care about the Jews? There are two probable

---

160. Simon, *Verus Israel*, 153. See also Augustine, "Letter XXVIII;" Augustine, "Letter LXXI;" and Jerome, "Letter LXXV," chapters 3–4, 13 and chapter 7, 22.

161. Graves, "'Judaizing' Christian Interpretations of the Prophets," 143.

162. Simon, *Verus Israel*, 93–94. See also Augustine, "Letter XXVIII," chapter 3, 3. It should be noted that Jerome's interpretation of the Galatians is incorrect while Augustine's is more closely and exegetically sound.

163. Jerome, "Preface to the *Book of Hebrew Questions*." Work is found in Rebenich, *Jerome*, 95–96. Rebenich apparently cites the 1868 translation by P. deLagarde or the translation of D. Vallarsi.

164. Rebenich, *Jerome*, 93 and Rebenich, "Vir Trilinguis' and the 'Hebrew Veritas,'" 52.

165. Jerome, "Preface to the Vulgate." See also Kelly, *Jerome*, 157.

166. Itzkowitz, "Jews, Indians, Phylacteries," 563.

answers to Itzkowitz's question as well as the core question of this section—was Jerome anti-Jewish in sentiment? The first answer can be found in his words and approaches towards the Jewish people. Jerome saw Judas as the representative symbol of Judaism but yet engaged their rabbis and scholars to help him learn the original text language.[167] He responds angrily to his contemporary Rufinus against charges that he regretted using Jewish materials and being influenced by their teachings;[168] yet, his commentaries of Old Testament books are filled with images identifying the Jewish people with wretchedness in Zephaniah, harlotry in 1 Kings, and being the true face of Edom in Obadiah.[169] However, the most honest answer to answering the question of whether Jerome was anti-Jewish can be found in his exchange with Augustine ("Letter LXXV") when he writes the following statements:

> If, however, there is for us no alternative but to receive the Jews into the Church, along with the usages prescribed by their law; if, in short, it shall be declared lawful for them to continue in the Churches of Christ what they have been accustomed to practice in the *synagogues of Satan*, I will tell you my opinion of the matter, they will not become Christians, *but they will make us Jews.*[170]

He adds, "I, on the contrary, shall maintain, and, though the world were to protest against my view, I may boldly declare that the Jewish ceremonies are to Christians both hurtful and *fatal*; and that whoever observes them, whether he be Jew or Gentile originally, *is cast into the pit of perdition.*"[171] And while it might be argued that Jerome was responding in his typical way of utilizing hyperbolic attacks in his communication with Augustine, it is difficult to make that argument when Jerome compares any attempt by Jewish believers to maintain their heritage through observing the ordinances as nothing more than being guilty of Ebionism.[172] In addition, his allegorical approaches to interpreting the books of the Tanakh as reflecting poorly on the Jewish people and the fact that he was—according to Kelly—an admirer of Tertullian (and by whom it could be rationally argued that he was

---

167. Simon, *Verus Israel*, 230–31. See also Newman, "Jerome's Judaizers," 444. Newman's specific point is that while Jerome threw around the term "Judaizer," it was his relationship with the Jewish people that could best be decribed as "Jew-friendly."

168. Jerome, *Apology against Rufinus*, book 2, 24. See also Kelly, *Jerome*, 253.

169. Kelly, *Jerome*, 166, 222, and 253.

170. Jerome, "Letter LXXV," chapter 4, 13 (emphasis added). See also Jacobs, "Forgiveness and Perfection," 261.

171. Jerome, "Letter LXXV," chapter 4, 14 (emphasis added).

172. Jerome, "Letter LXXV," chapter 4, 16.

influenced),[173] the argument of literary exaggeration is difficult to make. Some might argue that Jerome was not anti-Jewish in sentiment; however, it is hard to argue against that fact when his own commentary on Haggai argues that the synagogue has been replaced (i.e., supersessionism) by the church.[174] Perhaps it would be accurate to surmise that his relationship to the Jewish people is much like his relationship with everyone—difficult and uncertain.

John Chrysostom

The young man who will become praised as one of the great orators of Christian history and reviled in Jewish history for the words which he spoke had a rather inauspicious beginning when he was born in the middle of the fourth century. John Chrysostom was raised by a widowed Christian mother (Anthusa) after his Roman officer father was killed when John Chryststom was a baby.[175] His early educational efforts at rhetoric and plans to become a lawyer changed when he decided to adopt the life of a monastic, despite the opposition which came from his family.[176] He lived for several years as an ascetic before becoming a deacon and then priest and one of Diodore of Tarsus's foremost students (along with Theodore of Mopsuestia). He also became one of the leading voices of a more literal interpretation of Scripture via the School of Antioch.[177] Kannengiesser describes Chrysostom as having an "idealistic disposition [that] was permeated by his intense familiarity with scripture."[178] Ultimately, Chrysostom became the bishop of Constantinople and it is here that some of the more interesting aspects of his biography must be limited for the sake of space. However, it should be noted that he was exiled from his pastoral post and died in exile in September 407.[179]

---

173. Kelly, *Jerome*, 33.

174. Kelly, *Jerome*, 166.

175. Kannengiesser, *Handbook of Patristic Exegesis*, 783 and Hall, *Reading Scripture*, 93.

176. Thurén, "John Chrysostom as a Rhetorical Critic," 183 and Hall, *Reading Scripture*, 93.

177. Kannengiesser, *Handbook of Patristic Exegesis*, 783 and Froehlich, *Biblical Interpretation in the Early Church*, 19.

178. Kannengiesser, *Handbook of Patristic Exegesis*, 783.

179. Hall, *Reading Scripture*, 96 and Kannengiesser, *Handbook of Patristic Exegesis*, 783.

What is essential as it relates to the life of the "Golden Mouth" of John Chrysostom are the words which relate to the Jewish people and their relationship with God. Most of the surviving homilies that are available for inspection today are from his days in Antioch and do indicate his Antiochene exegetical view; however, they also indicate something more profound and ominous as well.[180] From Chrysostom's *Adversus Judaeos*, one can analyze two statements for both their anti-Jewish comments as well as their supersessionistic contents. The first provides evidence of the continuing argument that the Jews are not simply complicit in the death of Jesus but that this act has cast them into the realm of Satan worshipers: "If, then, the Jews fail to know the Father, if they crucified the Son, if they thrust off the help of the Spirit, who should not make bold to declare plainly that the synagogue is a dwelling of demons? God is not worshipped there. Heaven forbid! From now on it remains a place of idolatry."[181] The second statement of the future bishop of Constantinople is not only anti-Jewish in its denigration of the people but also disparages feasts that were commanded in Lev 23, for Chrysostom saw them as both unnecessary and replaced by Christianity[182]:

> The festivals of the pitiful and miserable Jews are soon to march upon us one after the other and in quick succession: the feast of Trumpets, the feast of Tabernacles, the fasts ... Yet some of these are going to watch the festivals and others will join the Jews in keeping their feasts and observing their fasts. I wish to drive this perverse custom from the Church right now.[183]

Marvin Wilson has sought to redeem Chrysostom to a point by arguing that the pastor was seeking to fight against the Judaizers that were seeking to infiltrate his congregation[184]—and perhaps there is a certain amount of leeway that should be granted to the fourth-century pastor from our twenty-first century perspective. However, as Daniel Cohn-Sherbok correctly

---

180. Kannengiesser, *Handbook of Patristic Exegesis*, 784–87.

181. John Chrysostom, "On the Jews," Homily III.

182. Ben Ezra, "'Christians' Observing 'Jewish' Festivals of Autumn," 67 and Simon, *Verus Israel*, 217–23. Simon acknowledges that a portion of Chrysostom's invective is toward Judaizers; however, he still views the bishop's main focus of vitrolic language as towards the Jewish people themselves.

183. John Chrysostom, "On the Jews," Homily I.

184. Wilson, *Our Father Abraham*, 95. This same argument is held by Robert Wilken's work, *John Chrysostom and the Jews* (Wipf & Stock, 2004). And while both Wilson and Wilken could have a point to make as it relates to Chrysostom's rhetorical approach to the issue of Judaizers, later generations took the bishop's words seriously towards the Jewish people. See also Smelik, "John Chrysostom's Homilies against the Jews," 194–200.

points out, it is difficult for a Jewish audience to do so when their faith and heritage have been accused of sacrificing children for religious rituals (i.e., blood libels) by church fathers.¹⁸⁵ It is also difficult when John Chrysostom himself writes these words regarding the Jewish people:

> But the Jews neither know nor dream of these things. They live for their bellies, they gape for the things of this world, their condition is not better than that of pigs or goats because of their wanton ways and excessive gluttony. They know but one thing: to fill their bellies and be drunk, to get all cut and bruised, to be hurt and wounded while fighting for their favorite charioteers.¹⁸⁶

RISE OF THE DARK AGES AND EXPULSIONS (C. 500 TO 1290)

As Augustine witnessed the fall of Rome to the Visigoths, the medieval period began. A period of political, theological and social confusion abounded in all parts of Europe. Intellectual darkness in many ways reigned supreme and theological superstition was the norm and not the exception of the day. These experiences of confusion, darkness, and superstition did not encompass all members of society, as sparks of intellectual brightness flickered across monasteries to the people in the Jewish enclaves. However, one question was still predominant in many minds—who had the right to claim sonship as the "Chosen People of God"? The people to whom it was first given or the people to whom now claimed the right, the Roman Catholic church?¹⁸⁷ I could argue that much that will occur religiously and socially in this period will truly revolve around that very question.

Formulation of Catholic Dogma in Regards to Judaism

Michael Frassetto overstates the argument when he says that the Jews of the medieval period were "defined as the diabolical enemy of Christendom and associated with heretics, witches, the minions of Antichrist, and the

---

185. Cohn-Sherbok, *Paradox of Anti-Semitism*, 152.

186. John Chrysostom, "On the Jews," Homily IV.

187. Berger, "Roots of Anti-Semitism," 5. Berger notes the arguments that others have made, including Robert Chazan in the inter-familial dialogue found in the Gospels but notes that the medieval period took it a step further with this observation: "But Christianity reached outside the Jewish faith, and internal criticism was transformed into external condemnation." See also Chazan, "Medieval Anti-Semitism," 53.

devil."[188] However, within this period the church established a pattern of assumptions and presumptions regarding the Jewish people that follows them to this day, as well as enables the Jewish people themselves to develop a defense mechanism and a philosophical leader, Maimonides, to defend their theological moorings and values. This establishment of theological moorings and values will prevent them from seeing the truth of the Messiahship of Jesus.

For it was in the medieval period that codification of the view that the Jewish people were solely responsible for the death of Jesus (i.e., deicide) was affirmed.[189] Indeed, even the sympathetic Bernard of Clairvaux viewed the medieval Jews as guilty of deicide, even if he did not want them severely punished for their crime.[190] It was also in this period that the Catholic dogma of deicide was fleshed out for the masses in the form of "Passion Plays": frescoes, icons, and stained glass windows which depict the Jewish people as responsible for the death of Jesus, regardless of Jesus's own testimony in John 10:18.[191]

However, it was not only the Catholic dogma of deicide that the church established in this period. Fears such as the outlandish, imaginary "Jewish-Mongol Plot of 1241" that Sophia Menache described, encouraged Christians and the church to establish both eschatological demarcations and possible identifying badges for the Jewish people of Europe.[192] The badge of identification established by the Fourth Lateran Council of 1215 was one such means of identification, separation, and isolation for the Jewish people, all established as a dogma of the Roman Catholic Church.[193] Similar badges will reappear in Europe in the 1940s for a far more sinister purpose.

Medieval Papal Attitudes toward the Jewish People

The popes of the medieval period cast a long shadow on the lives of the Jewish people, from often choosing their livelihood to the daily existence

---

188. Frassetto, "Heretics and Jews in the Writings of Ademar," 1–2.

189. Cohen, "Robert Chazan's 'Medieval Anti-Semitism,'" 68–71; Mégier, "Jewish Converts in the Early Church," 6–7; Chazan, "Medieval Anti-Semitism," 53; and Frassetto, " Heretics and Jews in the Writings of Ademar," 3.

190. Kroemer, "Vanquish the Haughty and Spare the Subjected," 56, 58–59, 62.

191. Epstein, "Frescoes of the Mavriotissa Monastery near Kastoria," 26–28 and Bale, "Christian Anti-Semitism," 24–26.

192. Menache, "Tartars, Jews, Saracens," 319–42.

193. Cohen, *Under Crescent and Cross*, 38–40; Telushkin, *Jewish Literacy*, 185–86; and Chazan, "Medieval Anti-Semitism," 60–61.

of their very lives. Rebecca Rist notes that while many followed both the Augustinian "Jewish Witness" and the Theodosian Code of the fifth century which promised them the protection of life, each pope varied in the approach he might take in regards to the quality of their lives.[194] The most positive papacy towards the Jewish people is interestingly led by one that has been given the title, "the Great," Gregory (590–604). Gregory opposed forced conversion of the Jewish people and sought to win the Jewish people to Jesus by means of persuasion and apologetics.[195] And while D. N. Makuja might argue that Gregory's largesse was perhaps because of his interest in speeding up the eschaton, nevertheless, his papal decrees regarding providing compensation to Jewish individuals for lost and/or seized property is not something that will necessarily be seen in other papacies.[196]

There were other "good" popes towards the Jewish people during the medieval period. For example, Calixtus II (1119–1124) confirmed the Gregorian codicil of the Theodosian Code of fair treatment towards the Jewish people.[197] However, many of the popes either displayed an attitude of apathy or antipathy towards the first people of "The Book." Two examples of "bad" popes as it relates to Jewish-Christian relations are Innocent III (1198–1216) and Gregory IX (c. 1127–1241). Each of these popes played a role in establishing a demarcated dividing line between reconciling the Jewish people to the Jewish Messiah.

Innocent III is known not only for the decision of the Fourth Lateran Council (1215) in which European Jews were required to wear yellow badges to delineate them from the rest of society but also for allowing, via the *Sicut Judaeis*, for Jews to be attacked if they were even suspected of verbally denigrating Christianity.[198] He acknowledged Augustine's call for personal protection; however, he also followed Augustine's Sarah/Hagar typology and believed that Jews should live in a subservient position.[199] Gregory IX took the antipathy towards Judaism one step further and called for the burning of the Talmud and other Jewish extra-biblical sources following accusations made by Jewish believer Nicholas Donin against his own Jewish countrymen (c. 1239).[200] Each event and occurrence was seemingly isolated

---

194. Rist, "Through Jewish Eyes," 643.

195. Makuja, "Gregory the Great, Roman Law and the Jews," 36; Cohen, *Under Crescent and Cross*, 36; and Berger, "Roots of Anti-Semitism in Medieval Visual Imagery," 8.

196. Makuja, "Gregory the Great, Roman Law and the Jews," 53–56, 61–63.

197. Berger, "Roots of Anti-Semitism in Medieval Visual Imagery," 16.

198. Berger, "Roots of Anti-Semitism in Medieval Visual Imagery," 16.

199. Klepper, "Historicizing Allegory," 309–10.

200. Grayzel, "Talmud and the Medieval Papacy," 224–27; Rose, "When was the Talmud Burnt at Paris,?" 325–28, 336–39; Rist, "Through Jewish Eyes," 647–48; and

in many ways; however, they built upon a legacy of antipathy between the Christian church and its Jewish roots even to this day.

Crusades and the Jewish People

In this already brief summary of almost eight hundred years of Jewish-Christian history, only a few words can be allotted to the blood-soaked era known as the Crusades. A period often romanticized and mythologized by those outside of Judaism, the Crusades are a time of sorrow and lamentation for those who call Abraham the father of their faith. It is a time of loss and grief often directed toward the physical descendants of Jesus by those who carried the flag and cross of the Messiah as their clarion validation for their actions.[201]

It is known that in 1095, Pope Urban II called for the Christians of Europe to reclaim the Holy Land from the Muslim pagans. This sermon by Urban II began a series of Crusades of individuals leaving the relative security of a darkened Europe to travel to the mysterious East to liberate a land they had only heard about in homilies and seen on stained-glass windows.[202] However, it was what happened during the Crusaders' travels to Palestine that is often undiscovered unless one opens the pages of musty historical tomes. For it was the murder of Western European Jews that has left an indelible stain on the spiritual hearts of Jewish people that not even a millennia can erase.[203]

While one may argue with Norman Roth that French Jews were left unscathed by the First Crusade, French Jews were most definitely touched by the massacres as seen by the efforts of sanctuary by such clerics as Bernard of Clairvaux.[204] However, it was the Jews of Germany who experienced wrath from Crusaders determined to both liberate Jerusalem and massacre

---

Berger, "Roots of Anti-Semitism in Medieval Visual Imagery," 21, 23–24.

201. See Telushkin, *Jewish Literacy*, 183–84. While the above sentences were written from my own hand, it should be acknowledged that my common knowledge of this concept comes from reading diaries and Jewish evaluations of the period such as from Telushkin who writes, "For more Jews, the word 'Crusades' has two very different associations: murder and forced baptism."

202. Shepkaru, "Preaching of the First Crusade," 93–94 and Telushkin, *Jewish Literacy*, 183–84.

203. Much more could be written about this period than even a hundred books could contain. Therefore, it is my decision to simply highlight key points of loss and consequence of this period with appropriate documentation as necessary.

204. Berger, "Roots of Anti-Semitism in Medieval Visual Imagery," 13–14 and Kroemer, "Vanquish the Haughty and Spare the Subjected," 62.

the Diaspora of Zion while on their journey.²⁰⁵ Many German Jews chose the path of martyrdom (i.e., suicide) while others chose the path of least resistance, a forced conversion that had little impact on their eternal soul.²⁰⁶ "The Chronicles of Solomon Bar Simson" provide a detailed report of martyrdom and false conversions that were "reversed" as soon as possible or as the narrator puts it "until the day of indignation passed."²⁰⁷

Therefore, due to the ultimate failure of the Crusades, one may ask: what was ultimately accomplished by these failed raids of the Holy Land and pogroms of European Jewry? Did it accomplish some need for "blood lust" of vengeance for the death of Jesus as Shmuel Shepkaru hypothesizes?²⁰⁸ Or, was it for some misguided attempt at evangelism as proposed by David Berger?²⁰⁹ The only thing accomplished was apparently more death. As Susan Weingarten reports, it was following the Crusader period that the urban legends of blood libels (Jewish communities killing Christian children for their blood to be used in rituals) began, which only led to more killing of European Jews by Christians.²¹⁰

Early Inquisitions and Jewish-Christian Disputations

While Cullen Murphy is correct that the earliest Inquisition by Gregory IX was directed towards the Cathars of France in 1231, the word itself stirs the imagination of abuse and misuse towards European Jewry for a great portion of the medieval period.²¹¹ Therefore, a Jewish approach to protecting rabbinic Judaism from the natural temptation of a quasi-conversion or a self-defeating martyrdom was often to engage in polemical apologetics and disputations with the Catholic Church that was seeking what rabbinic Judaism perceived to be its destruction.²¹² As will be illustrated in later chapters,

---

205. Rubenstein, *Armies of Heaven*, 49–53; and Kroemer, "Vanquish the Haughty and the Spare the Subjected," 67–72.

206. Telushkin, *Jewish Literacy*, 184 and Rubenstein, *Armies of Heaven*, 49–53.

207. "The Chronicle of Solomon bar Simson," 67–68.

208. Shepkaru, "Preaching of the First Crusade," 105–6, 110, 117–18, 121, 123, 127–28.

209. Berger, "Mission to the Jews," 577.

210. Weingarten, "'In Thy Blood Live,'" 2–3.

211. Murphy, *God's Jury*, 8–9.

212. Lasker, "Jewish Critique of Christianity," 121, 123–24. Berger in "Mission to the Jews," 579–85, notes that some Christian scholars were reticent to engage in polemical arguments with scholars but that they were an exception to the rule and sometimes their reticence was because, as in the case of Adam of Perseigne, they believed Jews turning to Jesus was "reserved for the *eschaton*."

Maimonides was such an individual; however, it is David Blumenthal who provides a modern explanation for the medieval Jewish rationale:

> The true meaning of the sacred texts was up for discussion. The true path to God and Torah was at issue. Often the coherence of the Jewish community—religiously and socially—was a major concern. In the interfaith disputations, the very existence and safety of the community was frequently at stake. And so was God's honor, and Israel's. The intellectual had no choice but to respond. It was his sacred duty.[213]

Two of the most well-known apologetic Jewish polemics, outside of the time period known by Maimonidean thought and philosophy, were written by Rabbi David Kimhi (*Sefer ha-Brit*) and Rabbi Judah Loew who sought particularly to negate Christian interpretation of messianic prophecies from the Hebrew Scriptures such as Ps 22 and Gen 49:10.[214]

And it was from these works that the most well-known disputations such as in Paris (c. 1240s) and Barcelona (1263) were based, as well as the lesser known Ceuta Disputation (1179) in North Africa.[215] Often the disputations engaged the thoughts and arguments of leading Jewish scholars such as Nachmanides and Jewish believers in Jesus such as Paul Christiani (Barcelona).[216] The decision of the debates were often pre-set, as the judges were Catholic kings and/or Catholic bishops; however, the purpose was not truly for evangelism but ultimately for triumphalism on the one hand and survival on the other. Therefore, little was accomplished but further separation between the church and its Jewish roots.

---

213. Blumenthal, "Religion and the Religious Intellectuals," 126. Blumenthal also provides an excellent description of his understanding of the Jewish intellectual during the medieval period that notes the isolation of such individuals as well as the necessity of such men to be "autodidactic" in all areas of life (119).

214. Bokser, "Religious Polemics in Biblical and Talmudic Exegesis," 710–13 and Berger, "Christian Heresy and Jewish Polemic," 289. See also Trautner-Kromann, "Jewish Polemics Against Christianity," 640–41, which notes that the works of Jacob ben Rueben (c. 1170) and Joseph Hamekane (c. 1270) were particularly acerbic in tone and posture. They are also mentioned by Berger (290–91, 293, 297).

215. Stemberger, "Elements of Biblical Interpretation," 579–80 and Soifer, "'You Say that the Messiah Has Come . . .,'" 288, 293, 296.

216. Roos, "Paul Christian," 50–51, 56; Stemberger, "Elements of Biblical Interpretation," 580–81; and Telushkin, *Jewish Literacy*, 187–89.

Jewish Expulsions in Medieval Europe

There is an adage in Judaism that states, "Someone tried to kill us, God saved us, let's eat." The Jewish people were accustomed from the Babylonian Diaspora onward to trials, calamities, and expulsions. Therefore, the expulsions from various areas and countries of Europe during the medieval period was not necessarily new; however, the tinge of religious and economic prejudice that these expulsions took on was what could only be described as somewhat new and unusual.

In France, expulsions began in various regions of the country beginning as early as the ninth century by the archbishop of Sens.[217] In 1182, King Philip II expelled Jews from the Bourges-en-Berry region of France for financial benefits to his coffers.[218] His actions encouraged other French fiefdoms to follow suit with Jewish expulsion for financial gain throughout the thirteenth century.[219] So even though there had been a French Jewish presence since at least the fourth century in Gaul, financial benefits cast them from the land in a matter of days.[220]

The evidence of a German Jewish presence in medieval times is obvious by not only the calls for expulsion by the archbishop of Mainz in the middle of the tenth century and their actual expulsion from the city in 1012, but also by the discovery of *Responsa* (a rabbinical document providing a halakhic evaluation of the Torah) on whether Jewish merchants could sell to Germans on Christian holidays.[221] However, it is the 1290 expulsion from England that is the most well-known and most infamous, as it combined both religious and financial rationales in the choice to dispel a people who had become accustomed to expulsion.[222]

Cecil Roth reports that as early as the Crusades, Richard the Lionheart sought the personal services of Maimonides which validates an influential Jewish presence on the British Isles as early as the recognized date of 1066.[223] However, Gabriel Sivan argues for an even earlier date for Jewish

---

217. Roth, "Bishops and Jews in the Middle Ages."

218. Jennings, "Cathedral of Bourges," 3 and Jordan, "Jews, Regalian Rights, and the Constitution in Medieval France," 2.

219. Jordan, "Jews, Regalian Rights, and the Constitution in Medieval France," 2.

220. Handley, "'This Stone Shall Be a Witness,'" 240–41, 243–44.

221. Ta-Shma, "Judeo-Christian Commerce," 11–22 and Roth, "Bishops and Jews in the Middle Ages."

222. Brown and McCartney, "Living in Limbo," 169 and Telushkin, *Jewish Literacy*, 189–90.

223. Roth, "Maimonides and England," 209; Mundill, "Out of the Shadow and into the Light," 572; and Stacey, "Crusades, Martyrdoms, and the Jews of Norman England," 235.

immigration to England, even if their total population never grew to more than 10,000 by the time of their expulsion in 1290.[224] Regardless of the exact settlement date of British Jews in medieval times, the presence of multiple synagogues throughout England indicate a communal presence that was strong and "tight-knit."[225]

Therefore, the blood libel accusation after the death of William of Norwich in 1144 and the subsequent accusations created an environment of danger for the Jewish people that was unaccustomed to British Jews.[226] However, the power of greed also created a financial danger for the Jewish people, for by 1290 the influence they had once extended as moneylenders had evaporated. Their presence was no longer necessary and Edward I ordered their expulsion.[227] This was an expulsion that was to last for almost four hundred years until they were allowed to return under the auspices of Oliver Cromwell in the 1650s.[228]

CHAPTER SUMMATION

Any attempt to cover thirteen hundred years of Jewish-Christian history in one chapter will by necessity leave some events covered in a summary fashion.[229] However, the importance of this summary cannot be overlooked as it relates to the overall focus of this book. The background that estab-

224. Sivan, "Hymns of the Isles," 326.

225. Hillaby, "Beth Miqdash Me'at," 183, 186, 188–91, 194. Hillaby provides in the article a complete list of not only synagogues but also examples of expulsion lists from these houses of worship.

226. Menache, "Faith, Myth, and Politics," 353–54. Menache provides a detailed list of further blood libel accusations beyond the more well-known Norwich case including one in Northampton in 1279, just eleven years before the actual expulsion order. See also Rokéah, "State, the Church, and the Jews in Medieval England," 106–11. Unfortunately, space prevents a complete detailing of the William of Norwich blood libel accusation; however, the following sources can provide a thorough examination of the case including the lack of any evidence to accuse any Jewish individual much less the Jewish community of Norwich for the death of the young boy: Cohen, "Flow of Blood in Medieval Norwich," 41–46, 64–65; Weissberger, "Motherhood and Ritual Murder," 7; and Rokéah, "State, the Church, and the Jews in Medieval England," 104–6.

227. Barnett, "Edward I and the Expulsion of the Jews," 224–25, 229, 235 and Brown and McCartney, "Living in Limbo," 170–71.

228. Telushkin, *Jewish Literacy*, 190.

229. Schaff, *History of the Christian Church*, 442–57. The reason for this footnote placement is that even while Schaff laments the treatment of the Jewish people during this period, he also seeks to provide some sense of rationale and/or justification for it. Schaff writes, "Some explanation is afforded by the conduct of the Jews themselves." He then goes on to fall into the basest of stereotypical traps regarding Jews and wealth, etc.

lished Maimonides as a Jewish philosopher, scholar, and theologian would not have been possible without the millennia of Jewish-Christian history that proceeded him. The antipathy of gentiles that bubbled to the surface after the death of the disciples towards the Jewish people who still resisted the gospel, the overt animosity of some of the patristic leaders towards rabbinic Judaism, and the urban legends and hostility of the medieval period all created an environ in which the Sephardic scholar was allowed to create a Judaism that was designed around the construct of negation and separation from the God of Israel.

3

Moses Maimonides the Man (1135/38–1204)

As I stood under the oppressive sun of an Andalusian Spanish summer in 2015, it was not difficult to imagine a young Jewish boy running the streets of the Jewish section of Cordoba towards home and his daily rabbinical studies with his father and teacher.[1] I could imagine him running past the Mezquita de Córdoba, one of the great mosques of twelfth-century Sephardic Spain, which runs parallel to the Jewish Quarter. I could imagine him seeing the opulence that was Islamic Spain while running to the more simple life of Jewish Spain. The boy's name in actuality was Moshe ben Maimon, and the real world would eventually know him by other names as well, such as Rambam or more commonly Maimonides.[2] Eventually, albeit not without a great deal of early opposition, much of the real world of rabbinic Judaism would view him as the greatest leader of modern Judaism.[3]

---

1. Nuland, *Maimonides*, 30–33; Arbel, *Maimonides*, 15. See also Hoffman, *Wisdom of Maimonides*, 6. Arbel and Nuland conflict on the relationship between Maimonides and his father. Arbel presents an idealized portrait of the relationship while Nuland is perhaps more honest about the unique dynamic present between father and son. Nuland perhaps built his perception of the strained relationship between father and son from the work of A. Benisch, who wrote in a quite literary manner of the scholar's early years of being less than an admirable student in his nineteenth-century work. Benisch, *Two Lectures*, 2–4.

2. Telushkin, *Jewish Literacy*, 176. Rambam is an acronym for Rabbi Moshe ben Maimon.

3. Bokser, *Legacy of Maimonides*, 12.

This chapter will argue that the legacy that the very real Rambam created is one of both spiritual confusion and theological division between the "Mother Faith" of Judaism and its child, Christianity—confusion and division about perhaps the core issue of faith and the possibility of a personal relationship with God himself. As I stood there in the summer of 2015, I could not help but wonder—could the boy running home for Torah study imagine the legacy that lay before him?

FROM BIRTH IN CORDOBA TO EXPULSION FROM ANDALUSIA

Moshe ben Maimon was born c. March 1135/38 in Cordoba, Spain;[4] however, the legacy and history of Jews in Spain had long preceded this son of Sephardic (or Jews of the Mediterranean, Spanish, and Iberian worlds) Jewry. Indeed, some will attempt to date the arrival of Jews in Spain to the time of the Babylonian Diaspora (i.e., Obad 20) but most assuredly to the times of the Roman Diaspora.[5] Maimonides himself attempted to trace his family's lineage in the *Commentary on the Mishnah* back at least seven generations and, according to Kraemer, believed in the Obadiah 20 legend.[6] Consequently, perhaps the most thorough work on the subject appears to be done by Mariona Vernet Pons who believes the location of Obadiah 20 is Lydia, Sardis, but will acquiesce to the likelihood that Sephardic Jews lived in Spain as early as AD 70.[7] Martin Cohen describes the Jews of Spain as truly a phenomenon and notes that for most of the two millennia of the Common Era, the Sephardim outnumbered the Ashkenazi (German and

---

4. Sachar, *History of the Jews*, 178; Papademetriou, "Moses Maimonides' Doctrine of God," 306–7; Bokser, *Legacy of Maimonides*, 2; and Telushkin, *Jewish Literacy*, 175. Some of the preliminary biographical information was also completed in a paper I did during my MATh experience at Southwestern Baptist Theological Seminary; see Downey, "Maimonides' *Via Negativa*, 1, 3; see also van der Heide, "'Their Prophets and Fathers Misled Them,'" 35, which provides the anecdotal story that Maimonides was born on the fourteenth of Nisan (i.e., Passover) which will play an important role in the legacy of Rambam throughout time.

5. Nieman, "Sefarad," 128–32; Roth, "Jews in Spain at the Time of Maimonides," 1; Gray, "Diaspora of Israel and Judah in Obadiah v. 20," 53–59; and Cohen, "Sephardic Phenomenon," 3, 9–10. Cohen utilizes the New Testament texts as a source material when he writes, "By the middle of the first century, however, the Jews had apparently attained sufficient importance to induce Paul of Tarsus, who had been preaching his message to Jews in many other parts of the Greco-Roman world, to consider a visit to the Iberian Peninsula" (9).

6. Kraemer, "Moses Maimonides," 11 and Halbertal, *Maimonides*, 16.

7. Pons, "Origin of the Name Sepharad," 297–313 (esp. 310–11).

Eastern European Jews).[8] However, the question at hand is not the population statistics but the introductory and lasting influence the Jews of Spain have played on religious and philosophical thought, especially the influence of Maimonides.

The term "Convivencia" refers to the period in Spanish medieval history in which Christians, Jews, and Muslims lived in what was allegedly a time of peace and harmony.[9] The concept and utopian idealism of such a term is highly suspect as even Benjamin Gampel will acknowledge; however, he also notes that for Spanish Jewry the idea of attempting to live in relative harmony and not acrimony was the norm whether it be Roman pagans, Muslims, or Christians, dating at least back to the third century.[10] However, it was the triad of Muslim, Jewish, and Christian under the aegis of the Islamic Umayyads that allowed for the flowering of a Sephardic Jewish religion and culture in which the ancestral family of Maimonides found their place in Cordoba and Andalusia.[11] María Rosa Menocal describes this idealistic period as a time when the language of the synagogue Hebrew was allowed to breathe again even while Maimonides himself prayed in both Hebrew and Arabic, as both were available to him.[12] Ruth Birnbaum notes that for Jews in Spain, they experienced two unique features that would be unheard of throughout the rest of Europe. The first was freedom of travel and the second was living among Christians and Muslims and outside a ghetto-proper environment.[13]

However, this bastion of relative safety for both Spanish Christians and Jews changed when the Umayyads were overthrown by the Almohads at the conclusion of the eleventh century, with an approximate date given by Norman Roth of 1090, or approximately forty-five years before the birth of Rambam.[14] The Almohads invaded from North Africa and brought with them a more ascetic and observant brand of Islam that contravened with

8. Cohen, "Sephardic Phenomenon," 3–5.

9. Wolf, "*Convivencia* in Medieval Spain," 72 and Gampel, "Jews, Christians, and Muslims in Medieval Iberia," 11.

10. Gampel, "Jews, Christians, and Muslims in Medieval Iberia," 11–13.

11. Wolf, "*Convivencia* in Medieval Spain," 77–78; Cohen, *Under Crescent and Cross*, 52; and Gampel, "Jews, Christians, and Muslims in Medieval Iberia," 14–18. Both Cohen and Gampel note that the Muslims continued to view non-Muslims as *dhimmis* but also a "protected minority" as long as they did not seek to overthrow Islamic rule.

12. Menocal, *Ornament of the World*, 161.

13. Birnbaum, "Maimonides, Then and Now," 67. I would disagree with Birnbaum's idealistic assessment of the living situation as I have visited the Jewish Quarter of Cordoba; however, she is correct that it was not a ghetto in the strictest sense of the word.

14. Roth, "Jews in Spain at the Time of Maimonides," 15. See also Telushkin, *Jewish Literacy*, 174.

the Umayyad Islamic faith that was more tolerant of art, diverse faiths, and lifestyles.[15] Therefore, and anywhere between Maimonides's eighth and thirteenth year, the family followed the southern exile path to Morocco around 1150.[16] This was an exile that Ilil Arbel describes as lasting for Rambam the remaining years of his life.[17]

YEARS IN MOROCCO AND NORTH AFRICA

The years in Morocco and North Africa can be described in many ways for Maimonides as his "wilderness" years.[18] Additionally, in many ways these years will prove to be among the most controversial years of his life because of what is shrouded in mystery and for what is sometimes brought to life. For while many of the fleeing Sephardic Jews of Spain chose to travel north to Europe, Moshe's father chose the less-traveled route into the heart of Islamic territory.[19]

Ben Zion Bokser acknowledges that they settled in Fez, Morocco, for twelve years but he calls it a period "without a fixed home."[20] Both Abram Leon Sachar and Martin Cohen focus on the continent and the scholar's youthful intellectual achievements while mentioning the city of Fez only in passing.[21] Joseph Telushkin continues the ambiguity regarding the years of North Africa, but does include a mention of his brief time in Palestine.[22]

The mysterious years of Maimonides, albeit revealed somewhat by his intellectual accomplishments and writings, will in some measure be subsumed by a question that has challenged Jewish scholars for nearly a millennium. This is a question that is not completely answerable and a

15. Dodds, "Mudejar Tradition and the Synagogues of Medieval Spain," 119; Gampel, "Jews, Christians, and Muslims in Medieval Iberia," 20; and Telushkin, *Jewish Literacy*, 174. Telushkin notes the Almohads followed an obscure teaching that ordered all Jews to convert to Islam if the Jewish Messiah had not arrived within five hundred years from the date of Mohammad's edict.

16. Telushkin, *Jewish Literacy*, 174; Bokser, *Legacy of Maimonides*, 2; and Sachar, *History of the Jews*, 178–79.

17. Arbel, *Maimonides*, 22. See also Halbertal, *Maimonides*, 16

18. The utilization of terminology in some of the sections related to Maimonides's biography is intentional due to the nature of the topic as well as to what is revealed in both Rambam's view of himself as well as how many within Judaism view the scholar as a "savior" of Judaism, i.e., including the legend that he was born on Passover in 1135/1138.

19. Gampel, "Jews, Christians, and Muslims in Medieval Iberia," 21.

20. Bokser, *Legacy of Maimonides*, 2 and Cohen, "Sephardic Phenomenon," 21.

21. Sachar, *History of the Jews*, 178–79.

22. Telushkin, *Jewish Literacy*, 176.

question that is perhaps not fair to ask from the relative safety of a twenty-first century purview. However, it is a question that needs to be considered not only for understanding but also for the implications to Rambam's own theological underpinnings—did the family Maimon convert to Islam during their "wilderness" years?

RUMORS OF POSSIBLE CONVERSION TO ISLAM

Bokser and Sacher, while noting Maimonides's sojourn in Morocco and North Africa, also hastily mention one of the most controversial areas of his life—the accusation of his conversion to Islam.[23] Telushkin avoids the subject altogether and instead argues that Rambam's family traveled throughout North Africa in essence one step ahead of forced conversion.[24] Marc Shapiro notes that Maimonides exhibits little respect for the first prophet of Islam, Muhammad, and referred to him by a number of negative terms.[25] However, it is Norman Roth who offers the counter-factual perspective to the whole legend and argues that no one in Fez was forced to convert to Islam.[26] The preponderance of the evidence lies against Norman Roth, especially when one considers the story provided by D. S. Margoliouth.

Margoliouth in an article for *The Jewish Quarterly Review* not only recounts the legacy of Maimonides and his family's conversion to Islam, including stories of how Rambam faked reading from the Qu'ran and reciting prayers during Ramadan, and also went to great lengths to ensure his economic backstory to preserve his conversion story.[27] However, one does not need anecdotal proof such as Margoliouth's research to find possible evidence. Maimonides's and his father's own writings called for compassion for those who felt compelled to "fake a conversion" for physical safety for a period of time.[28]

---

23. Bokser, *Legacy of Maimonides*, 2 and Sachar, *History of the Jews*, 178–79.

24. Telushkin, *Jewish Literacy*, 176.

25. Shapiro, *Studies in Maimonides and His Interpreters*, 151–53.

26. Roth, "Jews in Spain at the Time of Maimonides," 17 and van der Heide, "'Their Prophets and Fathers Misled Them,'" 35.

27. Margoliouth, "Legend of the Apostasy of Maimonides," 539–41. The overarching purpose of Margoliouth's article was to discount the strong efforts of Maimonidean defenders such as Grätz and Friedländer who sought to debunk Maimonides's Marrano period.

28. Roth, "Jews in Spain at the Time of Maimonides," 17–19. See also Netanyahu, *Origins of the Inquisition*, 163; Hoffman, *Wisdom of Maimonides*, 9–10; Kraemer, "Moses Maimonides," 16–17; and Cohen, *Under Crescent and Cross*, 182–83.

We also have the possible inference of his own experience that he provided to the Moroccan Jewish community, after he was safely ensconced in Cairo, who were once again being pressured to choose. However, this choice came from a rabbi who was encouraging them to choose death rather than undergo a false conversion and telling them any acts of Judaism they performed as "converts" would be nothing more than "a sinful act."[29] Maimonides wrote to the Moroccan Jewry these words that if one chooses to read between the lines, one can sense almost a self-identifying word of testimony about his own time of spiritual exile while on the way from Spain to Egypt:

> If a person wishes to fulfill the 613 commandments of the Torah in secret he can do so. He is not guilty of anything unless he happens to desecrate the Shabbos without being forced to do so. This oppressive regime does not force anyone to do any prohibited act, just to make an oral affirmation [of faith]. They know very well that we do not mean what we say, and that the person is only doing so to escape the king's wrath and to satisfy him with a recitation of meaningless incantations.[30]

Therefore, one can safely assume a lot of presumptions from these words, despite the protestations of many Jewish scholars that struggle with the thought that Maimonides might have went through a period in which he prayed, albeit falsely, toward Mecca.[31] While this period of false conversion does not change who Maimonides was to the Jewish community, it certainly does raise the question—how much influence did Islam have on Rambam himself?

---

29. Boušek, "Polemics in the Age of Religious Persecutions," 57 and Maimonides, *Rambam*, 67.

30. Maimonides, *Rambam*, 96. It should be noted that I found a form of this original quotation in the Boušek article; however, I am seeking to go to primary sources as much as possible. Additionally, I have included a sentence on the observance of the Sabbath that Boušek omitted, as the Sabbath would be sacrosanct to Maimonides and rabbinic Judaism—regardless of the circumstances one might find themselves in at the moment.

31. Boušek, "Polemics in the Age of Religious Persecutions," 58–59. Boušek also takes the time in his article to go into great detail regarding the accusation brought against Maimonides by Ibn al-Qiftī, in the rabbi's later years, about his earlier conversion and the corroborated Islamic sources from the Cairo hospital.

Influence of Islam on Rambam

Menachem Kellner writes a telling statement that is accurate on one level; however, it misses a key influence on the theological view of Rambam on another level. He writes:

> Moses Maimonides (1138–1204) expressed a vision of Judaism as a remarkably naturalist religion of radical responsibility; a religion in which concrete behavior serves the needs of abstract thought; and a religion in which that abstract thought is to be understood as the deepest layer of the Torah and is a system which, at least in Maimonides' day, could be most clearly and accurately expressed in the vocabulary of the Neoplatonized Aristolelianism which Maimonides accepted as one of the highest expressions of the human spirit.[32]

Yes, Maimonides was influenced by Aristoleanism and the thoughts of others as will be examined later in this book; however, I would argue that the beginning influences of Rambam's thought related to concreteness and an incorporeal God began in his hometown of Cordoba as he viewed from a distance the magnificent, mysterious, and powerful arches of the Mezquita Mosque.

Perhaps Lawrence Berman better expresses the amalgamation of this perspective when he notes Alexandrian influences but sees that they were "absorbed into the writings of some of the most well known names of the eastern Islamicate intellectual tradition . . ."[33] I myself stood within the shadow of those arches and was overwhelmed by the power and the mystery of medieval Islamic thought as row upon row and column and column lay before me. I then considered how young Moshe must have seen the power of Islam, itself a religion that he viewed as a monotheistic religion, with a God who exhibited distant-like qualities, and wondered if he had a twinge of both jealousy and aspiration on how to develop within Judaism that sense of power and presence. It has also been suggested that Maimonides saw within Islam, given that they were truly monotheistic—unlike Christianity in Maimonides's view—a system that had the potential to become Jewish with proper instruction and teaching.[34] However, I would still maintain the better question to ask and answer is, how did the medieval Islamic teachings

---

32. Kellner, "Maimonides' Disputed Legacy," 245.
33. Berman, "Ethical Views of Maimonides," 13.
34. Novak, "Treatment of Islam and Muslims," 235–38 and Boušek, "Polemics in the Age of Religious Persecutions," 47–48, 62–64.

Moses Maimonides the Man   57

regarding the singular God influence Maimonides's view of the *via negativa* Jewish God?

The first observation would perhaps be considered somewhat banal in light of all that has been and will be discussed; however, it is more consequential than might be realized at first glance. Oliver Leaman and Gideon Lideon both note that Rambam's writing style and approach to his evaluation of the Torah and its talmudic sources are Islamic in approach.[35] Leaman writes that Rambam's choice in taking this approach was "to provide the Jewish community in the Islamic world with a series of texts that would help them cope with the difficult conditions in which they found themselves."[36] I argue that this is an idealistic summation of the argument and would surmise that Maimonides was drawn to the structure and organization of the Islamic world as will be shown, a structure that Hassan Hanafi would argue can even be found in his division of works based on the number fourteen as it corresponds to the "Divine Imperatives to Prescriptions and Proscriptions."[37] This structural comparison to Islam could be called a stretch but it is an interesting observation.

The second observation is to note that Rambam was not hesitant to note the influence that the writers and scholars of Islam had on his teachings, even if he disagreed with them.[38] However, it is the work of such scholars as Ibn al-Farabi (aka Ibn 'Arabī) and Al Ghazali and their impact on the "God-Scholarship" of Maimonides that is worthy of brief and special attention. Lenn Goodman writes of this period of Islamic scholarship that it "represents the most open, and so the most creative phase in the history of Islamic thought. And it was Maimonides's openness to their ideas that made possible the *philosophical synthesis* [Goodman is speaking specifically on the subject of theophany] that he achieved" (emphasis added).[39]

---

35. Leaman, "Maimonides and the Development of Jewish Thought," 189, 191 and Libson, "Parallels Between Maimonides and Islamic Law," 209–48 (esp. 211–13).

36. Leaman, "Maimonides and the Development of Jewish Thought," 191.

37. Hanafi, "Maimonides' Critique of the Mutakallimūn," 270.

38. Stroumsa, "Elisha ben Abuyah and Muslim Heretics," 183–93. Stroumsa takes the analogy from the Talmud of four scholars who are taken to Paradise and are driven mad, driven to the Talmud, etc., as a personal analogy for some of the Islamic scholars that Rambam cites in *Guide of the Perplexed*. Tangential to this discussion but nevertheless interesting, is the story of Elisha ben Abuyah who many believe became a Christian and is purported in the Talmud to go insane.

39. Goodman, "Maimonides and the Philosophers of Islam," 282–83.

Influence of Islam on Maimonidean Judaism

In using primary sources such as *Teshuvot ha-Rambam*, Albert van der Heide argues that according to Maimonides, Muslims are true monotheists as opposed to Christians whose Trinitarianism "always confused the other monotheists."[40] Additionally, Alfred L. Ivry relates a series of Islamic philosophers and scholars that Maimonides was not only influenced by in his writing of *Guide of the Perplexed* but also recommended as secondary resources to one of his translators Samuel ibn Tibbon as good scholarship material.[41] I also argue (and maintain this argument elsewhere) that the concept of the incarnation created a God-dynamic for Maimonides that was unfathomable and untenable. Even if Shapiro is correct about Rambam's disrespect for the first Islamic prophet, the Allah of Islam more closely resembles the incorporeal, unattainable, and inaccessible God of Maimonidean thought than the Triune God of the Christian faith that would come in human form to be the Messiah of humanity. Therefore, and as mentioned previously about the specific influence of al-Farabi and al-Ghazali, we should compare and contrast what—if anything—those two Islamic teachers taught Rambam and if their teachings continue to influence modern (i.e., Maimonidean) Judaism today.

Pines will argue that Rambam's basic premise of epistemology that "the divine science, with regard to whose object matter no certainty is possible for man" was perhaps influenced by al-Farabi's *Commentary on the Ethics* as much if not more than as by the thought of Aristotle.[42] The concept of epistemology and the idea of the true knowledge of God is the cornerstone of all of Maimonides's work, but none more so than his *Guide of the Perplexed*. Aydogan Kars points out that there are a plethora of sources—early Greek but most importantly Islamic—who "intersect and crystallize in Maimonides' critical philosophy."[43] He points out that both al-Farabi and Maimonides allow for "no [sense of] potentiality for God" and "positive ascriptions in reference to God are nothing but implicit profanity and blas-

---

40. van der Heide, "'Their Prophets and Fathers Misled Them,'" 43–46.

41. Ivry, "*Guide* and Maimonides' Philosophical Sources," 59–64; Shiffman, "Differences between the Translations," 47; Ivry, "Strategies of Interpretation,'" 113–16; and Kraemer, "How (not) to Read the *Guide of the Perplexed*," 359. The article by Shiffman was interesting in the sense that I felt as if I was reading the introductory explanation of a textual criticism explanation between literal, word-for-word translation (Ibn Tibbon) versus the dynamic equivalence rational of other early translators.

42. Pines, "Limitations of Human Knowledge," 109. See also Fackenheim, "Possibility of the Universe," 303–34. Fackenheim takes the argument that Maimonides imbues Al-Farabi's concept of creation and builds upon it.

43. Kars, "Two Modes of Unsaying," 265.

phemy;" however, Rambam did not go as far as al-Farabi in the delimitedness of God.[44]

In relation to Al-Ghazali (1058–1111), Amira Eran writes a rather compelling case that Maimonides garnered some of his views regarding the resurrected body and the incorporeality of angels from the teachings of this Islamic scholar.[45] Al-Ghazali did not believe that angels "experience sensuous pleasures like those of mating and eating" because they have an "insight into the realities of things." He also wrote that the greatest pleasure that a man can attain is ". . . getting the secret information of an emperor. God is the most high and most honorable. So the divine knowledge is the best of all kinds of knowledge."[46] These all reflect Maimonides's concept of the incorporeality of angels and the idea that the reality of eternity is not about temporal pleasures but to gain complete knowledge of God apart from the body itself. Ultimately, Eran writes that Al-Ghazali's views gave Rambam "a cover in his struggle against the naïve interpreters of the Torah."[47] I argue that this Islamic philosopher gave the Cairo rabbi another rationale for his attempt to create a God that was distant, inaccessible, and impossible to become the incarnate Messiah Jesus. For as has been shown in this section, medieval Islam influenced and continues to influence Judaism in ways that no one could have anticipated. In essence, it is still a little known secret today.

YEARS IN EGYPT ("OUT OF EGYPT, I CALLED MY SON")

Perhaps it could be seen as pseudo-heretical to utilize a perceived messianic prophecy (Hos 11:1) as a subheading for a section dealing with one of the leading influences on modern Judaism that rejects Jesus as Messiah. However, I have chosen to do so because in many respects Rambam serves as a pseudo-messianic figure for many within medieval and even modern Judaism. There is a Jewish cliché related to Maimonides that states, "From Moses to Moses, there were none like Moses."[48]

This statement even appears as an epitaph on his tombstone in Tiberias,[49] which creates an allusion to the prophecy in Deut 18:15 which

44. Kars, "Two Modes of Unsaying," 267, 268, 269.
45. Eran, "Al-Ghazali and Maimonides," 137–43.
46. Eran, "Al-Ghazali and Maimonides," 144.
47. Eran, "Al-Ghazali and Maimonides," 138.
48. Sachar, *History of the Jews*, 178.
49. I have been to Maimonides's Ohel in Tiberias and have seen Jewish souls paying

reads, "The LORD your God will raise up for you a prophet like me from you, from your countrymen, you shall listen to him." Indeed, Moshe ben Maimon and his teachings regarding the accessibility of God in the lives of individuals have become in many ways almost "Gospel" to the Jewish people who are searching for meaning, purpose, and spiritual presence in their lives. Therefore, Maimonides's years in Egypt are vitally important as they play a key role in establishing the religious legend of the rabbi who influences Judaism even to this day.

Physician to the Court

Maimonides and family arrived in the land of Egypt in c. 1165 after sojourns in Morocco, North Africa, and Palestine. He remained the rest of his life in the land of the ancient Pharaohs surviving religious controversies, familial calamities, and political upheavals; however, as Mark R. Cohen notes, he always considered himself a Sephardic (aka Spanish) Jew and a pilgrim longing for home in Andalusia.[50] Upon the family's arrival in Egypt, the original plan was for Rambam to be permitted to occupy himself with Torah and talmudic studies while his younger brother financially provided for the family; however, this all changed when David died while traveling abroad in c. 1169/1173.[51] After a period of grief that perhaps extended as long as a year, Maimonides took responsibility for the family finances and became a physician of some renown in Egypt.[52] It was also during this time that Rambam married and became father to his son Abraham; however, little is known about his family life, including his wife's name, beyond his son's legacy who followed after him in rabbinical studies.[53]

---

homage and praying to the supposed remains of a man who has been deceased for over 800 years.

50. Cohen, "Maimonides' Egypt," 21 and Halbertal, *Maimonides*, 16.

51. Lowney, *Vanished World*, 93–94; Meyerhoff, "Jewish Physicians," 138; Shivtiel, "'Contribution' of Maimonides," 97; Birnbaum, "Maimonides, Then and Now," 67; Cohen, "Maimonides' Egypt," 25; Kraemer, "Moses Maimonides," 27; and Bokser, *Legacy of Maimonides*, 2. Birnbaum, 70, also notes that one of Rambam's claims to fame was that he was actively involved in the practice of holistic medicine.

52. Meyerhoff, "Jewish Physicians," 138.

53. Halbertal, *Maimonides*, 34–36; Benisch, *Two Lectures*, 11; Russ-Fishbane, "Maimonidean Legacy in the East," 190–223; Harvey, "Obligation of Talmud on Women," 122–30; and Kraemer, *Maimonides*, 230–32. It would be tempting to write a great deal about Rambam's misogynistic attitudes (see chapter 8); however, the purpose of this topic prevents such an endeavor. However, one can refer to his views on women in the *Mishneh Torah* and the Laws of Marriage to ascertain his feelings on the subject. Another interesting subject would be Abraham's devotion to continuing his father's legacy

Maimonides's ability as a doctor, and the long-standing practice of the Fatimid Dynasty to employ Jewish medical experts, eventually brought him into the circle of the last caliph of the ruling Fatimid, al-Adid, and ultimately as the court physician for the Emperor Saladin and his son al-Afdhal after the Fatimid Dynasty fell.[54] Maimonides's medical aptitude and approach to healing could be described in modern vernacular as holistic in perspective in that he viewed a healthy soul as key to a healthy body.[55] Interestingly, and within his role as court physician, the legend of an invitation by Richard the Lionheart and perhaps even Amalric to join the ranks of medical doctor by the invading Crusaders began to grow.[56] The question of the legend's authenticity is debatable; however, we do know that Maimonides served as a physician to the emperor, medical advisor to the Jewish people of Egypt,[57] rabbinical scholar as this was when much of his scholarship was written, and Jewish leader during his "wilderness years."

Chief Rabbi of Cairo

From the Avignon Papacy during the medieval period to the Reformation's conflict between Calvin and Arminius, church squabbles can be legendary and even deadly. Whether it is my mother's childhood memory of the police being called out to break up a West Texas gunfight at Calvary Baptist to a secret business meeting to dismiss the pastor when he is on vacation, churches have diminished their witness over control issues. Interestingly enough, Maimonides himself was involved in such a battle of religious control and influence during his years in the Egyptian "wilderness." However, for Maimonides, the "spiritual" mêlée only raised his stature in the eyes of the people.

Much historical backstory involving the internecine struggle for rabbinical power could be written in these pages; however, only a summary description is possible as it is both convoluted and as Jacob Lavinger himself would summarize in one word, "confusing."[58] Ultimately, it appears to be

---

and the ongoing struggle that the son had with the ha-Levi family as well.

54. Harvey, "Maimonides in the Sultan's Palace," 47; Meyerhoff, "Jewish Physicians," 131–38; Bokser, *Legacy of Maimonides*, 2; and Lowney, *Vanished World*, 146.

55. Lowney, *Vanished World*, 147–56 and Nuland, *Maimonides*, 154–85.

56. Lewis, "Maimonides, Lionheart, and Saladin," 70–75; Meyerhoff, "Jewish Physicians," 139; and Roth, "Maimonides and England," 209.

57. Shivtiel, "'Contribution' of Maimonides," 97

58. Lavinger, "Was Maimonides 'Rais al-Yahud' in Egypt?" 83–93. The term "Rais al-Yahud" as Lavinger describes it would be considered as "the official head of Egyptian Jewry," and describes it as "one of the most difficult problems in his biography" (83).

a struggle between the heart and soul of rabbinic Judaism and two men, Sar Shalom ha-Levi and Maimonides.[59] Ancient documents in which Sar Shalom ha-Levi appears to be referred to by the offensive term *Zuta* only exacerbate the confusion, as well as why Maimonides would be so opposed to the religious rulings of the Babylonian (Geonim) faction led by the ha-Levi family.[60]

Ultimately, we do know that Maimonides appeared to serve as "Chief Rabbi of Cairo" in two separate periods: from c. 1171 to 1177 as well as from 1195 to his death in 1204, with ha-Levi serving in the role in the intermediate period.[61] We can also ascertain from documents found in the Cairo Genizah that Maimonides was often sought after for decisions (*Responsa*) on a variety of difficult biblical and talmudic decisions. In fact, S. D. Goitein compares Maimonides's *Responsa* work to that of being a "chief justice."[62] Therefore, and despite Lavinger's confusion, there can be no doubt that Maimonides's role in Egypt was that of rabbi, advisor, and spiritual judge.

CHAPTER SUMMATION— LIFE, DEATH, AND LEGACY OF RAMBAM

Any individual who is still being discussed and written about 800 years after his death in 1204 and apocryphal burial in Tiberias, Israel, will have such words as legacy, controversy, and mystery attached to his name.[63] Maimonides is no exception. Ben Zion Bokser wrote a fitting if idealistic tribute

---

59. Ben-Sasson, "Maimonides in Egypt," 13–15, 22–28; Lavinger, "Was Maimonides 'Rais al-Yahud' in Egypt?," 87–91; and Kraemer, *Maimonides*, 227.

60. Lavinger, "Was Maimonides 'Rais al-Yahud' in Egypt?," 83–93; Ben-Sasson, "Maimonides in Egypt," 3–30; and Kraemer, *Maimonides*, 261–68. Robert Brody in a presentation and an appendix that were compiled into a chapter on Maimonides's life explains in great detail, as it relates to talmudic laws involving the monthly cycle of a woman, as to why Rambam had no respect for the ha-Levi family and why he went out of his way to discredit them at every opportunity. Brody, "Maimonides' Attitudes," 183–208.

61. Lavinger, "Was Maimonides 'Rais al-Yahud' in Egypt?," 84, 92; and Kraemer, *Maimonides*, 222–23.

62. Goitein, "Maimonides as Chief Justice," 191–204. See also Saperstein, *Jewish Preaching*, 378–80; Halbertal, *Maimonides*, 47; and Shivtiel, "'Contribution' of Maimonides," 95–97.

63. Kraemer, "Moses Maimonides," 47. I utilized the word apocryphal here as there is a tomb that is alleged to hold the body of the rabbi; however, and while many make pilgrimage to the burial site, there is no concrete proof that Rambam is actually buried in this location. Kraemer in this article also takes the opportunity to draw the allusion to the "first Moses" with the allusion to Deut 34:6.

about Rambam with these words: "The controversy faded after a time. It is the lot of every pioneer in thought that the world's first reaction is to ignore him, then to vilify him, and finally to acclaim. Maimonides was too great a man to be ignored."[64] Yes, his works were burned by the Catholic Church at the instigation of French rabbis less than three decades after his death.[65] However, it is interesting to note that P. B. Fenton observes that some of the "most factual contemporary accounts" of Rambam's life come from Muslim sources, including a letter detailing his interaction with a young child.[66] It is also invaluable to note that by the early part of the fourteenth century, the Jewish communities in certain parts of Spain were basing all their talmudic decisions, except for "two questions of halakhah," on the scholar's *Mishneh Torah*.[67]

Controversial in his time? Yes. Controversial today? Yes. However, the influence of the Sephardic Jewish scholar who spent a great deal of his formative years fleeing from Spain across North Africa to Egypt cannot be denied. Telushkin notes his influence on both Christian and Muslim thought to the point that the United Nations hosted a conference in 1985 to honor and celebrate the 850th anniversary of his birth.[68] Jacob Minkin writing in 1957 correctly writes: "His appeal is universal. The only Jewish scholar whose prestige and influence extend far beyond the confines of his own people, Christian and Moslem theologians recognized—and disputed with—him."[69] However, it is his influence on modern Jewish thought and the souls of Jewish people that is of particular interest and concern to this book and myself. For while there is merit and validity to the Jewish adage, "From Moses to Moses there were none were like Moses," the missing presence of Messiah Jesus in the phrase should cause Christians and churches to pause in great concern.

---

64. Bokser, *Legacy of Maimonides*, 12.

65. Telushkin, *Jewish Literacy*, 177; Menocal, *Ornament of the World*, 231; and Bokser, *Legacy of Maimonides*, 12.

66. Fenton, "Meeting with Maimonides," 1–3. What is unique about this information is that it indicates Rambam's influence even within Islamic thought at this time, thereby, affirming the concept that I raised earlier.

67. Shmidman, "On Maimonides' 'Conversion' to Kabbalah," 380.

68. Telushkin, *Jewish Literacy*, 178.

69. Minkin, *World of Moses Maimonides*, 14.

4

Maimonides the Theologian and His Writings

IT WOULD BE IMPOSSIBLE to examine each letter of correspondence, *Responsa*, sermon, and treatise of Rambam. Therefore, this chapter will examine four major writings of Maimonides that relate to the presence and availability of God and to his understanding of the identity and purpose of the Messiah. Maimonides was definitely prolific and his writings—even while most of them were burned and subjected to censorship by both Christians and other rabbis after his death—managed to survive and be reproduced even though Gutenberg's transformative invention was still almost four hundred years in the future.

COMMENTARY ON THE MISHNAH

Rabbi Marc Angel in his summary explanation of the young Maimonides's (c. 1161) purpose behind writing his first major work, *Commentary on the Mishnah* or *Siraj*, explains it in a way that is significant but often not understood from a Christian perspective. He writes, "Since the Mishnah is the foundation stone of Jewish law, Maimonides felt the need to study it thoroughly, to explain it to students of Jewish law, and to incorporate the talmudic discussions on each passage."[1] What is significant is twofold:

---

1. Angel, *Maimonides*, xiii. Arbel, *Maimonides*, 81, describes it as a "life-long ideal—bringing order and system into the immense body of Jewish law..."

1. the Torah is not mentioned at all in the rabbi's sentence but the Mishnah is considered the foundation of Jewish law and
2. Rabbi Angel does not indicate that Maimonides refers to the Tanakh but to the Talmud for his commentary source.

This is important not only for this chapter but also for the rest of the book as it serves to illustrate that rabbinic (or modern) Judaism depends more upon outside Jewish sources than The Source for its understanding of the Jewish religion and beliefs. This concept did not begin with Rambam but it could be argued that it received it credence from him.

The Mishnah is the "codified core of the Oral Law" and is "considered as "equally authoritative" in rabbinic Judaism to the "Written Law, or the Scriptures."[2] While the Mishnah was a law code, it became an amalgamation of arguments and interesting sociological insights into Jewish thought and history than the Talmud was intended to clarify.[3] Therefore, the young Maimonides in c. 1168 completed the work in Egypt, while allowing for constant revisions throughout his life, to repair the clarity issue from his perspective and, naturally, also to create additional controversy.[4]

Two primary issues of controversy that deserve a small amount of attention, especially the second one as it will be amplified and illustrated in the following section, are

1. Rambam's preference for the Jerusalem Talmud over the Babylonian Talmud and
2. his division and/or categorization of Jewish scholarship into an approach that almost resembles the allegorical approach of the Christian Origen from earlier centuries.

As it relates to the issue of the Talmud preference issue, we should begin at the beginning of Rambam's actual commentary where he wrote the following:

> It should be understood that every mitzva that the Holy-One-blessed-be-He gave to Moshe Rabbaynu [Moses our Teacher],

---

2. Arbel, *Maimonides*, 81, 82.
3. Arbel, *Maimonides*, 82.
4. The exact date of the publication is flexible. The primary understanding is that it was written before, during, and after his father's death and completed around the time of his brother's drowning in c. 1169/1173. Sachar, *History of the Jews*, 179; Halbertal, *Maimonides*, 92–93; Kraemer, *Maimonides*, 164; Nuland, *Maimonides*, 54–62; and Kraemer, "Moses Maimonides," 21–22. Nuland devotes considerable time in his evaluation of this work to examining how Rambam's opposition to Karaites could have played a role in the work.

> peace unto him, was given to him together with its Explanation. G-d would tell him the mitzva, and afterwards He would give its Explanation, its substance, and all the wisdom contained within the Torah's verses.[5]

This statement by Maimonides should be understood to reflect the rabbinic view that a commandment in the Torah was not seen as sufficiently self-explanatory but required additional material (i.e., Oral Law) that was to be passed down until it was written down by Judah the Prince and the compilers of the talmudic literature. This passing down of the Oral Law was understood by Maimonides in his commentary the *Pirkei Avot* (*Ethics of Our Fathers*):

> [1:1] Moses received the Torah from Sinai and passed it on to Joshua; Joshua [passed it on] to the elders; the elders to the Prophets; the Prophets passed it on to the Men of the Great Assembly. They [the men of the Great Assembly made three statements: Be deliberate in judgment; raise up many students; and make a fence around the Torah.
>
> [*Commentary of the Rambam*] In the introduction to this text, we already explained the order of the [Oral] Tradition, and how it was transmitted. Therefore, my intent [in these notes] will be merely to explain these ethical statements, to encourage the acquisition of these qualities, for they are of great value . . . And make a fence around the Torah—institute decrees and ordinances that will separate a person from sin.[6]

This idea of "institut[ing] decrees and ordinances" from his commentary on the *Pirkei Avot* fits in perfectly with Kraemer's supposition that Rambam viewed Jewish law as "evolve[ing] over time, as every generation of sages derives new legislation from the Oral and Written Law."[7] New legislation that will be validated and confirmed by Talmudic references as the need arises and rabbinic bodies decree.

Interestingly, in his *Pirkei Avot* 1:3 commentary, we find a reference to the Jerusalem Talmud and not to the Babylonian Talmud.[8] Therefore, and because the Babylonian Talmud was and is the default rabbinic resource for

---

5. Maimonides, *Maimonides' Introduction to the Talmud*, 35.

6. Maimonides, *Pirkei Avot with the Rambam's Commentary*, 62. Perhaps some might see this particular section as extraneous to the issue; however, it is important groundwork to future chapters, especially as I examine apologetic approaches to presenting the gospel. We must understand their perspective if we are to be effective witnesses of Messiah Jesus.

7. Kraemer, *Maimonides*, 172.

8. Maimonides, *Pirkei Avot with the Rambam's Commentary*, 63.

Jewish scholars, we can speculate over the primary reasons why Maimonides developed an affection for the Jerusalem Talmud. First, I propose that the Babylonian Talmud was the resource of his religious opponents. The Sar Shalom ha-Levi family in Egypt were of the Geonic lineage and one could argue that he disrespected their rabbinical abilities with such statements as "For, if you should ask any of the great *Geʾonim* for the explanation of a certain law of a Mishna, he would be unable to tell you a thing unless he would know the Gemora on that Mishna by heart...."[9] Second, Rambam had written a work, *Precepts of the Jerusalem Talmud*, and scholars recognize that he appreciated its succinctness and its usage of "explaining the reasons for normative legal decisions," and this led to him defaulting to Jerusalem over Babylon in particular instances.[10] This put Rambam at odds with many of the Geonim rabbis of his day but it was his next controversial action that is especially relevant to the question at hand.

According to Arbel, Maimonides divided the Jewish people into three groups as it related to understanding the Torah and the meaning of *Olam Haba* ("the world to come" or what Christianity would call heaven or the afterlife)—literalists, non-literalists but avoiders of deeper study, and allegorists who sought out the deeper meaning of the text.[11] As will be illustrated further, Maimonides ultimately was an allegorist in much the same way as Origen. Rambam wrote in his introduction to the *Commentary on the Mishnah*, "Altering the *Oral Law* in any way is equally as well a manifestation of false prophecy, even if the prophet is ostensibly supported by a literal interpretation, as opposed to its *actual meaning* (emphasis added)."[12] It could also be argued that Maimonides was an elitist if one agrees with Arbel and Sherwin Nuland who wrote, "Much of the holy writings, he said, are in the form of metaphor, with the deeper meaning only to be understood by those with the proper training and intellect."[13] Rambam himself refers to

---

9. Maimonides, *Maimonides' Introduction to the Talmud*, 181. See also, Halbertal, *Maimonides*, 98. Halbertal spells out succinctly the four goals that Rambam elucidated in his introduction while I have only given you the first goal above; however, I stand by my perspective that there was a hidden agenda by the overt statement of the Geonim especially since the first struggle with the ha-Levi was occurring during the time the commentary was being completed.

10. Kraemer, "Moses Maimonides," 22; Halbertal, *Maimonides*, 95; and Kraemer, *Maimonides*, 150.

11. Arbel, *Maimonides*, 84 and Angel, *Maimonides*, 150. Angel does not go into the explicit detail that Arbel does; however, the general concept is present.

12. Maimonides, *Maimonides' Introduction to the Talmud*, 50.

13. Nuland, *Maimonides*, 70. See also Klein-Braslavy, "Maimonides' Exoteric and Esoteric Biblical Interpretations," 163. This thought is present throughout Klein-Braslavy's work; however, it is most overtly stated, albeit in the most tactful of wording

this metaphor concept as "Secrets": "It is thus improper for a scholarly person to reveal what he knows of the Secrets, unless it is to one who is greater than, or at least equal to, him. For, if he reveals it to an unknowledgeable person, even if this person will not discredit it, he will still not appreciate it properly."[14] Therefore, Rambam's allegorical views in his first work will allow him to establish a God, a Messiah, and a Judaism that reflects himself and not the God who is there.

EPISTLE TO YEMEN

Today, Yemen is not a locale that one imagines as a Jewish region; however, during the Middle Ages this area was such an expanse. In his biography of Rambam, Kraemer notes the importance of the port of Aden to trade routes and a place where Jewish travelers could study "the Torah of Moses," and hold "fast to his covenant."[15] Therefore, when Maimonides received the letter in 1172 from Yemenite leader Jacob ben Nethanel detailing the desperate conditions of Yemenite Jews, the newly-minted *Ra'īs al-yahūd* of Egypt responded not only to the leader but also to the whole of Yemenite Jewry as well.[16] The response to the three conditions are very telling to both Maimonides's perspectives on the Messiah and his understanding of Jesus's claim to divinity.

The three "emergencies" related to

1. Islamic attempts to forcibly convert the Yemenite Jews;
2. the attempt of a Jewish convert to Islam to spread the message that Muhammad was prophesied in the Torah; and
3. the rise of a messianic claimant who was attracting a large following.[17]

Obviously, Rambam could understand the emotional toil of the first and second issues given his upbringing in Islamic Spain and residual questions over his own pseudo-conversion experience. Therefore, the messianic issue became an issue of paramount concern to Maimonides and this is reflected in his response to the Yemenite Jewry and because he sought to develop "an

---

on page 163.

14. Maimonides, *Maimonides' Introduction to the Talmud*, 151.
15. Kraemer, *Maimonides*, 253.
16. Kraemer, "Moses Maimonides," 33; Halbertal, *Maimonides*, 47; Kraemer, *Maimonides*, 233–34; and Arbel, *Maimonides*, 95.
17. Eraqi-Klorman, "Yemeni Messiah in the Time of Maimonides," 132–38; Mazuz, "Identity of the Apostate in the Epistle to Yemen," 363–66; Kraemer, *Maimonides*, 234; Halbertal, *Maimonides*, 47–50; and Arbel, *Maimonides*, 94–96.

active Messianism built on natural preparation, not a passive Messianism based on eschatological visions of divine interventions."[18]

This idea of "natural preparation" included a rather elaborate analysis based on his own family tradition of Num 23:23 which allowed for the restoration of prophecy and advent of the messianic era to begin in c. 1216.[19] One could argue that Maimonides was himself making a prophetic utterance, or as Jewish scholars today call simply a prediction. However, he was not called to account for his error due to his death prior to the missed date and what could only be called "hedging his bets" with the wording— "Although I have spoken out against making such calculations and strongly opposed the publicizing the date of his arrival, I have done this in order to keep people from [falling into despair], thinking that his coming is in the distant future. I have mentioned this to you earlier. Blessed is Hashem Who knows [the truth]."[20]

This idea of "natural preparation" also necessitated dealing with the historical claims of other supposed Messiahs, in particular and most importantly the subject of Jesus of Nazareth. Kraemer argues that Maimonides never believed Jesus sought to establish a new religion but instead blamed the Apostle Paul for the natural outcome of Christianity and that by happenstance the errors of Christianity and Islam would create the avenue for the Messiah to arrive.[21] One finds it difficult to find a Pauline fault line in Maimonidean thought; however, the concept that two negatives could make a positive for Rambam is present when he wrote:

18. Kraemer, "Moses Maimonides," 34 and Halbertal, *Maimonides*, 50. Halbertal would not agree with my assessment for he wrote, "At the heart of the work is Maimonides' effort to provide the Jews living under Muslim rule with a credible historical picture that would preserve the historical sense of time that was now threatened with collapse." However, I stand by my assessment of the letter not only because of Rambam's utilization of Danielic prophecies but also because of his date setting for the arrival of redemption.

19. Kraemer, *Maimonides*, 236; Arbel, *Maimonides*, 95; and Kraemer, "Moses Maimonides," 34.

20. Maimonides, *Rambam*, 52.

21. Kraemer, *Maimonides*, 239–40. The rationale behind Kraemer's view is his translation of the phrase, "A long time after Jesus a religion ascribed to him became prevalent among the descendants of Esau [the Christians], although this was not his aim" (238). The translation by Finkel reads as "Long after he lived, the descendents of Eisav created a religion and traced its origins to him. He did not establish a new faith, . . ." Another translation reads as "Quite some time later, a religion, which is traced to him by the descendants of Esau, gained popularity. Although this was the aim he hoped to realize . . ." Therefore, the competing translations as well as the animosity towards Jesus by Maimonides in other places negate Kraemer's argument.

They [Jesus and Muhammad] will enable the masses and the elite to acquire moral and intellectual qualities, each according to his ability. Thus, the godly community becomes preeminent, reaching a twofold perfection. By the first I mean man's leading his life under the most agreeable and congenial conditions [Messianic Age]. The second will constitute the gain of the intelligibles, each in accordance with his native powers.[22]

It is also impossible to agree with Kraemer's view that Maimonides had a sympathetic inclination towards Jesus when one reads: "The first to institute this plan was Jesus the Nazarene, may his bones be ground to dust. He was Jewish because his mother was a Jewess although his father was a gentile, and our principle is that a child born of a Jewess and a gentile or slave, is legitimate. *Only figuratively do we call him an illegitimate child*"[23] (emphasis added). Thus, we find in this short segment not simply the negation of any possibility of divinity, but also the renewal of the bastard claim against Jesus. There is no sympathy or positivity in Maimonides's view towards Jesus, even if Rambam did hold Christianity in slightly higher esteem than Islam, which is disputable.[24] Additionally, the concept of his attitude towards Jesus's divinity will be considered in greater detail in the introductory section on Maimonides's *Mishneh Torah*.

MISHNEH TORAH

In many respects, Rambam's *Mishneh Torah* and *Guide for the Perplexed* are what could only be described as the magnum opuses of his writing career. Haym Soloveitchik refers to the *Mishneh Torah*, while also praising the *Guide for the Perplexed*, as a "work of art" that is "a work of crystalline clarity and protean ambiguity."[25] However, it is to his *Mishneh Torah* that we now turn, for it is here that much of the Maimonidean concept of the *via negativa* God is found. In his biography, Halbertal notes that Rambam sought to render "his spiritual and religious positions binding status" and it is here that his "voice shook the rafters in its day and posed a lasting challenge to all later Jewish thought."[26] Isadore Twersky describes this perception and reality in this both elegant and necessarily lengthy way:

22. Maimonides, *Epistles of Maimonides*, 100. See also Shamir, "Allusions to Muhammad," 212–16.
23. Maimonides, *Epistles of Maimonides*, 98.
24. Halbertal, *Maimonides*, 53.
25. Soloveitchik, "Mishneh Torah," 335, 337.
26. Halbertal, "What is the *Mishneh Torah*?," 81–83; Genack, "Rambam's Mishneh

> The Mishneh Torah, the first serious attempt, since the redaction of the Mishnah by R. Judah the Prince, at a comprehensive survey, classification, and codification of Jewish law, changed the entire landscape of rabbinic literature. Although it did not attain its goal—it was not adopted as the universal Jewish code nor were its really novel features (scope and arrangement) imitated by later codifiers—the Mishneh Torah did become the pièce de résistance of all Talmudic study through the ages . . . The Mishneh Torah was like a prism through which practically all Talmudic study had to pass.[27]

It has already been mentioned that Maimonides viewed the *Mishneh Torah* as not merely sufficient but also necessary for understanding both the Oral and Written Law; however, the rationale for his perception should also be noted:

> On these grounds, I, Moses the son of Maimon the Sefardi, bestirred myself, and, relying on the help of God, blessed be He, intently studied all these works, with the view of putting together the results obtained from them in regard to what is forbidden or permitted, clear or unclean, and the other rules of the Torah—all in plain language and terse style, so that thus the entire Oral Law might become systematically known to all, . . .[28]

The theological history has already been explained by Rambam himself; however, a quasi-historical backstory does need a further examination and understanding. One is left with somewhat of a conundrum as to the date of the compilation of the *Mishneh Torah* and we can only estimate a date range of between 1175–1180 which would place him firmly in Egypt; however, we

---

Torah," 78–84 and Halbertal, *Maimonides*, 53. The significance of the title according to Genack is that it is the Hebrew name for Deuteronomy. Menachem Kellner raises an interesting question while acknowledging the sense of binding status in a religious sense for *Mishneh Torah*—does the binding spread across all areas of Jewish life including areas of science given that Maimonides wrote at a time when Ptolemaic thought was still triumphant? Kellner cites that there are some ultra-Orthodox, and I have heard some as well, who will argue in the affirmative. Kellner, "Maimonides on the Science of the *Mishneh Torah*," 169–94 (esp. 173, 176).

27. Twersky, *Introduction to the Code of Maimonides*, 33.

28. "Introduction" to *Mishneh Torah*, cited in Maimonides, *Maimonides Reader*, 39, 40. It should be noted that I added the parenthesis of [earlier] because I argue that some of what was written and the purpose behind it was also an attempt to confront and degrade the ha-Levi family in Egypt. See also Twersky, *Introduction to the Code of Maimonides*, 9 and Halbertal, "What is the *Mishneh Torah*?," 95–96.

do know that it took at least ten years for him to codify and compile all his arguments and writings together.[29]

The division of the book into fourteen books was significant as the number itself is the "numerical value of the Hebrew word for 'hand' which earned the work its secondary title of *ha-Yad ha-hazaqah* or *The Mighty Hand* based on Deut 6:21—"then you shall say to your son, 'We were slaves to Pharaoh in Egypt, and the LORD brought us from Egypt with a mighty hand.'" Both Arbel and Kraemer also note that Maimonides was born on the fourteenth of Nisan (aka Passover); however, it is only Arbel that draws the connection to the "Moses to Moses" adage as well as the inclusion of two anecdotal legends which tie the two Moseses together even further.[30] One could argue that Moses Maimonides did indeed see himself as another Moses and as I will argue additionally in later sections that he developed somewhat of a quasi-messianic complex, or at the very least a forerunner mentality, about himself. For as both Halbertal and Arbel will argue, Maimonides saw his *Mishneh Torah* as something that would serve as a "transparent, accessible system" that would one day "serve as the Israeli Constitution."[31]

This is a controversial and perhaps arrogant thought when one considers not only the almost millennia of Jewish thought that preceded Rambam's compilation but also dangerous in many ways and one of the reasons why his writings were so controversial in the medieval period. However, Halbertal considers this question as valid to be asked in his biography. He concludes that Maimonides saw the *Mishneh Torah* as "halakhah itself, and the composition is a replacement for the halakhic literature that preceded it" but that he sought to "conceal that stance" as he was aware of the controversy that such an overt stance would create.[32] Isadore Twersky is more effusive in his praise of Rambam's effort: "It is, as we shall see, unprecedented in terms of scope and structure, and although it did not have the precise impact which Maimonides envisaged, it is decidedly unique in its multifaceted influence."[33]

Therefore, it should surprise no one that within Rambam's *Mishneh Torah* we find such definitive stances on the corporeality/incorporeality of God, the person of Jesus, and the identity and role of the Messiah. These

---

29. Kraemer, *Maimonides*, 316–17 and Arbel, *Maimonides*, 115.

30. Kraemer, *Maimonides*, 24 and Arbel, *Maimonides*, 120–22.

31. Trigano, "Conventionalization of Social Bonds," 51–52; Halbertal, *Maimonides*, 164 and Arbel, *Maimonides*, 119–20.

32. Halbertal, *Maimonides*, 194. It should be noted here that I agree with Halbertal's position.

33. Twersky, *Introduction to the Code of Maimonides*, 20.

Maimonides the Theologian and His Writings 73

clear stances leave no room for disagreement or bifurcation in the eyes of the Sephardic rabbi living in Egyptian exile. For as it relates to the concept of personhood and the existence of God, it is clear from the inception of *Mishneh Torah* that the two are not mutually compatible. Warren Zev Harvey writes in this way, "God is One means both that God is incomparable and that He is incorporeal."[34] For Maimonides, the cliché of never the twain shall meet is quite apropos. However, Kraemer is correct that Maimonides does it in a most Aristotelian way[35]:

> The basic principle of all basic principles and the pillar of all sciences is to realize that there is a First Being who brought every existing thing into being. All existing things, whether celestial, terrestrial, or belonging to an intermediate class, exist only through His true existence . . . If, however, it were supposed that all other beings were non-existent, He alone would still exist . . . For all beings are in need of Him; but He, blessed be He, is not in need of them nor any of them. Hence, His real essence is unlike that of any of them.[36]

Interestingly, both Halbertal and Kraemer who wrote fascinating and invaluable biographies of Maimonides, both struggle to define and explain how the rabbi sought to rationalize the command of loving a God that was existent but also distant in his definition of the *First Being*.[37] Rambam first seeks to create a God that is not only incorporeal in the intransigent sense but also one that is intractable. Phrases in chapter 1 of the "Book of Knowledge" include the following:

> He alone is real, and nothing else has reality like His reality . . . And whoever permits the thought to enter his mind that there is another deity besides this God, violates a prohibition . . . and denies the essence of religion—this doctrine being the great principle on which everything depends . . . That the Holy One, blessed be He, is not a physical body, is explicitly set forth in the Pentateuch and in the Prophets . . . and a physical body is not in two places at one time . . . If He were body,

---

34. Harvey, "Maimonides' Monotheism."

35. Kraemer, *Maimonides*, 326. Kraemer specifically follows the argument that I also noted earlier that Rambam follows "Aristotle's cosmology as formulated by al-Farabi and Ibn Sina." The Islamic influence on Maimonidean thought is definitely worthy of further study. See also Halbertal, *Maimonides*, 197–98.

36. Maimonides, *Mishneh Torah*, book 1, chapter 1, secs. 1–3. Source is from Twersky translation as noted above (*A Maimonides Reader*) and most all further references will be from this translation.

37. Kraemer, *Maimonides*, 326–31 and Halbertal, *Maimonides*, 197–208.

> He would be like other bodies ... But God's essence as it really is, the human mind does not understand and is incapable of grasping or investigating ... If God were sometimes angry and sometimes rejoiced, He would be changing. All these states exist in physical beings that are of obscure and mean condition, dwelling in houses of clay, whose foundation is in the dust."[38]

Maimonides then seeks to command the Jewish people to love an unattainable God who cannot be understood regardless of how much investigation is undertaken—"This God, honored and revered, it is our duty to love and fear..."[39] I argue that Kraemer, Halbertal, and other Jewish scholars since Rambam struggle with this dichotomy that the rabbi created because they do not recognize that in many regards this first chapter is not only an attempt to define God as First Being but also to undefine the possibility of Jesus and the incarnation.

Maimonides's emphatic pronouncements, including: that God alone is real; that whomever allows for the idea of other deities has denied the essence of religion; that there is the absence of a body because a body cannot be in two places at once; that the presence of a body would make God just like anyone else; and that for God to express emotions is nothing more than a reaction of a vapid, mercurial individual are all attempts to negate the person of Jesus as will be illustrated in concluding sections of his *Mishneh Torah*. I propose that Rambam began in his definition of God as *via negativa* because he needed to refute any attempt that Jesus could be God Himself. Many Jewish scholars miss this nuance;[40] however, it can be seen if one reads the words of Maimonides:

> And what is the way that will lead to the love of Him and the fear of Him? When a person contemplates His great and wondrous works and creatures and from them obtains a glimpse of His wisdom which is incomparable and infinite, he will straightway love Him, praise Him, glorify Him, and long with an exceeding longing to know His great name; ... If the Creator lived as other living creatures live, and His knowledge were external to Himself, there would be a plurality of deities, namely: He himself,

---

38. Maimonides, *Mishneh Torah*, book 1, chapter 1, secs. 4, 6, 8, 9, 12.

39. Maimonides, *Mishneh Torah*, book 1, chapter 2, sec. 1.

40. Halbertal, *Maimonides*, 196 and Kraemer, *Maimonides*, 326. Kraemer even notes that the *Mishneh Torah* "did not begin, as we expect in a Jewish theology, with the Exodus from Egypt or the revelation at Mount Sinai." And because Rambam did not begin this way, Kraemer acknowledges that "It transforms Judaism from a religion rooted in history, in great events, to a religion implanted in nature and knowledge of the existent beings, God's works rather than God's words."

His life, and His knowledge. This however, is not so. He is One in every aspect, from every angle, and in all ways in which Unity is conceived. Hence the conclusion that God is the One who knows, is known, and is the knowledge (of Himself)—all these being One. This is beyond the power of speech to express, beyond the capacity of the ear to hear, and of the human mind to apprehend clearly.[41]

If the concept of God to Maimonides should be defined by acknowledging that "one should not say that God exists in the usual sense of the term; all we can say that God is not non-existent" and that one should "attempt to express knowledge of God by what God is not, rather than by describing what God is,"[42] then we have both created the ultimate of negation theology and a God in which the incarnation through Jesus is impossible.

And I argue that this was Rambam's ultimate objective in his writing of the *Mishneh Torah* as well as the *Guide for the Perplexed*. He needed to create a God in which not only could Jesus not be God the Son, but also not be the Messiah of the Jewish people.[43] Therefore, he wrote a statement about Jesus in book 14, chapter 11 that was often "suppressed by Christians censors" for generations but that is available today.[44]

> Even of Jesus of Nazareth, who imagined that he was the Messiah, but was put to death by the court, Daniel had prophesied, as it is written, "And the children of the violent among your people shall lift themselves up to establish the vision; but they shall stumble" (Dan. 11:14). For has there ever been a greater stumbling than this? All the prophets affirmed that the Messiah would redeem Israel, save them, gather their dispersed, and confirm the commandments. But he caused Israel to be destroyed by the sword, their remnant to be dispersed and humiliated. He was instrumental in changing the Torah and causing the world to err and serve another besides God.[45]

However, Rambam sought to find a silver lining in the person of Jesus. He believed that through the "false teachings" of Christianity and Islam, the path would be made for the real "King Messiah, to prepare the whole world to

---

41. Maimonides, *Mishneh Torah*, book 1, chapter 2; secs. 2, 10. I would speculate that perhaps even an anti-Trinitarian response could be found in his words as well.

42. Kraemer, *Maimonides*, 156.

43. Twersky, *Introduction to the Code of Maimonides*, 452.

44. Kraemer, *Maimonides*, 353 and Twersky, *Maimonides Reader*, 226 (Twersky note).

45. Maimonides, *Mishneh Torah*, book 14, chapter 11 (uncensored version).

worship God with one accord, . . ." because when the real one finally arrives "they will forthwith recant and realize that they have inherited naught but lies from their fathers, that their prophets and forebears led them astray."[46]

The concept of a personal, relational God was an impossibility for Maimonides, ergo no possibility for the incarnation. Additionally, Rambam denounced the messianic claim of Jesus. Therefore, who for the Cairo rabbi could fit his select definition of Messiah? Halbertal writes of Maimonides's Messiah—"By concluding his halakhic treatise with the messianic concept, Maimonides makes the point that the messianic age will be within the *halakhah* purview, not beyond it. Moreover, the Messiah will *institute full halakhic governance* (emphasis added)."[47] For while the Messiah will live, die, and be succeeded by a messianic lineage in Rambam's purview, the Torah but most especially the Talmud must always be preserved and sustained.[48] Therefore, one can find certain stock definitional parameters for the Messiah within the pages of any Maimonidean biographer:

1. restoration of the Davidic kingdom to its original and former glory;
2. rebuilding the temple and regathering the people;
3. reinstating all original sacrifices (whether he believed it was necessary or not);
4. complete fulfillment of the Torah;
5. end of strife and restoration of harmony between man and nature; and
6. unusually long life for all people.[49]

Many of these are parameters that many Christians, especially of those premillennial eschatological perspective, would affirm; however, we would

46. Maimonides, *Mishneh Torah*, book 14, chapter 11 (uncensored version). See also, Twersky, *Introduction to the Code of Maimonides*, 452–53.

47. Halbertal, *Maimonides*, 223.

48. Halbertal, *Maimonides*, 400. Halbertal quotes from the *Pereq Heleq* which is chapter 10 in his *Commentary on the Mishnah*. The original source is available from Maimonides, *Ethical Writings of Maimonides*, 167.

> The messiah will die, his son will succeed him, and then his grandson, God has explained that he (the messiah) will die. He said: *He shall not fail nor be crushed until he establishes justice in the earth, etc.* His kingdom will last an extremely long time. The duration of life will also increase, because with the removal of grief and hardship the duration of life increases. It would not be surprising if his dominion lasted for thousands of years. For the wise men have said that if the virtuous community comes into existence, it is unlikely that it disintegrate.

49. Arbel, *Maimonides*, 119; Kraemer, *Maimonides*, 354–56, 397–99; and Halbertal, *Maimonides*, 223–28. The notation regarding Rambam's ambivalence towards animal sacrifices will occur in *Guide to the Perplexed*.

state that these come in the Messiah's second coming and not in his first arrival.

However, and as already stated in the uncensored section of *Mishneh Torah*, book 14, chapter 11, the Messiah is not allowed to be killed in Rambam's definition, thereby, negating the possibility of Jesus of Nazareth. However, this is contradictory to a basic talmudic statement regarding a Messiah who would indeed die—Messiah ben Joseph and then be succeeded by Messiah ben David:

> What is the cause of the mourning [mentioned in the last cited verse]? R. Dosa and the Rabbis differ on the point. One explained, The cause is the slaying of Messiah the son of Joseph, and the other explained, The cause is the slaying of the Evil Inclination. It is well according to him who explains that the cause is the slaying of Messiah the son of Joseph, since that well agrees with the Scriptural verse, And they shall look upon me because they have thrust him through, and they shall mourn for him as one mourneth for his only son; . . . Our Rabbis taught, The Holy One, blessed be He, will say to the Messiah, the son of David (May he reveal himself speedily in our days!), "Ask of me anything, and I will give it to thee", as it is said, I will tell of the decree etc. this day have I begotten thee, ask of me and I will give the nations for thy inheritance. But when he will see that the Messiah the son of Joseph is slain, he will say to Him, "Lord of the Universe, I ask of Thee only the gift of life". "As to life", He would answer him, "Your father David has already prophesied this concerning you", as it is said, He asked life of thee, thou gavest it him, [even length of days for ever and ever].[50]

Perhaps this is why he himself did not cite differing opinions from himself that were in the Talmud,[51] especially one that related to such an important concept as one that dealt with the identity of the Messiah. He also contradicted the messianic promises of Isa 11:6 and 35:5 as they relate to the power of the Holy One when he wrote:

> Do not think that King Messiah will have to perform signs and wonders, bring anything into being, revive the dead or do similar things. It is not so . . . Let no one think that in the days of the Messiah any of the laws of nature will be set aside, or any innovation be introduced into creation. The world will follow its normal course. The words of Isaiah: "And the wolf shall dwell

50. *Babylonian Talmud* (BT) Sukkah 52A. http://juchre.org/talmud/sukkah/sukkah3.htm#52a.

51. Kraemer, *Maimonides*, 324.

with the lamb, and the leopard shall lie down with the kid" (Is. 11:6) are to understood figuratively, meaning that Israel will live securely among the wicked of the heathens who are likened to wolves and leopards, . . .[52]

For Rambam, complete observation of the Written and Oral Torah by a kingly ruler of the Davidic throne was sufficient to be declared Messiah:

> If there arise a king from the House of David who meditates on the Torah, occupies himself with the commandments, as did his ancestor David, observes the precepts prescribed in the written and the Oral Law, prevails upon Israel to walk in the way of the Torah and to repair its breaches, and fights the battles of the Lord, it may be assumed that he is the Messiah. If he does these things and succeeds, rebuilds the sanctuary on its site, and gathers the dispersed of Israel, he is beyond all doubt the Messiah.[53]

Ultimately, Maimonides created a Messiah in his own image, for he sought to create a Messiah because he could not accept the truth of Messiah Jesus. I argue that Rambam created a messianic idol much like the statue of himself that resides currently in Cordoba, Spain, a statue that does not talk, speak or offer eternal hope to the Jewish people. He also created a negative God because of his rejection of the true God and the true Messiah.

GUIDE FOR THE PERPLEXED[54]

As I was walking through the cobbled-stone streets of the Jewish Quarter of Cordoba in the summer of 2015, I stopped at the statue of Rambam to take a few pictures. I encountered a Reform Sephardic rabbi and her California family who were there on vacation. As we discussed the statue that stood before us, the rabbi stated that she had a love/hate relationship with Rambam and it all stemmed from what he wrote in *Guide for the Perplexed*. For her it represented perplexity, irritation, and the overwhelming sense that rabbinical Judaism was something that could never be accomplished or understood wholly. The Jewish scholar Shlomo Pines writes as well of this conundrum when he states: "There is a question whether the *Guide* was meant to be an apologetic attempt to render religion intellectually respectable by exposing the limitations of human reason; or, alternatively, whether it meant to

---

52. Maimonides, *Mishneh Torah*, book 14, chapters 11, 12; sec. 3, 1 (respectively).

53. Maimonides, *Mishneh Torah*, book 14, chapter 11, sec. 4.

54. It should be noted that there are variations in the title with the preposition alternating between "of" and "to" and "for." I will use all three interchangeably.

demonstrate that religion has a purely practical use."⁵⁵ I would argue that in many ways, this was Maimonides's ultimate attempt—not to clear up the confusion for the rabbinically perplexed, but to establish his own guide so that his stamp would forever mark the face of modern Judaism.

Therefore, let me, as I did with the explanation of *Mishneh Torah*, divide the evaluation of *Guide for the Perplexed* into two arenas—a historical summary and a theological evaluation. Kraemer in his article for Seeskin's *Cambridge Companion* refers to Rambam's *Guide of the Perplexed* as the final volume of what might be called "the third stool leg of Rabbinic Judaism" around 1190 when the rabbi was 52 and exhausted after completing a five-year writing journey.⁵⁶ It is different from both the first two legs—*Commentary on the Mishnah* and *Mishneh Torah*—in two distinct ways:

1. it serves as more of a series of letters between Maimonides and a student, Joseph ben Judah (aka Joseph ibn Aknin) and

2. its purpose was to reveal to his student, who he believed was capable of understanding, "the hidden meanings of Scripture and the metaphysical tradition" behind the text.⁵⁷

While much could be written about Joseph ben Judah, the best information about the student of Rambam comes from Islamic tradition and includes that he as well once experienced the "Jewish sorrow" of having to undergo a

---

55. Pines, "Maimonides," 130; Harvey, "Maimonides in the Sultan's Palace," 52–55; and Kraemer, "How (Not) to read the *Guide of the Perplexed*," 389. Kraemer will argue that the purpose of the *Guide* is to explain two parables found within the pages of his work. However, Rambam himself will argue that he does not want everyone to understand the work and that it is not for everyone. Therefore, I argue generally that Kraemer and Harvey's premise is wrong as Jonathan Ray illustrates through a quotation (not included here as I was not able to find the primary source). He includes from the original translator Samuel Ibn Tibbon that he wanted to preserve Judaism's teaching against the "inherent challenge to Judaism and its stature in Christian Europe." However, Ray did note that it was Ibn Tibbon and not Maimonides who took Rambam's teachings to the masses. Ray, "Reconquista and the Jews," 170.

56. Kraemer, "Moses Maimonides," 40.

57. Manekin, "Belief, Certainty and Divine Attributes in the Guide," 133; Frank, "Elimination of Perplexity," 130–35; Halbertal, *Maimonides*, 65; Arbel, *Maimonides*, 152–55; Nuland, *Maimonides*, 131–35; Kraemer, *Maimonides*, 361–66; and Kraemer, "Moses Maimonides," 40–41. Manekin uses forms of the word "apprehend" a great deal in his article. Perhaps the best example is found in this statement—"Yet because Maimonides singles out the inability of the ignorant to approach an apprehension of the divine essence, one may infer that the learned *can* approach this apprehension." Frank takes a slightly different approach to the instruction for Joseph ben Judah, as he sees Maimonides first wanting to temper the upstart student, or in other words, "tear him down so that he can build him up" into the mold of who Rambam wants him to be.

forced conversion.⁵⁸ Therefore, one could surmise that perhaps Maimonides saw within the Jewish merchant and student touches of himself and his beloved brother David, who had died more than a decade earlier.

Regardless of why Judah ben Joseph was chosen as the recipient of what will become *Guide of the Perplexed*, the letters reveal a rabbi who wanted to pass down not simply biblical information but also the deeper meaning of the text so that the law would be "respectable to philosophy and to make philosophy compatible with the law."⁵⁹ However, this passing down of information was something that Maimonides wanted to keep self-contained to what I would call a select and elite few.⁶⁰ It was not Rambam's intention for the *Guide* to reach a broad audience; however, the broader audience was the ultimate outcome of the work and his worst fears were realized as both Jewish and Christian audiences burned the work in Paris in 1232.⁶¹ It also reached the broadest of audiences in the latter parts of the thirteenth century and beyond when Frederic II requested a Latin translation of the work, and by the 1800s it was a recognized literary masterpiece in European thought.⁶² However, I propose this was because one could relate its ideas and/or interpret them as early quasi-Enlightenment as it related to his view of God and the absence of the possibility of miracles.⁶³ This idea will be explored in greater detail in a later chapter.

Ivry punctuates the overarching thrust of Maimonides's purpose of *Guide of the Perplexed* with this not-so-succinct but still important paragraph from Seeskin's *Cambridge Companion*:

58. Kraemer, *Maimonides*, 363–64.

59. Kraemer, *Maimonides*, 366–67.

60. Ravitzky, "Secrets of the *Guide to the Perplexed*," 159 and Halbertal, *Maimonides*, 66. Halbertal cites a letter from Maimonides to Joseph ben Judah in which he writes: "I am here sending you sending six booklets of the Guide which I have taken from the others, and they complete the first part . . . They have been copies only the pious *dayyan* and Abu al-Mahasin, so treat them carefully and do not lose them, so I am not harmed by the gentiles or by the many wicked Israelites." Original source is from Yizchack Shailat's translation of *Iggerot ha-Rambam* (Ma'aleh Edomim: Ma'Eliyot, 1987), 310–11.

61. Halbertal, *Maimonides*, 67.

62. Arbel, *Maimonides*, 159–60.

63. Frank, "Maimonides and Medieval Jewish Aristotelianism," 136 and Arbel, *Maimonides*, 160. This is not Arbel's position but my own since she mentions the influence that *Guide* had on Baruch Spinoza, Friedrich Hegel, and Moses Mendelssohn. Frank also mentions Maimonides's influence on Spinoza. Rambam was skeptical of the validity of miracles and it has influenced Judaism today (see Isaacs, *Miracles*, 64–70. Please note this statement from the *Guide of the Perplexed*: "For a miracle cannot prove that which is impossible; it is useful only as a confirmation of that which is possible, as we have explained in our Mishneh-torah" (Maimonides, *Guide for the Perplexed*, part 3, chapter 24).

> Maimonides' first concern in the *Guide* is to educate the reader how to read the Bible. He does so forcefully and dogmatically, for the first seventy(!) chapters of the book. This section of the *Guide* is primarily devoted to an unorthodox hermeneutic of the biblical text. Maimonides' basic conviction is that the canon is not to be taken literally when it speaks of God. In as thorough a manner as possible, Maimonides removes every human and personal aspect of the Deity, every attribute by which He is conceived and depicted.[64]

Ivry goes on to explain his view as to why Rambam chose to take this path which agrees to a limited but not complete extent with my original perspective as well—". . . predicating attributes of God introduces *plurality* and corporeality into the unique simplicity of God, thereby returning Judaism to the pagan world from which it came (emphasis added)."[65] I agree with Ivry on Maimonides's concern about the issue of plurality, but I argue that it is more related to the Christian and trinitarian concern of Jesus as God the Son than a return to paganism "from which it came." There is no evidence in Maimonidean thought that he viewed Judaism as coming from pagan roots; however, there is ample evidence throughout Rambam's writings that he was concerned about Jesus of Nazareth. Therefore, he would need to turn "the historic God of Israel into an ahistoric Deity."[66]

Kraemer notes that Rambam began his *Guide to the Perplexed* with the following poem that I argue reveals an individual who thought of himself destined to be responsible for the future of the Jewish people (i.e., pseudo-messianic or a forerunner of the individual himself):

> *My knowledge goes forth to point out the way,*
> *To pave straight its road.*
> *Lo, everyone who goes astray in the field of Torah,*
> *Come and follow its path.*
> *The unclean and the fool shall not pass over it;*
> *It shall be called the Sacred Way.*[67]

The accepted and readily available introduction to Joseph ben Judah also reveals that Maimonides saw the need to introduce his allegorical

---

64. Ivry, "*Guide* and Maimonides' Philosophical Sources," 64. Aside from direct references to primary sources, I am attempting to keep block quotes to the bare minimum; however, this was too important of a statement for the overarching theme to edit down and so I left it as it was.

65. Ivry, "*Guide* and Maimonides' Philosophical Sources," 64.

66. Ivry, "*Guide* and Maimonides' Philosophical Sources," 64.

67. Kraemer, *Maimonides*, 368.

hermeneutical premises to the intended select audience regardless of the anger that it might incur. He believed it was necessary for the future of Judaism and for the protection of a negative God that was created more in the image that Rambam wanted to preserve than the One that actually exists. He wrote this to his student:

> Lastly, when I have a difficult subject before me—when I find the road narrow, and can see no other way of teaching a well-established truth except by pleasing one intelligent man and displeasing ten thousand fools—I prefer to address myself to the one man, and to take no notice whatever of the condemnation of the multitude; I prefer to extricate that intelligent man from his embarrassment and show him the cause of his perplexity, so that he may attain perfection and be at peace.[68]

Beginning with the very first chapter of *Guide of the Perplexed*, Maimonides takes on one of the most difficult hermeneutical and theological issues related to the issue of corporeality versus incorporeality in Scripture—Gen 1:26 and the question of the *Imago Dei* or *tzelem* in Hebrew. How is man created in the image of God? Is it bodily? Is it spiritual? Is it a combination of the two? Another question that should also be asked is why did Rambam begin here with this passage and at this point?

While Shoshanna Gershenzon's PhD dissertation of Abner of Bergos deals with a Jewish believer's trinitarian apologetic—which includes the usage of midrashic argumentation in the latter part of the of the thirteenth century, almost one hundred years after Rambam's death—it still indicates that the Christian argument that Gen 1:26 pointed to a plurality of the Godhead was present in the years of Maimonides.[69] In fact, she writes that the scriptural origins of the Trinity "already had a long polemical history," and it is this history that I argue that Rambam sought to negate in the first pages of his allegorical, hermeneutical, perplexing, guide to Hebrew Scriptures.[70] Rambam wrote, "The incorporeality of the Divine Being, and His unity, in the true sense of the word—for there is no unity without incorporeality—will be fully proved in the course of the present treatise."[71]

---

68. Maimonides, *Guide for the Perplexed*, 15. Both Kraemer's biography and Twersky's supplemental source have more "entertaining" translations; however, and for the sake of continuity, I will continue utilizing the Friedländer source. However, usage of words such as "ignoramuses" and "creatures" was entertaining.

69. Gershenzon, "Study of *Teshuvot Le-Meharef*," 86–94.

70. Gershenzon, "Study of *Teshuvot Le-Meharef*," 94. Harry Wolfson would concur with Gershenzon in his article; however, he spends too much energy wondering if Rambam is attacking Islamic thought rather than Christian doctrine. Wolfson, "Maimonides on the Unity and Incorpeality of God," 112–36 (esp. 132–33).

71. Maimonides, *Guide for the Perplexed*, part 1, chapter 1 (19).

Therefore, Maimonides in *Guide of the Perplexed*, will have to create a hermeneutical understanding of *tzelem* that will allow for a non-corporeal understanding of the word. In other words, he will have to allegorize what is understood on a surface level throughout the Hebrew Scriptures (specifically as it relates to concept of the image of the visible idols—Num 33:52; 1 Sam 6:5; 6:11; 2 Kgs 11:18; 2 Chr 23:17; Ezek 23:14; Amos 5:26) as something visible and tangible. He sought to do so by translating *tzelem* as something that "constitutes the essence of a thing, whereby the thing is what it is, the reality of a thing in so far as it is that particular being."[72] Understandably, and as will be discussed in the next chapter related to Thomas Aquinas, Christians can affirm the Maimonidean concept of "Divine intellect with which man has been endowed"[73] but the imperative purpose behind Rambam's design was to eliminate the possibility of any future incarnate reality of the Godhead through Jesus the Son. This is something that we in the Christian faith cannot affirm.

Ivry writes of Maimonides that his goal was to "reform his society and educate those capable of understanding him to the path he believed led to happiness required him to expose the esoteric dimension of the Bible as much as he dared."[74] He further wrote that "Maimonides' allegorical treatment of the Bible extends . . . toward understanding the entire text as imaginative human construct, not to be taken literally as God's spoken word."[75] Rambam himself wrote in *Guide of the Perplexed*:

> Therefore bear in mind that by the belief in the corporeality or in anything connected with corporeality, you would provoke God to jealousy and wrath, kindle His fire and anger, become His foe, His enemy, His adversary in a higher degree than by the worship of idols . . . I do not consider those men as infidels who are unable to prove the incorporeality, but I hold those to be so who do not believe it, especially when they see that Onkelos and Jonathan avoid [in reference to God] expressions implying corporeality as much as possible. This is all I intended to say in this chapter.[76]

---

72. Maimonides, *Guide for the Perplexed*, part 1, chapter 1 (19–20).

73. Maimonides, *Guide for the Perplexed*, part 1, chapter 1 (21). See also Lorberbaum, "Imago Dei in Judaism," 59, 69–70. It should be noted that Lorberbaum comes across as much more sympathetic to the kabbalistic thought than to the Maimonidean concepts of *Imago Dei*.

74. Ivry, "*Guide* and Maimonides' Philosophical Sources," 66.

75. Ivry, "*Guide* and Maimonides' Philosophical Sources," 66–67.

76. Maimonides, *Guide for the Perplexed*, part 1, chapter 36 (93). Onkelos was a gentile convert and will be briefly mentioned later in this section.

The incorporeality of Maimonide's Yahweh will take on many shapes, forms, and approaches throughout his *Guide of the Perplexed* which will only create a more perplexing God for the Jewish people, and a more distant and remote God causing humanity to have a more deistic perception of Him. The concepts of God's speech and the possibility of knowing God personally by an individual will take precedence as they relate to the question of both the possibility of the incarnation and negating the issue of possible Jewish deism in Maimonidean thought.[77] Additionally, the usage of the phrase "possible Jewish deism" that I myself used in the previous sentence is idealistic. For if Maimonides was so concerned about any tinge about the personification or perhaps even the humanization of God that he utilized allegory as a hermeneutical device throughout *Guide* "wherever the Bible describes God anthropomorphically,"[78] he must have recognized the ramifications of what it would mean if it was present. This is why *Guide of the Perplexed* began with a hermeneutical analysis of Gen 1:26.[79]

The purpose of Rambam's *Guide* has been described by Halbertal as one that was "primarily an exegetical book that administers therapy to religious language."[80] This is a clever turn of phrase by Halbertal but accurate in many ways. Maimonides could not allow the obvious expression of God to stand, for it might turn the Jewish people in a direction towards the Islamic or Christian faith. Such a turn towards this direction would be politically expedient as I have shown, for the oppressive winds of the Crusades in Europe were blowing and the pressures of conversions were always prevalent. Therefore, he took the path that had been laid out earlier by the Roman proselyte Onkelos and sought to remove the "humanity," the closeness, the tangible relationship an individual could have with God.[81] We will examine

77. From this perspective, Kraemer, *Maimonides*, 376–82, focuses more on the knowledge aspect, while Halbertal, *Maimonides*, 293–311, focuses on both. I argue that both are of equal importance for one cannot know God if one does not hear and speak with God, and one speaks and hears God in order to know Him. Others might add aspects to this list; however, I am focusing on these two areas as the primary issues of concern.

78. Ivry, "*Guide* and Maimonides' Philosophical Sources," 65.

79. Kreisel, "*Imitatio Dei* in Maimonides' *Guide of the Perplexed*," 179–81. Kreisel describes the *Imago Dei* for Maimonides of Gen 1:26 as the "theoretical intellect" in which "humans distinguish between truth and falsehood, i.e., attain knowledge of the sciences culminating in the knowledge of God" (180). However, it is interesting that despite Rambam's best efforts to dissuade his Jewish audience, words such as "knowledge" still creep into the conversation. See also Cohen, "Figurative Language, Philosophy, Religious Belief," 385.

80. Halbertal, *Maimonides*, 291.

81. Kraemer, *Maimonides*, 377. Kraemer notes that Onkelos would substitute the words *memra*, *shekhinta*, and *yeqara* for the word God. A brief historical explanation

the cost of this approach and the possible Christian apologetic approach to re-engagement with the Jewish people later; however, the remaining section of this chapter will include Rambam's allegorical exegesis in his *Guide for the Perplexed*, as it relates to speech and knowledge, of the *Akedah* of Gen 22, the "angel" of Gen 32, the name of God in Exod 3, the encounter with God and Moses and the elders in Exod 24:10–11, and the desire of Moses to see God's face in Exod 33.[82]

In many ways, the rabbi from Cairo's concern about direct speech and knowledge coming from God to individuals relate to the idea of what he called prophecy.[83] Whereas one can seemingly find a plethora of individuals in Scripture—including Amos the shepherd and Hosea the husband of a harlot, who were not considered the "best and brightest" of Israel—Maimonides seems to express what could only be considered as an elitist mentality toward the subject. For while a biographer might summarize (i.e., clean up) the rabbi's wording, "Prophecy, he said, rests upon only a sage, great in wisdom, heroic in character, whose reason overcomes his passion, and who has a broad and sound mind."[84] Rambam's own words in part 2, chapter 32 speak for themselves:

> Among those who believe in Prophecy, and even among our coreligionists, there are some ignorant people who think as follows: *God selects any person He pleases, inspires him with the Prophecy, and entrusts him with a mission.* It makes no difference whether that person be wise or stupid, old or young; provided he be, to some extent, morally good . . . As for the principle which I laid down, *that preparation and perfection of*

---

of Onkelos the Roman proselyte to Judaism is appropriate without devoting an inordinate time and space to the man. According to most historical accounts, Onkelos was a member of the Emperor Hadrian's royal family who converted to Judaism during the second century. He is credited with translating the Torah into Aramaic and credited with the *Targum Onkelos*. This brief explanation is from http://www.chabad.org/library/article_cdo/aid/112286/jewish/Onkelos.htm.

82. Kraemer, *Maimonides*, 376 and Halbertal, *Maimonides*, 306, 326. Obviously, more examples from both Scripture and *Guide of the Perplexed* could be examined; however, these have been chosen since they are obvious, from the Torah, and include either a patriarch or the prophet Moses himself.

83. Halbertal, *Maimonides*, 321. Halbertal specifically notes that Rambam focuses on prophecy in part 2, chapters 32–48, of the *Guide*. However, references dealing with the passages of concern will come from areas across a wide spectrum of the work.

84. Kraemer, *Maimonides*, 387. The philosophic vs. miraculous nature of prophecy in the mind of Rambam is not easily explained or understood even today. Could someone fit Rambam's criteria and not be a prophet? Is prophecy a miracle or philosophical in nature? These were all questions that later Jewish scholars sought to ascertain without much success. Kaplan, "Maimonides on the Miraculous Element in Prophecy," 233–56.

moral and rational faculties are the sine quâ non, our Sages say exactly the same: . . . There are, however, numerous passages in Scripture as well as in the writings of our Sages, which support the principle that it depends chiefly on the will of God who is to prophesy, and at what time; *and that He only selects the best and the wisest. We hold that fools and ignorant people are unfit for this distinction* . . . We must not be misled by the words of Jeremiah (i.5), . . . Nor must we be misled by prophecies like the following: "I will pour out my spirit over all flesh, and your sons and your daughters shall prophesy"; since it is distinctly stated what is meant by "prophesy" in this place, viz., "Your old men will dream dreams, your young men shall see visions . . ." Since we have touched upon the revelation on Mount Sinai, we will point out in a separate chapter what may be inferred as regards the nature of that event, *both from the Scriptural text, in accordance with reasonable interpretation, and from the words of our Sages.*[85]

Additionally, Halbertal stated that Rambam will argue that all prophetic incidences of speech and knowledge that can happen between God and man will occur with an angel serving as an intermediary.[86] For example:

---

85. Maimonides, *Guide for the Perplexed*, part 2, chapter 32 (367–70, emphasis added). Unfortunately, it was necessary to have such a long block quote to point out several key perspectives of Maimonides:

1. revelation and/or inspiration from God is not open to any individual and this perspective will find itself come to a modern fruition in the sense that many Jewish people will respond to questions about faith with the adage, "I will need to ask my rabbi;"
2. the elitist mentality of Maimonides is evident in chapter 32 of his *Guide* and one wonders how he deals with the question of a sheepherder and a harlot's husband (see http://www.moshereiss.org/articles/26_hosea.htm for one possible approach); and
3. the perspective that allegorical exegesis and talmudic commentary is required for proper interpretation of Scripture as a plain reading of the text is insufficient at any level.

Trigano, "Conventionalization of Social Bonds," 48–49, utilizes and borrows from Max Weber to construct an interesting analysis of the end result of Maimonidean allegorialism. Unfortunately, space and time prevents a further examination of this "chart."

86. Leaman, "Maimonides, Imagination and the Objectivity of Prophecy," 73–74 and Halbertal, *Maimonides*, 325. Many of us in the Christian sphere acknowledge this intermediary angel of the Lord as a pre-incarnate encounter with Messiah Jesus. However, many rabbis will resort to developing a hierarchy structure of angels with the unknown Metatron being placed in the spot of angel of the Lord. Others will seek to explain Metatron in other ways; however, it is always an interesting deviation away from the truth of Messiah Jesus. For a brief list see Davila, "Of Methodology, Monotheism, and Metatron," 3–18; Blumenthal, "Maimonides on Angel Names," 357–69; and

> There are four different ways in which Scripture relates the fact that a divine communication was made to the prophet. (1) the prophet relates that he heard the word of an angel in a dream or vision; (2) He reports the words of the angel without mentioning that they were perceived in a dream or vision, assuming that it is well known that prophecy can only originate in one of the two ways, "In a vision I will make myself known unto him, in a dream I will speak unto him (Num. xii. 6). (3) The prophet does not mention the angel at all; he says that God spoke to him, but he states that he received the message in a dream or vision. (4) He introduces his prophecy stating that God spoke to him, or told him to do a certain thing, or speak certain words, but he does not explain that he received the message or vision, because he assumes that is it is well known, and has been established as a principle that no prophecy or revelation origins otherwise than in a dream or vision, *and through an angel*.[87]

My emphasis of the wording "and through an angel" was purposeful as it illustrates this perhaps unintentional but impactful deistic God that Maimonides will create for future Jewish thinkers. It is also impactful as it discounts an intimacy that God had with Abraham when He asked the first patriarch to do what on the surface seemed to be the unthinkable—sacrifice his son. And it is this intimacy that is key to this passage and to what it represents to the future of humanity.

The account of the *akedah* (binding) of Isaac in Gen 22 is read in every synagogue around the world on every Rosh Hashanah. It is considered both a linchpin of the Abrahamic Covenant for Judaism and a testament of Abraham's faithfulness to his relationship with God.[88] Rabbis will struggle with how to create a new sermon on a familiar tale just as Christian pastors try to find a new way to tell their parishioners to love their mothers on the second Sunday of May. They also struggle with two other issues in this passage—the apparent call of God for human sacrifice and what to do with this mysterious "angel of the Lord" in verse 11. Maimonides's answer was to simply call

---

Stroumsa, "Form(s) of God," 269–88.

87. Maimonides, *Guide of the Perplexed*, part 2, chapter 41 (394–95, emphasis added).

88. Maimonides, *Guide of the Perplexed*, part 3, chapter 24 (507–11). It should be noted in all fairness, especially since this book is highly critical of the overarching teaching of Rambam's views, that the rabbi presents a nice homily on the issue of faith despite what seems logical to human sensibilities in this letter to Joseph ben Judah. And while I might take issue with some of his insertions that are superfluous about the "unity of God," it is still a teaching that even Christians should examine as an example of how to respond to trials and understand God in the midst of them.

it a vision and/or a dream with the premise that the test was not actually for Abraham but was a model lesson for future generations on how to behave:[89]

> He [Abraham] sees an angel that speaks to him *in a vision*, as was the case when Abraham was addressed by an angel at the sacrifice of Isaac (Gen. xxii. 15) . . . But *it appears to be me improbable that a prophet should be able to perceive in a prophetic vision God speaking to him; the action of the imaginative faculty does not go so far*; and therefore we do not notice this in the case of the ordinary prophets; . . .[90]

However, the question still remains if Rambam was correct—did Isaac have this same vision? Was it Abraham's solely? Was this why Isaac did not return with his father, for we next see him living alone in Beer-lahai-roi (Gen 24:62)? These are issues which Maimonides never answers in his *Guide* and hence he leaves his readers only more perplexed.

The question of angels in the theology of Maimonides is one that has been only briefly discussed. However, there are some specific notations that should be noted as well for Rambam:

1. angels like God are non-corporeal not only because it fits with his view of God but also because it fits an Aristotelian concept as well;
2. angels are messengers whose purpose is missional in nature; and
3. angels can override man's free will if it serves the purposes of God.[91]

These notations are relevant as we consider the second relevant passage of Jacob's wrestling match with a man who is also an angel in Gen 32.

We have already confirmed Halbertal's argument that the Cairo rabbi would argue against the possibility of even seeing an angel since they are non-corporeal.[92] We must also examine three other aspects of Rambam's exegesis of this passage:

---

89. Feldman, "Binding of Isaac," 109–12.

90. Maimonides, *Guide of the Perplexed*, part 2, chapter 45 (408–9, emphasis added). The confusion over this exegesis is that the passage begins with a literal reading of God speaking directly to Abraham and then the angel of the Lord speaking directly to him. Why the "apparent" change of persons? Followers of Rambam would never address this confusion except to go back to the default four ways of divine communication found in chapter 32.

91. Maimonides, *Guide of the Perplexed*, part 2, chapter 6 (270–71). One of the largest objections to Jesus in modern Judaism is their argument that original sin denies the possibility of free will; however, Maimonides does the same thing as it applies to the freedom of angels to move men capriciously. This is something to consider for chapter 5 as an apologetic response.

92. Halbertal, *Maimonides*, 326.

1. was it a man or an angel that Jacob wrestled?;
2. if a non-corporeal angel in a vision, how was Jacob maimed?; and
3. what did Jacob mean when he said he saw the face of God?

These three crucial questions create a tension for Maimonides as they relate not only to the negation theology which he is creating but also to the question of whether God can ever become incarnate in human form.

His attempt to answer the first issue is found in this rather convoluted response:

> In such visions, a prophet either sees God who speaks to him, as will be explained to us, or he sees an angel who speaks to him, or he hears some one speaking to him without seeing the speaker, or he sees a man who speaks to him, and learns afterwards that the speaker was an angel. In this latter kind of prophecies, the prophet relates that he saw a man who was doing or saying something, and that he learnt afterwards that he was an angel... The same, I hold, is the case when it is said in reference to Jacob, "And a man wrestled with him" (Gen. xxxii.25); this took place in a prophetic vision, since it is expressly stated in the end (ver. 31) that it was an angel.[93]

What is so difficult to understand about this perplexing passage of Maimonides is what appears to be a desperate need to force an interpretation of a vision or dream into an event that left someone injured for the remainder of his life. Interestingly, this section of the rabbi's *Guide* never deals with the subject and one can only assume that—according to Rambam's own guidelines in part 2, chapter 3—the injury must have been psychosomatic and made Jacob no longer eligible to be a prophet.[94] These are two concepts that many would be uncomfortable assuming; however, this is what would be required if one follows the rabbi's guidelines that are designed to create a *via negativa* Jehovah that could not become personal and relational with His people either through a Christophanic encounter or through the incarnation of Messiah Jesus. Maimonides also took the same approach and referred back to Onkelos in dealing with the sticky issue of Jacob seeing God's face by re-translating *panim el-panim* as *panim lepanim* which takes God out of the equation and replaces it with "So went the present over

---

93. Maimonides, *Guide of the Perplexed*, part 2, chapter 42 (396–97).

94. I found an interesting article that affirms the statement that I made about psychosomatic injury if in perhaps a more delicate manner—Miller, "Jacob's Injury," download.yutorah.org/2014/1053/813251.pdf.

before him."⁹⁵ A clever approach but something that takes the meaning and purpose from the text, an intention which was deliberate.

The final three passages under examination in this book all relate to the person for whom Maimonides feels the greatest kinship—the prophet and leader of the exodus, Moses. The first passage deals with what appears to be a personal and intimate conversation between Moses and God as it reveals the personal name of God in Exod 3:13–14—"I AM WHO I AM." It is personal in a plain reading of the text; however, and based upon Rambam's guidelines (part 2, chapter 32), it was not even a real conversation but a vision, a dream. However, a plain reading of the entire context of Exod 3:1–14 reveals perhaps what could be described by some as a vision but something that is intimate, personal, and Christophanic in its dynamic:

Additionally, a vitally important question is how can one reconcile the statement in verse 2 in which we find the "angel of the LORD" appearing to him from the bush and Moses hiding his face in verse 6 out of fear to see the face of God, with Maimonides's view that God is non-corporeal and unable to possess our attributes at any time or place? For Rambam wrote, "Anything predicated of God is totally different from our attributes; no definition can comprehend both; therefore His existence and that of any other being totally differ from each other, and the term existence is applied to both homonymously, as I shall explain."⁹⁶ Maimonides's response is to hearken back to an Aristotelian response and attribute Moses's response to a literal fear of the very real light coming from the bush while also expressing humility during the visional manifestation.⁹⁷ However, such a reaction does not make sense if Moses was not yet sure whom he was addressing and it is curious why an allegorical vision suddenly needed a literal fire. It also does not answer the question of the Qal perfect verb tenses or the issue of the name given to Moses that is of utmost importance.

The name I AM WHO I AM is a question of pronunciation, mystery, and quandary for the Jewish people. The word *Adonai* is utilized instead of *Yahweh* in the synagogue. *Yahweh* is never used as it is considered too holy, too reverent, and too special. As Maimonides explains, "Every other name of God is a derivative, only the Tetragrammaton is a *nomen proprium*, and must not be considered from any other point of view."⁹⁸ The I AM WHO

95. Maimonides, *Guide of the Perplexed*, part 1, chapter 21 (55).
96. Maimonides, *Guide of the Perplexed*, part 1, chapter 35 (89).
97. Maimonides, *Guide of the Perplexed*, part 1, chapter 5 (28). The beginning of the exact statement reads as follows: "When the chief of philosophers [Aristotle] was about to inquire into some very profound subject, and to establish his theory by proofs, he commenced his treaty with an apology, . . ."
98. Maimonides, *Guide of the Perplexed*, part 1, chapter 61 (161).

I AM is called a tetragrammaton as it consists solely of the letters *yod*, *hé*, *vau*, *hé* and is a *nomen proprium* as it is a name that can only be applied to God alone.[99] Interestingly, and contrary to scriptural attestations from David, Hannah, and others, Maimonides will argue that "[T]his sacred name, which, as you know, was not pronounced except in the sanctuary by the appointed priests when they gave the sacerdotal blessing, and by the high priest on the Day of Atonement, undoubtedly denotes something which is peculiar to God, and is not found in any other being."[100] While even Christians could agree with the concluding statement that God possesses traits (i.e., "something") that is not found in any other aspect of His creation, there is contradictory evidence within the Hebrew Scriptures as to his claim that the name was reserved to the priestly class and was reserved to being pronounced only in the sacrificial blessings and holy days. Eli did not condemn Hannah for saying the name of Yahweh, he condemned her because of his assumption that she was intoxicated. David's relationship with God was often predicated on his choice of the word *Yahweh* or *Elohim* (Ps 23 or 51). This effort to segregate the name of God within Maimonides's *Guide* appears to be another effort to segregate understanding of biblical knowledge to the best and the brightest according to Rambam's standards.[101] Sadly, this is a segregation that will hamper the Jewish people's relationship with God in later centuries.[102]

The second of the third Mosaic passages that will be examined does not include Moses alone. It also includes the elders who also "saw God." In Exod 24:10–11—"*and they saw the God of Israel; and under His feet there appeared to be a pavement of sapphire, as clear as the sky itself. Yet He [God] did not stretch out His hand against the nobles of the sons of Israel; and they saw God, and they ate and drank*" (emphasis added).[103] What is unique about these two verses is that we have two words for the action of seeing God in these verses and they can both mean either the action of really see-

99. Maimonides, *Guide of the Perplexed*, part 1, chapter 61 (160).

100. Maimonides, *Guide of the Perplexed*, part 1, chapter 61 (160).

101. Chapter 62 of *Guide* offers the recounting of an interesting apocryphal legend that has been passed down in Jewish tradition about expanded ways to pronounce the mysterious name of God from the 4-word method to a 13-letter approach to a 42-letter pronunciation. Darren Aronfsky even produced and directed the movie *PI* (Artisan Entertainment, 1998) about this apocryphal legend, as some ultra-Orthodox Jews believe that if this name can be revealed it will bring about the advent of the messianic age.

102. I will list here only a brief snapshot of some articles that describe the conundrum over God's name and proper usage of it within Judaism. Fox, "Hashem's Names and Their Meanings," 8–9 and Berkovitz, "Two-fold Tetragrammaton," 45–52.

103. The actions of the elders are in the Qal imperfect. The action of *Elohim* is in the Qal perfect.

ing something or a vision. Therefore, one has a choice in interpretation and Maimonides has chosen the action which fits his overarching motif of vision or dream. However, he is forced to deal with two issues:

1. the elders are not worthy of such a vision according to his prescribed definition as laid out for the sight and knowledge of a prophet and
2. they do a very real action of eating and drinking. His conclusion is to condemn and punish them for both choices.[104]

> But the "nobles of the Children of Israel" were impetuous, and allowed their thoughts to go unrestrained: what they perceived was but imperfect . . . [t]he purpose of the whole passage is to criticize their act of seeing and to describe it. They are blamed for the nature of their perception, *which was to a certain extent corporeal*—a result which necessarily followed, from the fact that they ventured too far before being perfectly prepared. They deserved to perish, but at the intercession of Moses this fate was averted by God for the time . . . The nobles of the Children of Israel, besides erring in their perception, were, through this cause, also misled in their actions, for in their consequence of their confused perception, they gave way to bodily cravings . . . All we here intend to say is, that wherever in a similar connection any one of the three verbs mentioned above occurs, it has reference to intellectual perception, not to the sensation of sight by the eye; *For God is not a being to be perceived by the eye.*[105]

Three notations are worthy of further attention:

1. Maimonides recognized a corporeal encounter by the elders even if he struggled to reconcile the passage with his allegorical exegesis;
2. his allegory of the passage completely counters the passage itself and allows for a changing of God's mind even though in other passages of the *Guide*, he seeks to discount such a possibility; and
3. it appears sometimes that Rambam perhaps is not even aware that in his own struggles to create a *via negativa* God that is so distant from humanity, he is fighting against the incarnate Jesus himself.

104. Levine, "Maimonides' Philosophical Exegesis," 61–106. Throughout a reading of this attempted exegesis of the passage, Levine both acknowledges and attempts to excuse Maimonides's struggle to explain what she calls the elders "physics" and "metaphysics" encounter with God. She attempts to re-exegete the passage while maintaining a Maimonidean understanding of the passage which only creates more confusion.

105. Maimonides, *Guide of the Perplexed*, part 1, chapter 5 (29, emphasis added). Rambam also notes that most were later punished according to the Midrash at Taberah while Nadab and Abihu were punished for burning the strange fire in the tabernacle.

As I read the last statement I included from chapter 5, "for God is not a being to be perceived by the eye," I was drawn to many of the Johannine statements "I Am" of Jesus about himself and when he quoted Dan 7:13–14 before the Sanhedrin after his arrest. Maimonides could not allow the concept of anyone who could "hear and know" God in a personal, intimate, concrete way. There are innumerable times in which he stated at the end of his letters to Joseph ben Judah two words that are anything but simple because they take on an almost dictatorial-type decree now when one reads them in retrospect. They read simply—"Note it."[106] Today, as I discuss Jesus with Jewish people and I hear them say, "I will have to ask my rabbi," I believe I also hear those two words as well.

The final Mosaic passage under consideration, Exod 33:18–23, is controversial and confusing even within Christian circles, much less Jewish thought. What was Moses really asking of God? What did Moses see? How anthropomorphic, literal, and/or allegorical should this passage be taken?

I actually agree with Rambam's definition of God's glory and the idea of what it truly entails to engage in glorification to His name:

> For the true glorification of the Lord consists in the comprehension of His greatness, and all who comprehend His greatness and perfection, glorify Him according to their capacity, with this difference, that man alone magnifies God in words, expressive of he has received in his mind, and what he desires to communicate to others.[107]

However, this is where my agreement with the Cairo rabbi ends. For Maimonides returns to his "separation between God and man" motif by explaining that Moses's encounter in Exod 33 is a "perception" since it occurred without the "intervention of angel,"[108] that the rock is an allegorical representation and not literal,[109] and that Moses can only know the actions

---

106. There are too many instances of this phrase to footnote each one; however, I will note one in particular that relates to the issue of Dan 7:13. He begins part 2, chapter 44 (402–3) with this statement—"Prophecy is given either in a vision or in a dream, as we have said so many times, and we will not constantly repeat it." Halbertal writes in this way: "Once the reader learns that speech [in the writings of Maimonides] cannot be attributed to God, he has no choice but to reinterpret the meaning of prophecy" (*Maimonides*, 294).

107. Maimonides, *Guide of the Perplexed*, part 1, chapter 64 (170–71). Interestingly, Rambam goes on to relate that non-living organisms such as "minerals" can also glorify God (cf. Hab 2:11; Luke 19:40). I am not suggesting that Rambam had an intimate knowledge of all of Jesus's teaching; however, it is interesting.

108. Maimonides, *Guide of the Perplexed*, part 1, chapter 37 (94–95).

109. Maimonides, *Guide of the Perplexed*, part 1, chapter 16 (47).

of God and not who God is, which is key to the passage itself.[110] Sarah Pessin seeks to redefine Maimonides's own explanation of himself by presenting a hylomorphic apophasis interpretation of the meeting. Pessin describes Moses's vision as truly a philosophic encounter with the wonders of nature and therefore he did "see the face of God" via the rocks on Mount Sinai.[111] However, I would describe this as an even more allegorical interpretation than Maimonides (or even Origen) would be comfortable utilizing. I argue that Pessin recognizes that Maimonides stretched the boundaries of allegory and instead of drawing back from the edge, she stepped over the edge.

Halbertal provides an excellent explanation of illustrating what Moses was asking in verse 18. Moses wanted a relational connection to God that would be described as that of a friend and was only shown God's back.[112] In other words, in Rambam's perspective Moses and all of creation can only know what is unknowable of God. However, this is contradictory to what Moses told the people in Exod 20:20 after they expressed fear and sought to keep their distance from God in verses 18–19. The first Moses implored them with these words, "Do not be afraid; for God has come in order to test you, and in order that the fear of Him may remain with you, so that you may not sin." However, the second Moses with his *Guide to the Perplexed* preferred to keep the Jewish people rooted at a distance from God, unable to discover the true prophet that was indeed greater than Moses (Deut 18:15).[113]

CHAPTER SUMMATION

Why did Maimonides need for the Jewish Messiah to not fit the parameters of the Christian Messiah, Jesus of Nazareth? This question ultimately can serve as a summary section for this chapter because I believe that this question is the basis for Rambam's life and work from *Commentary on the Mishnah* to the struggling people in Yemen. What drove the Cairo rabbi to focus all his work, drive, and energy to create a God that was so distant and inaccessible that he was unattainable to the Jewish masses that needed Him most? What drove the young child in Cordoba who became the "Second

---

110. Maimonides, *Guide of the Perplexed*, part 1, chapter 54 (137–38). See also Halbertal, *Maimonides*, 304–5.

111. Pessin, "On Glimpsing the Face of God in Maimonides," 75–105.

112. Halbertal, *Maimonides*, 304.

113. Obviously, I could have written more on just the *Guide* alone. However, I have sought to restrain myself to the key issue at hand—that being the issue of *via negativa* present in the pages.

Moses of Judaism" to create a messiah that looks nothing like the Messiah of Isa 53 and elsewhere in Scripture?

Is it a drive to place Christianity and even Islam as subservient to Judaism in the sense that they are merely precursors to the ultimate Jewish messianic age?[114] After all, he did argue in the *Mishneh Torah* that Jesus and Muhammad served an ultimate purpose even if they were misguided. Is it a need to illustrate that the intellect and the mind is greater than emotionalism in religious discussion, as he did in *The Guide of the Perplexed*? To both of these questions, I argue in the affirmative. For I have sought to show throughout this chapter that to Maimonides, the Torah, and especially the Talmud, via his brand of Judaism was of greater value to him than any concept of "hearing, knowing, seeing" God. Aviezer Ravitzky writes this about Rambam: "While his Messianism is dictated not by his mind but by his faith, it is essentially his mind that directs, defines, and limits the object of his faith."[115] Ravitzky attempts to meld this definition of Maimonidean messianism by explaining his concept of an ideal society in almost Platonic/utopian terms as a melding of the ideal political state and perfection of spiritual society.[116]

For when one creates a rabbinic Judaism such as Maimonides sought to develop, it naturally creates a Judaism that will supersede Christianity and render Jesus of Nazareth moot. For when one creates a utopian Jewish world as Rambam sought to do through his *Mishneh Torah* and *Guide of the Perplexed*, the God of Judaism is by matter of form distant. However, the creation of a messiah whose appearing is still uncertain—"[f]or indeed there is no definite time assigned for the appearance of the Messiah and no one can state with any assurance whether his coming will be in the near future or at some remote period"[117]—creates an uncertainty that many Jewish people cannot live with any longer. They will ultimately turn away from Judaism either in form, function, or in apathetic non-compliance. How could they not? For as Arthur Cohen states it—"The view which Maimonides held of the divine attributes led him to the paradoxical conclusion that the greater

---

114. Poorthuis, "Messianism between Reason and Delusion," 66–67. This might not be the complete intention of Poorthuis's argument; however, I argue that the implication is present in his concluding paragraphs.

115. Ravitzky, "'To the Utmost Human Capacity,'" 221.

116. Ravitzky, "'To the Utmost Human Capacity,'" 222–30. To state that I completely understood Ravitzky's argument would not be entirely truthful; however, the basis of it corresponds to all that has been communicated throughout this chapter.

117. Stitskin, "Maimonides Letter on Apostacy," 110. Stitskin argues that this is the first public document produced by Maimonides in c. 1160. Interestingly enough, it was about the messiah.

our knowledge of God, the less we are able to affirm of Him."[118] This will be revealed in greater, modern detail in chapter 6, and an effort to develop an apologetic, evangelistic response to this spiritual crisis will be fleshed out in chapter 8. For ultimately we have no choice but to do otherwise if we believe that "to the Jew first" has any continuing validity.

---

118. Cohen, *Teachings of Maimonides*, 91.

5

Maimonides and His Reaction to Controversy and Christianity

A MAN SUCH AS Maimonides who was so prolific in his writings and opinions would naturally create controversies in his wake. Controversies within Judaism itself and antagonism against his archrival Christianity found a natural home in the words of Rambam's texts. However, and in many regards, the "Chief Rabbi of Cairo" was not concerned over how he was perceived. Therefore, one wonders whether the rabbi would be concerned with what he has wrought for Judaism today, but that will have to wait for later chapters as this chapter will focus on what he stirred up in the thirteenth century.

TREATISE ON THE RESURRECTION

I have a Jewish friend who would call herself a Conservative but practices more of a Reform Jewish lifestyle. In the more than a decade that we have known each other, we have had many discussions on the person and divinity of Jesus, whether one can remain Jewish if one believes in Jesus, the reality of anti-Semitism in the modern world, and other biblically related issues. In fact, until I sent her a Passover card with Isa 53:5 writtten inside and she literally "unfriended" me in the pages of the *Texas Jewish Post*, there was almost nothing we could not discuss except the question of what happens after we die. She steered away from the question because of the great unknown it presented to her and the mystery behind the veil of death. In fact, the adage of "ashes to ashes and dust to dust" seems to create a smokescreen for most Jewish people in the twenty-first century and I surmise that much of the enigma for it can be laid at the feet of Rambam himself. In seeking to solve the paradox, Maimonides himself seemingly made a more perplexing problem out of it than necessary when one examines the words of Dan 12:2—"Many of those who sleep in the dust of the ground will awake, these to everlasting life, but the others to disgrace *and* everlasting contempt."

"Belief in resurrection is one of Maimonides' thirteen principles of faith. It is mentioned in the main prayer of liturgy, the 'Amidah. Yet important as it is for Judaism, resurrection is even more for Christianity and Islam."[1] Perhaps these might be considered as startling words to hear from a Jewish scholar for many readers from a Christian purview; however, they are actually very accurate. The issue of the resurrection is a complicated issue within modern Judaism, an issue fraught with nuances and speculations and debate as to its relevance and necessity. However, this debate is not new and actually began in great earnest as an internecine struggle between the Geonim forces in Babylon and Maimonides in Egypt. And it began in earnest for what appears to be an omission in the rabbi's *Mishneh Torah* over what happens when we die.[2]

In the latter part of the twelfth century, and after the completion of the *Guide of the Perplexed*, the popularity of *Mishneh Torah* was creating a division within Judaism as to what should be the default source to follow—Maimonides's work or the Babylonian Talmud? The Geonim family in Baghdad led by Samuel ben Eli did not appreciate the challenge to their authority as well as the dissemination of Rambam's work throughout the region by his student, Joseph ben Judah. Therefore, the rumors began that the Cairo rabbi did not believe in a literal, physical resurrection and thus the controversy began that Maimonides was forced to address in 1191 with his *Treatise on the Resurrection*.[3]

Kraemer would argue that "[T]he doctrine of a literal resurrection was problematic for Maimonides, but he could not afford to let that be known."[4] If this was the case for Maimonides that he did not believe in a literal resur-

---

1. Kraemer, *Maimonides*, 408.

2. Halbertal, *Maimonides*, 143; Kraemer, *Maimonides*, 413; Arbel, *Maimonides*, 165; and Kraemer, "Moses Maimonides," 45.

3. Lerner, "Maimonides' 'Treatise on Resurrection,'" 144–45; Arbel, *Maimonides*, 163–67, Kraemer, "Moses Maimonides," 45; Halbertal, *Maimonides*, 143; and Kraemer, *Maimonides*, 412–15. It should be noted that there was an attempt by J. Louis Teicher to discredit the validity of this treatise; however, that debunking attempt did not go far. Sonne, "Scrutiny of the Charges of Forgery against Maimonides," 48–64.

4. Kraemer, *Maimonides*, 412. See also Silver, "Resurrection Debate," 79. Silver expresses an amusing turn of phrase related to Rambam's conundrum on the subject even as he relates the historical difficulties of many medieval Jewish scholars on the issue of the resurrection: "Maimonides affirmed even as he squirmed."

rection, it would rationalize his anger in the beginning pages of the letter as to why he referred to the first Moses—it was both a defense mechanism and a self-comparison.[5] However, these attacks will be something that Rambam will have to confront and respond to if Halbertal is correct in his understanding that the rabbi saw

1. "physical reward" as something to push man toward a "pursuit of his true purpose—knowledge of his Creator" and that
2. "the central purpose of the Torah is to elevate human life to a dimension that transcends worldly needs and fulfillment of basic material impulses."[6]

For this was not the teaching at the time of Rambam, and the Geonim family in Baghdad was drawing attention to the differences of opinion between Cairo's view and the rest of Judaism at the time.

Therefore, I will argue that it was crucial for Maimonides to establish several crucial tenets of his concept involving the meaning behind *Olam Haba* ("World to Come") before he established his own views of the purpose of resurrection and the afterlife, including the role of the messiah (all direct quotes from the treatise):

1. "The resurrection of the dead is a cornerstone of the Torah and that there is no portion for him that denies that it is part of the Torah of Moses our Teacher, but it is nevertheless not the ultimate goal";
2. "Separated existence is the true existence because it is not subject to any manner of change. These are (the wise) to whom it is absolutely clear that God is not corporeal nor a power within a body and, therefore, the level of His existence is the firmest of all"; and
3. "This situation is similar to one who thinks that he has achieved an understanding of the truth, in one moment, although he has very meager

---

5. Maimonides, *Moses Maimonides' Treatise on Resurrection*, I, 1–2. Rambam took the tactic that he should not be surprised that he would have to defend himself against such accusations if the prophet Moses had to defend the unity of God against "the false view" "of the dualists." Indeed, the whole first section (esp. I, 5) is a diatribe against "dualists" that one could surmise was an attack against Christianity when he writes—"Indeed, other people that I met from some lands unequivocally proclaimed Him to be corporeal and denounced as a heretic anyone who believes the opposite, and they call him a sectarian and an epicurean, and they cite many passages (in their support which they understand) literally."

6. Halbertal, *Maimonides*, 143, 145. It should be noted that as much as I have gleaned and appreciated Halbertal as a source that I do disagree with his supposition that Rambam taught a form of reincarnation/resurrection in his writing on the subject (p. 146). I have not been able to find such a teaching in this treatise.

knowledge and made only feeble attempts (at penetrating analysis) and neglected all wisdoms and contented himself with the simple interpretation of scriptures as if the Sages of blessed memory had never written in many places in the Talmud that the words of Torah have both revealed and hidden meanings, and that the hidden meanings are referred to as the "secrets of the Torah," and as if the Sages had never said anything about the secrets of the Torah."[7]

Indeed, and in many ways, Kraemer is correct that Maimonides is defending his previous works of *Guide of the Perplexed* and *Mishneh Torah*; however, I argue that Kraemer is wrong that he merely was writing to a general audience but also was talking down to the Geonim family in Baghdad.[8] For while one could argue that David Hartman's argument itself is pedantic in its devotion to the Cairo rabbi, I would not disagree with the sentiment that he expresses when he writes, "Rather than claim that Maimonides did not believe in rewards and punishments in general and in resurrection in particular, it is more correct to claim that he was embarrassed to talk at length about doctrines used to motivate observance of commandments by appeals to self-interest."[9]

Consequently, the question is simply—what did Rambam believe about the resurrection and the *Olam Haba*? Was it earthshaking? Was it groundbreaking? Ultimately, does it cast doubt on the idea and person of Jesus whether intentionally or unintentionally? He claimed to believe in a literal return of the soul to the body and that Dan 12:2 should be interpreted non-allegorically; however, the body is not the same as the one we once inhabited.[10] Interestingly, this Maimonidean concept is not "strikingly" different than the Christian concept of the resurrected body (Luke 20:34–36; 1 Cor 15:51–57). He writes of the eternal body: "Further, the life following which there is no death, is the life in the world to come because there are no (physical) bodies there. We firmly believe—and this is the truth which every intelligent person accepts—that in the world to come souls without bodies

---

7. Maimonides, *Treatise on the Resurrection*, part 2, chapters 8, 12, 14. Moises Orfali Levi of Bar-Ilan University (Israel) believes that there was an additional purpose to the treatise—to finally place an end within Judaism itself to the latent anthropomorphic tendencies some applied to God, as this had become an apologetic attack by medieval Christian apologists against rabbinic Judaism. Orfali Levi, "Anthropomorphism in the Christian Reproach of the Jews," 60–61, 71.

8. Kraemer, *Maimonides*, 418.

9. Hartman, "Discussions," 247.

10. Maimonides, *Treatise on the Resurrection*, part 3, chapter 16; part 4, chapters 22, 24; and part 7, chapters 40, 42, 43.

will exist like angels."[11] Yes, he believes in a bodiless existence in the *Olam Haba* while Christianity believes in a resurrected body that we struggle to define or understand; however, we both recognize that this human and sinful flesh is lost to something greater than we have now. The key difference between Maimonidean understanding of the resurrection and the Christian faith is twofold:

1. how does it unfold and
2. what is the place or role of the Messiah in all of it?

Interestingly, these two issues can be evaluated together in a unique way. For Maimonides, resurrection and the "World to Come" is an individual event in the life of each person and the messiah has nothing to do with resurrection, especially as it has already been noted that Rambam believed that the messiah will himself die.[12] Rambam argues that "It does not follow from this treatise that the Almighty, *at the time of His choice*, will not resurrect *those He wishes to resurrect*, whether during the era of the Messiah or before him *or after his death*" (emphasis added).[13] We have here three important qualifiers about Rambam's view of the resurrection:

1. resurrection is variable according to God's timing;
2. resurrection is capricious according to whom God will or will not resurrect; and
3. Maimonides wants to restate that the messiah will die.

This is emphatically important to the Cairo rabbi because it was necessary for Rambam to reemphasize that Jesus could not be the Messiah. My position is validated by his argument restated from the *Mishneh Torah* that the messiah will have nothing to do with performing "signs and wonders, bring anything new into being, resurrect the dead or do similar things."[14]

However, it is his closing statement of "Section VI," designed to be an apologetic against the Messiahship of Jesus, that will create spiritual disaster for the Jewish people. For in creating a God of negation and impossible incorporeality out of fear of the incarnate Jesus, he creates a God that was so deistic and so distant that many modern Jewish people cannot find Him. Maimonides wrote:

11. Maimonides, *Treatise on the Resurrection*, part 4, chapter 24. He goes on in this paragraph into an explanation of bodily functions that I omitted.
12. Maimonides, *Commentary on the Mishnah*, *Pereq Heleq*, chapter 10.
13. Maimonides, *Commentary on the Mishnah*, *Pereq Heleq*, chapter 10 (30).
14. Maimonides, *Commentary on the Mishnah*, *Pereq Heleq*, chapter 10 (30).

> It is well known that we are very opposed to changing the order of creation. Let those who precede or follow who are mistaken remain mistaken in that they cannot differentiate between miraculous events which do not endure and which are permanent but occur as a temporary necessity or to accredit a prophet—and natural events which always recur and which represent the laws of nature which the Sages of blessed memory explained by repeatedly stating "the world follows the laws of nature."[15]

One might ask—"If only the first portion of this statement was copied, could you discern if this was from the rabbi from Cairo or David Hume?" Ultimately, Maimonides sought to create a resurrection without meaning and a messiah without miracles but apparently he created, as will be illustrated in a later chapter, a twenty-first century Judaism without God.

THIRTEEN PRINCIPLES OF THE JEWISH FAITH

Many Jewish people today could not locate the book of Nahum in the Hebrew Scriptures or even tell you there was a prophet Nahum; however, even the most secular can tell you about Rambam's "Thirteen Principles of the Jewish Faith."[16] In the darkest days of the Holocaust, apocryphal stories abound of etchings on cellar walls where Jewish souls hid in fear but found the fortitude to write one or more of the Thirteen Principles to mark their place in the world.[17]

Today, when an evangelist shares the truth of Jesus the Messiah with a Jewish person, a common refrain will be, "But Jesus doesn't match Maimonides' criteria for the Messiah," which are found in another section of the *Commentary on the Mishnah* but is summarized in the Thirteen Principles: "The twelfth principle is the era of the *Mashiach*—i.e., to believe earnestly that the *Mashiach* will come, and not to say that the time for his coming has passed. Instead, if he tarries, wait for him."[18] In other words, one of the most powerful and influential legacies of Rambam's writings can be found

---

15. Maimonides, *Commentary on the Mishnah, Pereq Heleq*, chapter 10 (33).

16. Abelson, "Maimonides on the Jewish Creed," 24, 25. Abelson refers to this section in the *Commentary on the Mishnah* as both the "locus classicus" and as Rambam's design so that "every Israelite [could] know what exactly what were the things he was expected to believe, so as to be *entitled* to call himself a Jew, and expect others to do so" (emphasis added).

17. Schwarzschild, "Messianic Doctrine in Contemporary Jewish Thought," 237.

18. Maimonides, *Pirkei Avot*, 173–76, 179–82.

Maimonides and His Reaction to Controversy and Christianity 103

as a conclusion and an addendum, to his first work, *Commentary on the Mishnah*. Therefore, it deserves its own section of evaluation since it is so crucial to the question at hand.

The historical background to the *Commentary on the Mishnah* has already been provided in the previous chapter; therefore, this section will be devoted more to a theological and evaluative consideration of some of these principles. I would like to provide a complete translation of the Thirteen Principles; however, we will only examine those that relate to the question at hand.[19]

- "The second fundamental principle is His oneness, that this Cause of all being is one;"
- "The fourth fundamental principle is [His] primeval existence—i.e., that this unified Being exists above all concepts of time;"
- "The fifth fundamental principle is that it is fitting to serve and exalt God and publicize His greatness and the obligation to serve Him . . . Nor should these entitities [angels, stars, etc.] be considered as intermediaries through which one can reach God. Instead, we should direct our thoughts to Him alone, disregarding any other entity. This is the fifth fundamental principle, the warnings against the worship of false divinities . . . ;"
- "The seventh fundamental principle is the supremacy of the prophecy of Moses our teacher. This includes the belief that he is the master of all the prophets, those who preceded him and those who followed him, they are all beneath his level;" and
- "The ninth principle is that the Torah of Moses will never be nullified. There will never come another Torah aside from this."[20]

Many rabbis since Maimonides have attempted to explain or codify the concepts that have been laid out. Some will disagree or seek to expand upon aspects of his argument.[21] Others will present nothing more than a

---

19. A condensed version of all Thirteen Principles can be found in a variety of sources. Two examples are Nuland, *Maimonides*, 68–69 and Arbel, *Maimonides*, 86.

20. Maimonides, *Pirkei Avot*, 173–76, 179–82. Obviously, some of the added emphases have already been discussed in previous sections but I have noted them to show a consistency in Rambam's argument throughout the scope of his thought and life.

21. Goldman, "Halachic Foundation of Maimonides' Thirteen Principles," 111–18; Shapiro, "Maimonides' Thirteen Principles," 187–242; and Blau, "Flexibility with a Firm Foundation," 179–91. Goldman in his critique acknowledges that many of the Thirteen Principles are directly pointed toward the Christian faith (112). Shapiro provides a fascinating historical journey on rabbis and scholars who disagreed with Maimonides on

commentary on what each statement means without recognizing the often contradictory statements that Rambam himself presents within the statements themselves.[22] I argue that what one sees here, especially what has been emphasized, is in many respects the groundwork for the anti-Christian apologetic that he seeks to create with all his writings. Therefore, and while it is in many ways an addendum to the original work, I argue it is the most powerful addendum in post-Jesus, Jewish theological writings.

Louis Goldberg, a messianic Jewish scholar, brings out an important concept in the second principle over the usage of the word "one." Instead of the Hebrew word *echad* as found in Deut 6:4, which gives the connotation of a plural or unified one, Maimonides uses the alternative of *yachid* which can only be define as the singular (i.e., lonely) one. Goldberg writes this simple but clear statement—"With one neat statement, this Jewish philosopher undercut what the Council of Nicea sought to express: the Father, Son, and the Holy Spirit, each viewed as God, are one God, but in a Tri-unity. That is, God is one but in three persons."[23]

It has already been illustrated regarding the influence that Aristotle and Islamic-Aristotelian thinking played in Rambam's religious thought. Later in this chapter, I will also examine the influence and counter-influence that Thomas Aquinas and other Christian writers such as Gregory of Nyssa and John Philoponus had or could have had on the rabbi. However, as one considers the fourth principle of God's timelessness, one cannot help but be drawn to the thought of fifth-century Aristotelian philosopher Boethius, whose work on the concept of eternity and time appears to be reflected in this fourth principle.[24] Boethius wrote in his *The Consolation of Philosophy* some thoughts on the Creator and eternity that call to mind what Rambam himself wrote about God as well:

> . . . And, further, God, should not be regarded as older than His creations by any quantity of time but rather by the peculiar quality of simplicity in His nature . . . Thus if we would apply proper epithets to these subjects we would say, following Plato,

---

various facets of the "Thirteen Principles" but yet were still considered non-heretical. Perhaps this is why Blau, in his view of Marc Shapiro's work *The Limits of Orthodox Theology*, takes the writer to task for actually questioning Maimonides's thirteen principles as self-limiting for Judaism. He writes, "Either *mizvot* remain the royal to spiritual accomplishment or they do not (Christianity). *Either God takes human form (Christianity) or He does not*" (182, emphasis added). Obviously, Blau understands the point of Rambam's Thirteen Principles.

22. Angel, *Maimonides*, 151–72.

23. Robinson, *God, Torah, Messiah*, 92.

24. Boethius, "God Is Timeless," 136–39.

that God is eternal, while the universe is perpetual . . . God is the ever prescient spectator of all things, and the eternity of His vision, which is ever present, runs in unison with the future nature of our acts, dispensing rewards to the good, punishments to the evil.[25]

Maimonides himself notes that this fourth principle is not "original with him" as a later translator (Rav Kapach) added it in a content footnote to the principle that was found written by Rambam in the margins of his work: "One of the reasons I put so much emphasis on (the negation of the concept of) the world existing before time, as (some of) the philosophers maintain is because (the creation of the world from nothingness) proves God's existence absolutely, as I explained in the *Guide for the Perplexed*."[26] Maimonides interacted with the sources of Christian writers, even such Christian writers as Boethius, to the point that he knew their thoughts about time, creation, and God. He knew the concepts of existence and preexistence, and I argue that many of the arguments of the Thirteen Principles were engaged as an effort to disprove that God could be personal and active with humanity as a counter-point to the incarnate Jesus being God the Son. The fourth principle is such an example of this engagement. God alone created the universe out of nothing because nothing but God *alone* existed before creation. Michael Schwarz, while writing particularly in reference to a section in the *Guide*, speaks of this "atemporal" nature of God. He references the Islamic philosopher Ibn Sina (Avicenna), a philosopher worthy of further Maimonidean connection and consideration, but one can also see perhaps a Boethian influence as well with this statement from Schwartz—". . . His knowledge is identical with His essence; that through His own essence, He knows the principle and the cause of all existents; and that knowledge of the cause includes knowledge of the effect and, moreover, that this knowledge causes the existence of all things known."[27]

One of the great promises of the New Testament is found in 1 Tim 2:5–6: "For there is one God, *and* one mediator also between God and men, *the* man Christ Jesus, who gave Himself as a ransom for all, the testimony *given* at the proper time." However, Rambam will argue in his fifth principle that to believe in any sort of mediator is to believe in nothing but idolatry, as Rabbi Angel has argued.[28] Idolatry is a punishment worthy of death, a place in *Gehinnom*.

25. Boethius, "God Is Timeless," 136–39.
26. Maimonides, *Pirkei Avot*, 175.
27. Schwarz, "Some Remarks concerning Maimonides' Discussion," 193–94.
28. Angel, *Maimonides*, 155.

I personally have heard this charge brought against me many times; however, the most interesting example occurred several years ago in Bensonhurst Park, Brooklyn. A young anti-missionary named Daniel came to disrupt an evangelistic outreach that I was participating in when a thunderstorm disrupted the activities. Daniel and I found ourselves underneath an awning as shelter from the rain. We began to discuss just who was Jesus via the C. S. Lewis perspective—a lunatic, a liar, or the Lord. This fifth principle came up when I asked him about the eternal destiny of Christians such as Corrie ten Boom who are considered "righteous gentiles" for their actions during World War II. He was literally "stuck between a rock and a hard place" because condemning them to *Gehinnom* was wrong yet they believed in Jesus as God and in 1 Tim 2:5-6. Daniel was torn between Maimonides's fifth principle and the New Testament claims about Messiah Jesus at that moment. I do not know which he chose as he chose to go out into the rain rather than answering the question.

In Deut 18:15-18, a prophecy is given through Moses to the people that a prophet will come to the people that will be like Moses and he should be obeyed as Moses was—"The LORD your God will raise up for you a prophet like me from among you, from your countrymen, you shall listen to him." There is no implication in the Scripture that Moses was the pinnacle of prophecy. There is nothing within Scripture that says Moses advocated such a position. Moses was punished for his sins by not being allowed to enter the Promised Land; however, Moses was established by this "Second Moses" Rambam as the ultimate prophet of all Judaism. One might ask—for what purpose? Was the purpose to downgrade the next prophet who would come after him who was destined to ultimately fulfill Deut 18:15-18, Jesus of Nazareth? Rabbi Angel, again writing in almost sycophantic language on behalf of both the first and second Moses, explains this seventh principle in this way, "The Name, blessed be He, only communicated with other prophets through an intermediary; but with Moses, there was no intermediary" (cf. *BT Berakhot* 7a).[29]

The ninth principle is obviously a response to both what the Christian church calls the New Testament and Islam calls the Qur'an.[30] For if there is additional testimony which comes from God, the first eight principles from Maimonides can be called into doubt and the remaining principles,

---

29. Angel, *Maimonides*, 157. The Babylonian Talmud states at this point the following: "Moses was privileged to obtain three [favours]. In reward of 'And Moses hid his face', he obtained the brightness of his face. In reward of 'For he was afraid', he obtained the privilege that They were afraid to come nigh him. In reward of 'To look upon God', he obtained The similitude of the Lord doth he behold." (cf. Num 12:8)

30. Maimonides, *Pirkei Avot*, 180–81 (fn. 113).

especially as it relates to the person of the messiah, could be called into question as well. In many ways, this is one of the most important principles. However, it should be understood that this does not relate solely to the Tanakh but also, and in some respects especially, to the Oral Law as well.[31] As has already been illustrated throughout this section on the specific writings of Maimonides, the Oral Law is just as important to modern Jewish understanding to Jewish life and perhaps more. This is a reality that many Christians and churches do not understand; however, this must become a primary understanding of apologetics if we ever hope to reach the Jewish people with the truth that Jesus is the Messiah of us all.

KABBALAH[32] AND MYSTICISM

As I walked through the streets of Cordoba in the summer of 2015, I was amazed to see the number of hamsas hanging off the carts of market vendors. Hamsas, which are a standard amulet of modern kabbalists but also possess Islamic roots, can be found for sale almost anywhere in the world—from Hollywood for the red-stringed starlets to Safed, Israel, the mythical birthplace of kabbalah, for those on a spiritual quest.[33] I was curious as to why a city which corners the market for Jewish tourists and this writer would promote Jewish mysticism in the birthplace of a Jewish rationalist. However, there was a "rational" reason and cause for their promotion of a good luck amulet and perhaps explains why so many were also rubbing the foot of Rambam's statue.

There is a well-known debunked, but nevertheless persistent, legend within Jewish history that, in the latter stages of Maimonides's life, he converted to kabbalistic thought. After being introduced to the mystical teachings, he renounced the teachings of rationalism found within *Guide of the Perplexed* and became a follower of the writings of the *Zohar*.[34] Aside from

31. Angel, *Maimonides*, 160, 163.

32. A complete explanation of kabbalah cannot be defined in this setting; however, Telushkin defines it in broad tones: "Kabbalah is the name applied to the whole range of Jewish mystical activity. While codes of Jewish law focus on what it is God wants from man, kabbalah tries to penetrate deeper, to God's essence itself" (*Jewish Literacy*, 200).

33. This reference is based upon personal anecdotal experience as I have attended kabbalist workshops, visited Safed, Israel, and been to the Synagogue of Isaac Luria. Interestingly, hamsas also have an Islamic connection and history as well: http://www.myjewishlearning.com/article/hamsa/.

34. Shmidman, "On Maimonides' 'Conversion' to Kabbalah," 375–86; Altmann, "Maimonides' Attitude toward Jewish Mysticism," 201; and Shapiro, *Studies in Maimonides and His Interpreters*, 85–93. Both Shmidman and Shapiro do an excellent job of destroying the legend through historical analysis; however, it is the overarching

the theological unlikelihood of this happening, the *Zohar*—which functions in many ways as a commentary of the Torah—was not brought to public attention until well after Maimonides's death.[35]

Nevertheless, there is a strong argument that before Maimonides's death there existed what both Menachem Kellner and Moshe Idel might call elements of proto-kabbalism, which should be examined not only for what they could have brought to his teachings but to consider if he fought against these early teachings.[36] Kellner also provides two specific examples of proto-kabbalism in the period of Maimonides's life:

1. *Sefer Yetsirah,* which is the idea that human language can actually create things, which gave rise to the Jewish legend of the golem, and
2. *Heikhalot* literature, which is the idea that the use of God's name can ward off evil spirits (i.e., "God bless you" and amulets such as the hamsa).[37]

Perhaps Kellner has a point that the world of Rambam's day was deeply "debased and paganized,"[38] however, it should be recognized that Maimonides expressed a measure of mystical thought as well. Whether it was his attention to detail of having fourteen sections in the *Mishneh Torah* as it matched the numeral value for Hebrew word for "hand," which is nothing more than *Gematria* to the idea that Aaron, Miriam, and Moses died by the "kiss of God," the Cairo rabbi was not completely innocent as it relates to the idea of mysticism.[39] However, modern scholars will attempt to rationalize the

---

analysis provided by Altmann of Maimonidean thought that illustrates the inanity of such a proposal.

35. Telushkin, *Jewish Literacy,* 200–203; Halbertal, *Maimonides,* 365–66; Shapiro, *Studies in Maimonides and His Interpreters,* 86. Personally, I would refer to the *Zohar* as a mystical "decoder ring" for kabbalists; however, Telushkin puts its in more academic language.

36. Kellner, *Maimonides' Confrontation with Mysticism,* 5–11 and Idel, "Maimonides and Kabbalah," 33–35. Kellner coins the term primarily but he depends heavily on Idel's article for the language and thought behind it.

37. Kellner, *Maimonides' Confrontation with Mysticism,* 18–25. For a modern example of *Sefer Yetsirah* being dramatized, one can watch the Richard Gere movie about kabbalah entitled *Bee Season* (Fox Searchlight Pictures, 2005).

38. Kellner, *Maimonides' Confrontation with Mysticism,* 1.

39. Blumenthal, "Maimonides' Intellectual Mysticism," 41–42; Blumenthal, "Religion and the Religious Intellectuals," 132–33. Blumenthal provided the reference to Maimonides, *Guide for the Perplexed,* part 3, chapter 51 (637) "To this state our Sages referred, when in reference to the death of Moses, Aaron, and Miriam, they said that death was in these three cases nothing but a kiss." The rest of the chapter goes into greater detail to describe how each death occurred.

rationalist rabbi by explaining that it was a philosophical or "intellectualist mysticism."[40] Maimonides was a rationalist in all areas and would not have been a kabbalist in his approach to interpretation of Scripture; for while he saw hidden meaning to the Torah, it was not parabolic in nature as kabbalists seek to promote but allegorical as we have already explored.[41]

A primary summary example of this approach is how he responded to the question of astrology to the French Jewish rabbis of Provence in the early 1290s.[42] Throughout Southern France, a discussion had arisen over the claims of a messianic claimant in a distant land and whether any validity could be found in the claims of astrology—particularly what Maimonides will respond to in his letter as "judicial astrology."[43] Rambam's concern over "judicial astrology" takes on many forms and many judgments, and his concern is worthy of consideration as it relates not only to kabbalah then and now but also to his continual drumbeat against the concept that God could take on any aspect of corporeality (i.e., incarnate form).

The Cairo rabbi writes in 1294 that it was because of such foolishness —such as astrology and star gazing—that the Second Temple was lost: "They erred and were drawn after them, imagining them to be glorious science and to be of great utility. They did not busy themselves with the art of war or with the conquest of lands, but imagined that those studies would help them."[44] However, Rambam also wanted the French Jewish

40. Blumenthal, "Maimonides' Intellectualist Mysticism," 27, 28, and 35. See also Blumenthal, "Maimonides," 1–16.

41. Wolfson, "Beneath the Wings of the Great Eagle," 209–37 (esp. 211–12) and Altmann, "Maimonides' Attitude Toward Jewish Mysticism," 201, 203, 208, 210. Wolfson and Altmann come at this argument from completely different perspectives; however, Altmann's arguments carry the day based upon historical and theological arguments. Wolfson's perspectives are based upon a wish-fulfillment desire more than actual hard evidence. Additionally, you have an exegetical argument from Maimonides's issue with the prophet Moses himself, which illustrates that Rambam struggled with any example of "magical incantation" even in Scripture. The example of Moses striking the rock the second time in Num 20 is found by Maimonides as an example of disobeying God's order. See Milgrom, "Magic, Monotheism, and the Sin of Moses," 88–112. Primary sources for Maimonidean references could not be located at this time.

42. Kraemer, *Maimonides*, 426–38. The entire historical overview of this scenario is from the same source as the story and is consistent with all sources.

43. Maimonides, "Letter to the Community of Marseilles," 21. Rambam defines "judicial astrology" as the "(the science) by which man may known what will come to pass in this world or in this or that city or kingdom and what will happen to particular individual all the days of his life." Kraemer gives this form of astrology the technical term of genethlialogy or the "the technique of compiling a horoscope" (*Maimonides*, 428). See also Stitskin, "Maimonides on Refuting False Notions," 99–104.

44. Maimonides, "Letter to the Community of Marseilles," 21. Original source for this reference was from Kraemer, *Maimonides*, 433–34.

community to know that astrology is pointless because not only did God alone create the stars out of nothing (*ex nihilo*) but also that He did it alone and "whoever does not acknowledge this is guilty of radical unbelief and is guilty of heresy."[45]

Therefore, Hava Tirosh-Samuelson is correct when she argues that while Rambam "did not rid Judaism of myth" he sought to replace "it with a *logocentric myth*, the crux of which was that the Torah is a philosophic, esoteric text whose interpretation constitutes the happy life in this world and the bliss of immortality in the afterlife."[46] However, the question must be raised—is the thought and argument of Maimonides winning the day in the twenty-first century? This is an issue that will be explored further in later chapters; however, this is an issue that should be considered constructively and theologically in this chapter as well.

Halbertal writes that while the Cairo rabbi was "more or less" able to eliminate "the belief in a corporeal God" from Jewish thought, there is still a long battle to be fought from "reject[ing] all personification of the divinity."[47] Alan Yuter, in his review of Menachem Kellner's *Maimonides' Confrontation with Mysticism,* recognizes the battle that the modern Orthodox rabbi is seeking to fight within his own Jewish denomination to return from a kabbalistic tendency to Maimonidean thought but believes the battle is lost because Jewish people want to feel something and not just think about God.[48] And while Rabbi Kellner might believe that Maimonidean thought and practice today has been relegated to "largely ignored backwater" due to the wave of kabbalistic thought in modern Judaism, I argue that his first belief that Rambam is "one of the most influential Jews who ever lived" is still correct.[49] Jewish people are attempting to fit both the thoughts of Maimonides and mysticism today into a systematized Jewish box without realizing that neither fit the "God Box" of their lives because Messiah Jesus is the only one who can.

NOAHIDES AND CONVERTS

Conversion, proselytism, evangelism are not words that one associates with rabbinic Judaism. Indeed, the concept of someone becoming Jewish

---

45. Maimonides, "Letter to the Community of Marseilles," 22.
46. Tirosh-Samuelson, "Maimonides' View of Happiness," 189.
47. Halbertal, *Maimonides*, 366.
48. Yuter, "Menachem Kellner on Maimonides and the Mystics," 126–33.
49. Kellner, *Maimonides' Confrontation with Mysticism*, 1, 4.

by choice is even today the exception and not the norm.[50] However, the question of Noahides and the question of converts to Judaism was an issue during Maimonides's day and is actually a growing issue today. Therefore, a brief examination of the issue is worthy of consideration as it involves the questions of God's non-corporeal status and what a non-Jewish person must do with the identity of Jesus becomes very important for all parties involved.

The first and most obvious question that many have is simply—what is a Noahide? Rambam in the *Mishneh Torah* reaffirmed the definition of the Sages and set the following parameters for who is one:

> A heathen who accepts the seven commandments and observes them scrupulously is a "righteous heathen," and will have a portion in the world to come, provided that he accepts them and performs them because the Holy One, blessed be He, commanded them in the Law and made known through Moses our Teacher that the observance thereof had been enjoined upon the *descendants of Noah* even before the Law was given (emphasis added).[51]

Kraemer simplifies the definition by stating that "Noahide laws are the elementary moral standards of civilized behavior for all mankind. Six go back to Adam, and are thus ultimately Adamic or universal human laws, and one was added at the time of Noah."[52] Upon a first reading of this concept, many unsuspecting individuals might assume that this is a biblical concept; however, this idea of the Noahide Laws and its obligation was a later addition to the Talmud in post-Jesus times (*BT Sanhedrin* 56a). Therefore, it is important to understand two issues. The first is why Christians cannot affirm the Noahide Laws. The second is why the hidden meaning behind Maimonides's call for a form of universalism has another purpose behind it.

First, this talmudic concept was designed to offset the basic Great Commission of Christians to be evangelistic to the Jewish people and all the people of the world. If non-Jews can obtain a place in the "World to Come" by observing the following commands while the Jewish people are commanded to observe these and the additional 613 Commandments prescribed by Maimonides,[53] then there is no need for Christian evangelism of any kind:

---

50. Pew Research Center, "Portrait of Jewish Americans," 65. The survey noted that only 2 percent of those surveyed had actually converted to Judaism.

51. Maimonides, *Mishneh Torah*, book 14, chapter 8, sec. 11.

52. Kraemer, *Maimonides*, 352 and Frimer, "Israel, the Noahide Laws and Maimonides," 91.

53. One of the most important aspects of Jewish and Christian life is that we hear

> Six precepts were given to Adam: prohibition of idolatry, of blasphemy, of murder, of adultery, of robbery, and the command to establish courts of justice. Although there is a tradition to this effect—a tradition dating back to Moses our Teacher, and human reason approves of those precepts—it is evident from the general tenor of the Scriptures that he (Adam) was bidden to observe these commandments. An additional commandment was given to Noah: prohibition of (eating) a limb from a living animal, . . .[54]

Christians should and do observe precepts three through seven; however, according to Maimonides himself, we would be in violation of the first precepts by affirming the incarnation and stating that Jesus is God the Son. Therefore, to become a follower of what Kellner calls Rambam's "universalism" (i.e., Noahide) requires a renouncement of one's Christian fidelity.[55]

Second, we find an Islamic tenor rising up within the chords of Rambam's thought. For I argue, he dreamed of the day when his form of rabbinic Judaism would have the political weight of Saladin's empire and could force the issue of Noahide belief upon the gentiles. For while he wrote that no one should be forced to convert to Judaism, he did advocate the following:

> Moreover, Moses our Teacher was commanded by God to compel all human beings to accept the commandments enjoined upon the descendants of Noah. Anyone who does not accept them is put to death. He who does accept them is invariably styled a resident alien. He must declare his acceptance in the presence of three associates. Anyone who has declared his intention to be circumcised and fails to do so within twelve months is treated like a heathen infidel.[56]

---

about these 613 Commandments of Judaism; however, there is no place in Scripture in which they are laid out or counted. This is a talmudic addition of which there are several versions. Maimonides in his *Book of Commandments* (which we did not examine) is the one who spelled out the list we have today. Naturally, this list of 613 rules has overtones of *Gematria* and focuses on the unity and non-corporeality of God. For further information see Davidson, "First Two Positive Commandments," 113–45.

54. Maimonides, *Mishneh Torah*, book 14, chapter 9, sec. 1.

55. Kellner, *Maimonides' Confrontation with Mysticism*, 250. However, it should be noted that Kellner struggled with this concept even though he affirmed it (251–61). He qualified the statement ultimately that Rambam's universalism extended to those non-Jews who became what we might term as enlightened or "Noahides" for the sake of this discussion. See also Bleich, "Divine Unity," in 239–40. I believe it should be noted that Bleich begins his article with what could be called an unnecessary diatribe of Maimonides's view towards Christians that defeats the overall theme of the article.

56. Maimonides, *Mishneh Torah*, book 14, chapter 8, sec. 10. See also Halbertal, *Maimonides*, 251–53.

Maimonides and His Reaction to Controversy and Christianity   113

Consequently, there was a subtle call for a reverse form of "Jewish evangelism" by Maimonides to either become a Noahide or a full-fledged convert to the faith. However, those who did convert were faced with other questions that Rambam sought to answer as well.

Ben Zion Wacholder in expressing his understanding of Rambam's view on converts to Judaism writes an important statement as it expresses in a cogent manner the defined purpose and heart of the Cairo rabbi's mission of life, regardless of the cause—"To him conversion to Judaism meant not so much the acceptance of the commandments as the philosophical recognition of the unity of God. It is from the unity of God that the observance of the Torah naturally follows."[57] This philosophical approach to Judaism is important as it opens up the community of Abraham to a broader audience that extends beyond a genetic heritage but to a philosophical-religious component that includes anyone who affirms the Maimonidean tradition.[58] James Diamond takes this concept even further and develops "a pedagogical teacher-disciple" construct to replace "biological father-son model." Father Abraham is the father to the world (cf. Gen 12:1–3) because his responsibility was to bring Judaism to the planet. Therefore, if a convert wants to become Jewish by religion, he is ultimately a Jew in a ethno-religious-genetic sense as well.[59]

The test case in this whole situation as it relates to Maimonides and the issue of Jewish converts can be boiled down primarily to one convert from Islam—Obadiah the Proselyte. The dating of the correspondence is uncertain; however, the questions of the correspondence revolve around two issues:

1. could Obadiah pray as a Jewish man to the "God of Our Fathers," and
2. was Islam a monotheistic religion?

---

57. Wacholder, "Attitudes Towards Proselytizing in the Classical Halakah," 18. Wacholder argues that Rambam believed that teaching about the "oneness of God and the futility of idol worship" should take priority over any aspect of talmudic instruction.

58. Frydman-Kohl, "Covenant, Conversion and Chosenness," 66, 75. Obviously, Frydman-Kohl perceives of Maimonides's perspective in a much more amenable way than I do; however, the premise of the New York rabbi's statement, "In this examination, Maimonides will be shown to hold that *Judaism* is a philosophical community with common beliefs that entail common practices . . ." (66) has one consistent word—common. Uniformity is the word of the day in Maimonidean Judaism.

59. Diamond, "Maimonides and the Convert," 127–35. The question of "Who is a Jew?" today is an issue of great controversy both within the United States and in Israel proper. This approach of Diamond would never be accepted and I argue that he is presenting a somewhat idealized view of Maimonides's view; however, he is not completely off-base from what Rambam proposed—within limits.

These two questions were important to Obadiah as he had been confronted by his synagogue rabbi and told that as a convert he could not pray to God as "his Father," and that Islam was full of idolatry and pagan worship.[60]

Maimonides's response to Obadiah was unique in several ways. He wrote to Obadiah that

1. Abraham taught people about "the true faith and the unity of God;"

2. Abraham even now is the one "who converted them to righteousness" as they are under the umbrella of his teaching model because "he converts future generations through the testaments he left to his children and household after him;"

3. Abraham is "the father of his disciples and of all proselytes who adopt Judaism; and

4. "Do not consider your origin as inferior. While we are the descendants of Abraham, Isaac, you derive from Him through whose word the world was created."[61]

Aside from the perplexing statements regarding the idea that it is Abraham who is converting them and not God, one is left with the constant thought about the unity of God, which is a never-ending strain in Maimonidean thought.

However, as I was reading the letter, I was drawn in my mind to Rom 11:17–24 and elsewhere throughout the epistolary letters of Paul. There is a refrain present that sounds remarkably similar in tone, concept, and presentation. Was this intentional? Was this accidental? Did the philosophical rabbinical rabbi draw inspiration from the greatest Jewish-Christian evangelist as to the nature of conversion, discipleship, and affirmation? These are not questions that can necessarily be answered? However, it is interesting that he also wrote—directly after the conclusion of the thirteenth faith principle—this statement: "When a person believes in all these fundamental principles and has earnest faith in them, he accepts upon himself his Jewish identity. We are obligated to love him, have mercy upon him, and to conduct ourselves in relation to him in all the paths of love and brotherhood commanded by God."[62] Rabbi Kellner will tell you that a convert can deviate, fall into sin, and become debased in all sorts of manner but as long as

---

60. The summation of the background to this story came from both Halbertal, *Maimonids*, 81–83 and Kraemer, *Maimonides*, 311–13. It should be noted that we have examined Rambam's view that he saw Islam as a monotheistic religion in earlier parts of this chapter and so the focus of this section will be on the first question.

61. Maimonides, "Letter to Obadiah the Proselyte," 475–76.

62. Maimonides, *Pirkei Avot*, 182–83.

Maimonides and His Reaction to Controversy and Christianity

he holds to the Thirteen Principles of faith (especially those related to God's unity), he is Jewish and has a place in the "World to Come."[63]

MAIMONIDES'S NEGATION THEOLOGY ANALYZED IN RELATION TO THE CHRISTIAN FAITH

In examining the concept of Maimonides's negation theology (*via negativa*) that I have been discussing in broad strokes and statements, a brief definition at this point would prove helpful. However, even within the term itself there is not one simple definition; therefore, I will list here some of the more prominent ones with their author included:

1. Denys Turner—"An adequate theology has to be unremitting in its denials of theological language, for all talk about God is tainted with ultimate failure ... It is the encounter with the failure of what we must say about God to represent God adequately."[64]

2. Rowan Williams—"Thus the use of negation to characterize the divine life expresses not simply the retreat of the finite mind before infinite reality—thought it does at least that; it expresses the process of 'finding our way' within the life of the three divine agencies or subsistents."[65]

3. David Braine—"[T]heologies which regard negative statements as primary in expressing our knowledge of God, contrasted with 'positive theologies' giving primary emphasis to positive statements ... However, within their original theistic context, positive and negative statements about God are interdependent, the second indispensably qualifying the first, the negative statements taken alone are useless."[66]

4. Hilary Putnam (speaking in his estimation on behalf of Rambam in modern vernacular)—"There are no 'propositions' about God that are adequate to God."[67]

5. Diana Lobel—"Negative theology is built on the premise of the unknowability of God: we can only make statements about what God is not; we cannot ultimately know what God is. Negative Theology

---

63. Kellner, *Maimonides' Confrontation with Mysticism*, 232–33.
64. Turner, "Apophaticism, Idolatry, and the Claims of Reason," 16, 18.
65. Williams, "Deflections of Desire," 134.
66. Braine, "Negative Theology," 759.
67. Putnam, "On Negative Theology," 412.

belongs to two spheres: the sphere of epistemology—what can we know?—and the sphere of discourse—what can we say?[68]

The first two definitions are from Christian sources, albeit from the non-evangelical end of the spectrum. The third and fourth options fall within more of a philosophical construct. The fifth from the Jewish scholar is also the primary defender of the Maimonidean view. What each definition has in common is that they are different; yet they agree on the essential idea that in negation one cannot know God in a personal way.

Ehud Benor, who along with others have sought to soften this perception of Rambam, acknowledges that this can cause others to see the Cairo rabbi as appearing to offer an "austere theology" that creates an "absolute unknowability of God."[69] Benor will argue that this perceived sternness by Maimonides was an attempt to prevent the worship of

1. one's own imagination and
2. subjective rather than objective worship.[70]

The defense of Maimonides's emphasis on God as *via negativa* by modern scholarship is admirable and understandable in many ways, and will be found in some measure in the Christian thinkers that we consider as well.

One idea put forth by the modern defenders is that Maimonides wanted his fellow Jews to understand the "Who" they were worshiping and that they were not worshiping a feeling, an emotion, or a concept. Hannah Kasher considers Maimonides's focus on the negative attributes as recognition of the fact that God is a "self-cognizing intellect" and/or "absolutely other" that we are not; therefore, we should only speak of him in the negative.[71] Another idea is simply the idea of silence or what Benor refers to as "rational mysticism."[72] If one is silent before God, one is not tempted to engage in effusive and/or offensive language that could border on idolatrous language that detracts from "God's true reality."[73] Maimonides wrote about the idea of silence in the *Guide*:

68. Lobel, "'Silence Is Praise to You,'" 25.
69. Benor, "Meaning and Reference in Maimonides' Negative Theology," 339.
70. Benor, "Meaning and Reference in Maimonides' Negative Theology," 341.
71. Kasher, "Self-Cognizing Intellect," 468, 470, 472. See also Burrell, "Naming the Names of God," 27 and Lobel, "Maimonides on Negative Theology," 26. Interestingly, both Kasher and Burrell reference the words in Leviticus, "Be Ye Holy as I am Holy" as illustrations in their context of Maimonides.
72. Benor, "Meaning and Reference in Maimonides' Negative Theology," 344. See also, Lobel, "'Silence Is Praise to You,'" 27, who expresses it this way—"The only true expression of rational certainty about God is silence."
73. Rudavsky, *Blackwell Great Minds*, 47.

> You must bear in mind, that by affirming anything of God, you are removed from Him in two respects; first, whatever you affirm, is only in a perfection in relation to us; secondly, He does not possess anything superadded to this essence; His essence includes all His perfections, as we have shown . . . The idea is best expressed in the book of Psalms, "Silence is praise to Thee (lxv. 2). It is a very expressive remark on this subject; for whatever we utter with the intention of extolling and of praising Him, contains that cannot be applied to God, and includes derogatory expressions; . . . [74]

However, it is Lobel who is the most honest about the desire for silence in Maimonidean thought when she writes: "Nevertheless, one can represent God falsely by endowing Him with essential attributes, which is no different from the Christian affirmation of the Trinity. This position leads one on a dangerous road away from monotheism."[75] This is perhaps why Joseph Buijs in multiple articles on the topic focuses on the idea of Maimonides's negation providing an "indirect knowledge" of God through what he is not;[76] however, is this enough to satisfy the longing of an individual's heart? Do the Christian proponents of negation proponents both ancient and modern offer something more that we could offer to twenty-first century Jewish people?

Gregory of Nyssa

Born in 335, Gregory of Nyssa was one of the three Cappadocian fathers of Christian history along with his brother Basil and Gregory of Nazianzus. Before his death in c. 394, he became known not for pastoral gifts or oratorical eloquence but for the ability to express himself in writing and in his intellectual ability.[77] He also became known, along with St. John of the Cross, as an early advocate of a Christian *via negativa* that is counterintuitive to Maimonidean thought. Gregory's idea sought to compel the individual towards a closer, mystical union, vis-à-vis prayer or meditation,

---

74. Maimonides, *Guide of the Perplexed*, part 1, chapter 59 (152–53). Original source which directed me to this section of the *Guide* was Halbertal, *Maimonides*, 296.

75. Lobel, "'Silence Is Praise to You,'" 27.

76. Buijs, "Is the Negative Theology of Maimonides Intelligible?," 14; Buijs, "Attributes of Action in Maimonides," 85; and Buijs, "Comments on Maimonides' Negative Theology," 90, 92, 93.

77. Quasten, *Patrology*, 254–55.

with the unknown God in order that one might eventually know and love Him in a non-idolatrous way.[78]

This Christian *via negativa* of Gregory begins with a conceptually correct but awkwardly phrased understanding of the Tri-Unity of God with this statement from *On "Not Three Gods"*:

> But in the case of the Divine nature we do not similarly learn that the Father does anything by Himself in which the Son does not work conjointly, or again that the Son has any special operation apart from the Holy Spirit; but every operation which extends from God to the Creation, and is named according to our variable conceptions of it, has its origin from the Father, and proceeds through the Son, and is perfected in the Holy Spirit.[79]

Yes, on first reading it could read as if Gregory is advocating a God with emanations; however, I believe this confusion can be resolved upon a further reading—

> Since then the Holy Trinity fulfils every operation in a manner similar to that of which I have spoken, not by separate action according to the number of the Persons, but so that there is one motion and disposition of the good will which is communicated from the Father through the Son to the Spirit (for as we do not call those whose operation gives one life three Givers of life, neither do we call those who are contemplated in one goodness three Good beings, nor speak of them in the plural by any of their other attributes); . . .[80]

What Gregory made available through his understanding of the Trinity is a God who can be both unknowable on one level but yet accessible on another through the actions of Son and Spirit, as well as through the actions we ourselves take to know Him. This is most evident because we were created in the *Imago Dei* and our soul longing (i.e., mysticism realized) is to return to this relationship that has been lost.[81] Gregory explains in his *Sermon on the Beatitudes*, however, that this is not possible without a life-change on our part and the purification only made possible by God alone:

---

78. Braine, "Negative Theology," 759.
79. Gregory of Nyssa, *On "Not Three Gods."*
80. Gregory of Nyssa, *On "Not Three Gods."*
81. Quasten, *Patrology*, vol. 3, 292–93. Quasten writes lyrically about what I have attempted to summarize and explain: "Thus the image of God in man enables him to attain the mystic vision of Him and compensates for the deficiencies of human reason and the limitation of our rational knowledge of God" (293).

The Divine Nature, whatever It may be in Itself, surpasses every mental concept. For It is altogether inaccessible to reasoning and conjecture, nor has there been found any human faculty capable of perceiving the incomprehensible; for we cannot devise a means of understanding inconceivable things . . . For it is possible to see Him Who has made all things in wisdom by inference through the wisdom that appears in the universe . . . Thus also, when we look at the order of creation, we form in our mind an image not of the essence, but of the wisdom of Him Who has made all things wisely . . . For power, purity, constancy, freedom from contrariety—all these engrave on the soul the impress of a Divine and transcendent Mind.[82]

Gregory of Nyssa in essence filed a preemptive strike in the areas of God's unity within the confines of diversity as well as in the ability to know the unknowable and to have intimacy with the unattainable on Rambam. However, Maimonides was more interested in the writings of another Christian writer, John Philoponus, and there is no tangible evidence that he read the writings of Gregory of Nyssa.

John Philoponus

Augustine, Justin Martyr, and even Origin would be early Christian scholars that I would have expected to see in *Guide for the Perplexed*; however, I was proven wrong. It would be mere speculation as to why such writers were not found, especially the thoughts of Gregory of Nyssa, given their similar views on the presence of God. The only early Christian writer to be found by name is the relatively obscure philosopher and Christian monophysite, John the Grammarian (aka John Philoponus).[83] However, it was not in glowing terms that John Philoponus was mentioned but almost in a condescending tone: "When the opinions of John the Grammarian, of Ibn Adi, and of kindred authors on those subjects were made accessible to them, they adopted them, and imagined they had arrived at the solution of important problems."[84] Consequently, it is important to understand who John Philoponus was, what his opinions were, and why Rambam was so dismissive of his claims, especially as it related to the unity and knowledge of God.

John Philoponus (c. 490–575) was born in Egypt and became a Christian scholar who was highly influenced by the writings of Plato and

---

82. Quasten, *Patrology*, 294–95.
83. Maimonides, *Guide of the Perplexed*, part 1, chapter 71 (192).
84. Maimonides, *Guide of the Perplexed*, part 1, chapter 71 (192).

Aristotle. He also came of age during the height of the Chalcedonian controversy which revolved around the person and nature of Jesus.[85] What is most enlightening about Philoponus's biography was written in the abstract to L. S. B. MacCoull's article: "His intention was to provide the nascent Coptic church with a powerful set of tools for argument, with which Egyptian Monophysites could defeat their Chalcedonian opponents."[86] This serves to bring out a point and a further reality—the view of the Monophysites should be understood and the writings of John the Grammarian was apparently still available to the Cairo rabbi as evidenced by this statement just prior to John's mention: "they [Greek and Syrian Christians] commenced by putting forth such propositions as would support their doctrines, and be useful for the refutation of opinions opposed to the fundamental principles of the Christian religion."[87]

Therefore, what is Monophysite Christology? One of the easier definitions to understand is simply the "juxtaposition, mixture, compound/fusion—are what are analyzed in all discussions of how divinity and humanity formed the ineffable union of the one saving Christ."[88] Ultimately, however, it should be recognized that in his Christology, John Philoponus was creating a trinitarian system that was untenable to basic Christian thought. Uwe Michael Lang correctly refers to this concept as Tritheism—three natures, three substances, three godheads—because of the confusion of how Jesus "could become flesh apart from the Father and the Spirit."[89] Lang provides an example of this confusion from a translation of Philoponus's own words (*Arbiter*)—"If things that are united become one, things that have not become one are necessarily not united. Thus if there are two natures of Christ and not one, and if a duality . . . is indicative of a division, but what is divided is not united, then the natures of Christ are not united."[90] This confusion about the nature of Jesus, the nature of the Trinity, and the nature of God's unity as understood by Christianity is what Maimonides saw and expounded upon in his *Guide*. One can understand his perplexity,

---

85. MacCoull, "New Look," 49–50, 59; Wickham, "John Philoponus and Gregory of Nyssa's Teaching," 205; and Lang, "Notes on John Philoponus," 23–24.

86. MacCoull, "New Look," 47.

87. Maimonides, *Guide of the Perplexed*, part 1, chapter 71 (191).

88. MacCoull, "New Look," 51.

89. Lang, "Patristic Argument and the Use of Philosophy," 86, 88. See also Erismann, "Trinity, Universals, and Particular Substances," 287 and MacCoull, "John Philoponus," 199–200.

90. Lang, "Nicetas Choniates," 546 (chapter 10, 36:70.24–31). Lang notes that the extant version is in Syriac and provides a complete explanation of how it came to be translated into English (540–41).

for while Gregory of Nyssa was imperfect in places, he found a way to meld the truth of the Trinity and the concept of *via negativa* in a relational God as well. Rambam, unfortunately, apparently never saw this side of Christian thought.

Thomas Aquinas

Much more could be written about the person of Thomas Aquinas (1225–1275) than space will allow here or anywhere.[91] One might argue that the *Summa Theologica* personifies the term *magnum opus*. However, the point of this section is not to amplify Aquinas but to examine the similarities and differences of the *via negativa* between the Christian scholastic and the Jewish rabbi. Before I begin, it should be noted that Maimonides is mentioned often as a reference point in Aquinas's *Summa Theologica* under the name of Rabbi Moses.[92]

However, this does not mean that the two were kindred spirits on the concept of *via Negativa* in connection to the person of God and/or humanity's relation to Him. Yes, they agreed on some aspects as to this relationship being a special gift; but Aquinas did not believe it was deposed to only the spiritually elite.[93] Jacob Haberman argues that Aquinas seeks to find a balance between a form of Maimonidean agnosticism and polytheistic anthropomorphism through the usage of analogy; however, Haberman will ultimately argue that St. Thomas falls victim to what we might call nonsensical speech or "verbalism."[94] It was not that Aquinas was opposed to the usage of speaking of God in the negative, it is that he felt that humanity needed to recognize that God was "good, wise and the like."[95] Additionally, St. Thomas adds the following to elaborate on this analogical answer:

---

91. Saint-Laurent, "Avicenna, Maimonides, Aquinas and the Existence of God," 168–69, takes care of writing out a biography for me when he states the following:
> Thomas became a model for devout emulation as a priest, a mystic, and a saint. He became the source of rich spiritual nourishment as a poet, hymnographer, and exegete of Sacred Scripture. He became the object of intense admiration as an intellectual of giant proportions with an altogether extraordinary talent for synthesizing his penetrating analyses of reality into a self-consistent whole.

92. McGinn, "*Sapientia Judaeorum*," 210; Broadie, "Maimonides and Aquinas on the Names of God," 170; and Aquinas, *Summa Theologica*.

93. Altmann, "Maimonides and Thomas Aquinas," 10–15.

94. Haberman, *Maimonides and Aquinas*, 58, 76 and Miller, "Maimonides and Aquinas on Naming God," 71.

95. Wolfson, "St. Thomas on Divine Attributes," 676–77; Buijs, "Maimonidean Critique of Thomistic Analogy," 450; Aquinas, *Summa Theologica*, 1.13.2.

> Therefore we must hold a different doctrine—viz. that these names signify the divine substance, and are predicated substantially of God, although they fall short of a full representation of Him. Which is proved thus. For these names express God, so far as our intellects know Him . . . Therefore the aforesaid names signify the divine substance, but in an imperfect manner, even as creatures represent it imperfectly. So when we say, "God is good," the meaning is not, "God is the cause of goodness," or "God is not evil"; but the meaning is, "Whatever good we attribute to creatures, pre-exists in God," and in a more excellent and higher way. Hence it does not follow that God is good, because He causes goodness; but rather, on the contrary, He causes goodness in things because He is good; according to what Augustine says (De Doctr. Christ. i, 32), "Because He is good, we are."[96]

Idit Dobbs-Weinstein expresses this philosophical division between Rambam and Aquinas as a difference between a focus on the incorporeality of God and a focus on the "unity of all existing things in virtue of their first and final cause—the Good, irrespective of composition."[97] Taking this concept further, both Seeskin and Harvey will argue that Aquinas viewed Rambam's God as too limiting for humanity to ascertain.[98] In other words, Aquinas saw that people need a connecting point to God even if we do so in some form of *via negativa*.[99]

This idea of a connecting point is especially relevant in the closing paragraph of the section. For connecting to God in the form of redemption and repentance is at the core of both rabbinic (modern) Judaism and Christianity. However, the question of how and to whom is where the great divide begins and ends. Jonathan Jacobs expresses the rabbinic position quite well when he states that it is the duty of the community to come together in a covenantal action of repentance.[100] This Maimonidean thread via the

---

96. Aquinas, *Summa Theologica*, 1.13.2.

97. Dobbs-Weinstein, "Matter as Creature," 227.

98. Seeskin, "Sanctity and Silence," 8 and Harvey, "Maimonides and Aquinas on Interpreting the Bible," 66. Harvey also notes that Aquinas takes issue with what I would call Rambam's rampant allegorical exegesis (65).

99. Buijs, "Negative Theology of Maimonides and Aquinas," 727, 731. It should be noted that the primary point of Buijs's article is to disprove Isaac Franck's premise and criticism of both Maimonidean and Thomistic *via negativa*. In doing so, Buijs creates a more convoluted and complicated article than necessary; however, the point that he makes is that the two scholars share similarities and differences in their approaches to the knowledge and negation of God.

100. Jacobs, "Forgiveness and Perfection," 232.

"Thirteen Principles," *Commentary on Teshuvah*, and other documents that we have examined have become a mainstay in Jewish life, even for the non-observant Jewish man or woman. However, Thomas Aquinas illustrates a more personal way that Jacobs himself notes even if he misunderstands the reference: "A person may repent of sin in two ways: in one way directly, in another way indirectly. He repents of a sin directly who hates sin as such: and he repents indirectly who hates it on account of something connected with it, for instance punishment or something of that kind."[101]

Therefore, sandwiched between John Philoponus's odd Tritheism, we find two Christian *via negativa* theologians who shared a similar concept as Maimonides as it relates to unknowability of God on a human plane but recognized that the search never ends, even while here on earth. Gregory of Nyssa and Thomas Aquinas are the individuals we must show to Jewish people who cannot let go of the idea that God is unknowable. Additionally, we in the Christian church who occasionally slip into bad trinitarian theology similar to Philoponus must disregard his thought if we ever hope to answer the hope that lies within us as it relates to the truth of God the Father, God the Son, and God the Holy Spirit.

MAIMONIDES CRITERIA FOR THE MESSIAH ANALYZED IN RELATION TO THE CHRISTIAN FAITH

There has been a great deal of discussion already in this chapter related to Maimonides's criteria for the Jewish messiah. Therefore, this section will seek to accomplish three primary goals:

1. a quick summary of his view;
2. a comparison and contrast of how Rambam's messianic figure is different and similar to the Christian Messiah; and
3. an analysis of why the Cairo's rabbi messiah needed to be different than Jesus of Nazareth from both a religious and sociological perspective in order for rabbinic Judaism to survive.

Amos Funkenstein states it well in explaining Maimonides's view of the messiah by stating that he "was the first theoretician of a 'realistic

---

101. Jacobs, "Forgiveness and Perfection," 232. The *Summa Theologica* reference specifically deals with the punishment of the damned. I find it interesting that Jacobs gravitates towards this reference as an example of interplay between Creator and humanity. Aquinas, *Summa Theologica*, Suppl. 3.98.2.

Messianism'; . . ."[102] This idea of a Maimonidean realistic messianic age "will be expressed through the rectification of the existing world . . . through the improvement of the social-political reality."[103] Rambam's messianic age will include a real person whose focus will be:

> King Messiah will arise and restore the kingdom of David to its former state and original sovereignty. He will rebuild the sanctuary and gather the dispersed of Israel. All the ancient laws will be reinstituted in his days; sacrifices will again be offered; the Sabbatical and Jubilee years will again be observed in accordance with the commandments set forth in the Law.[104]

I will again argue that the Cairo rabbi's perception of the messiah was influenced and tainted by the experience of a visual representation of Islamic power from his earliest childhood days with the Mezquita de Cordóba and this why he presented a kingly only messiah in the *Mishneh Torah*. There would be no need for a redemptive "Suffering Messiah," such as Messiah ben Joseph that even the Talmud mentions in *BT Sukkah* 52a but that Maimonides chooses to overlook in his reference to the passage—"The prophecy in that section bears upon the two Messiahs: the first, namely, David, who saved Israel from the hand of their enemies; and the later Messiah, a descendant of David, who will achieve the final salvation of Israel."[105]

In many ways, the answer to the question of how Maimonides's messiah is similar and different than Messiah Jesus might appear to be obvious. However, there are subtleties that should be considered, as it is important for understanding and evaluation. I have already brought forth from Maimonides's own words that he decried any need for the messiah to testify of his position through the use of miracles or mighty works, but needed a return of the people to the land of Israel and a return of the people to Torah observance. This is why some would key in on the term "historical

---

102. Funkenstein, "Maimonides," 82.

103. Ehrlich, "Hidden Apocalyptic Messianism in Late Medieval Jewish Thought," 75. Interestingly, Ehrlich provides a definition of apocalyptic messianism that he intends to reflect the teachings of another medieval Jewish scholar, Nahmanides, that actually could apply to Christian theology, at least dispensationalism, as well. For a similar explanation of what could be coined as "realistic messianism," see also Botwinick, "Maimonides' Messianic Age," 418–19, 425; Kraemer, "On Maimonides' Messianic Posture," 110–11; Novak, "Maimonides' Concept of the Messiah," 44, 46—47, 49—50; and Poorthuis, "Messianism between Reason and Delusion," 61.

104. Maimonides, *Mishneh Torah*, book 14, chapter 11, sec. 1.

105. Maimonides, *Mishneh Torah*, book 14, chapter 11, sec. 1 and Kraemer, "On Maimonides' Messianic Posture," 131. Please note that I provided the complete notation of *BT Sukkah* 52a in an earlier footnote.

success" and why today Jewish people will negate the possibility of Jesus being Messiah as there was no "historical success" to his actions.[106] Marcel Poorthuis acknowledges this conundrum albeit with a tinge of bias when he writes, "It is an old and stubborn prejudice of Christian origin that Jewish messianism is too political to be able to reach the spiritual heights of the Christian messianic message. But we do better to follow Maimonides in asking whether a religious expectation which denies political oppression may bear the predicate 'messianic.'"[107]

However, Christians would ask what kind of messiah are the Jewish people hoping for, if Maimonides only brings a human messiah that would one day die, as has already been shown? What kind of messiah brings a messianic age that brings sovereignty but not the hope for the "World to Come," as "The Sages said that the prophets only spoke of the days of the Messiah, but regarding the World to Come, *the eye has not seen* except for God"?[108] The response of Maimonides would also come from his *Commentary on Teshuvah* in which he states: "They will find rest [during the days of Messiah], and increase their wisdom in order that they inherit the life in the World to Come."[109] However, this is a promise that Christians will avow that we already have as well in the concept of the "already but not yet" of the Kingdom of God. Therefore, there are both similarities and differences in the sense of the messianic age, with the greatest difference being that Christians are no longer waiting while many Jewish people today have either given up or have allegorized the person into a messianic concept.

CHAPTER SUMMATION

Who ultimately was Maimonides as a theologian, a scholar, and a leader? He definitely was not one who shirked from expressing strong opinions. He believed he was saving the soul, the future, and the foundation of Judaism by doing so. He certainly was not one who saw in the person of Jesus anyone who possessed any redemptive value, either on the salvific or personal level. I would argue in fact that Rambam saw in the teachings and followers of

---

106. Klein, *Credo of Maimonides,* 109 and Botwinick, "Maimonides' Messianic Age," 425.

107. Poorthuis, "Messianism between Reason and Delusion," 62. See also Funkenstein, "Maimonides," 83: he is even less subtle as he refers to Christianity as growing "out of a Messianic heresy."

108. Maimonides, *Ways of Repentance,* 8.7.

109. Maimonides, *Ways of Repentance,* 9.2.

this Nazarene carpenter the greatest existential threat to Judaism that had ever existed.

Maimonides might have tread carefully around the question of the afterlife among his fellow rabbis. He would have expressed disdain for amulets and those who followed teachers of mysticism. However, the Christian belief of a personal God who could express such emotions as compassion and empathy for a fallen world, and the belief in a compassion and empathy that would extend to the incarnational appearance, death, and resurrection of Jesus the Messiah was a concept that needed to be philosophically defeated both subtly and overtly throughout his writings. Maimonides fought this view with every fiber of his being. I would go even so far to say it terrified him.

6

Maimonides's Impact on Modern Judaism

JEWISH SCHOLARS WILL DEFEND the theory of negation theology so as to prevent the creation of a "separate deity (i.e., because it would lead to dualism)."[1] However, I have sought to present the argument in the first chapters that the true fear is not dualism, because the "separate deity" issue is actually a straw man argument against the second person of the Trinity, God the Son. I would also argue this effort to create a *via negativa* God within Judaism and for the Jewish people ultimately created a God that was useless to many of these same people at the hour of their deepest theological and spiritual needs. Therefore, this chapter will examine five specific and concrete areas, historically and sociologically, of how Maimonides's impact on modern Judaism negatively impacted the Jewish people and their relationship with the God of Abraham, Isaac, and Jacob. Ultimately, this sixth chapter will serve as a springboard, along with chapter 7, for the final chapter which is designed to be an apologetic response of bringing the Jewish people back to a true Judaism and the true Messiah Jesus.

---

1. Englebretsen, "Logic of Negative Theology," 229. The overall point of Englebretsen's article is not to defend negative theology but he does present the point of Jewish scholarship while also showing that many negative theologians do speak of God in a positive manner even if by accident or happenstance.

UNDERSTANDING OF GOD IN PHILOSOPHY

Previously, I noted how even the most devoted Maimonidean biographer Ilil Arbel acknowledges the influence the Sephardic rabbi had on writers of the Enlightenment and beyond. And while I have often stated in public venues that rabbinic (modern) Judaism bears little resemblance to biblical Judaism, I also would argue that David Biale's statement that "Judaism as a religion is a modern invention" is an example of hyperbole. However, the question that this section will consider to some degree is by how much?[2] For Biale is again correct to a point when he argues that "secular Jewish thinkers seized these categories [of modern Judaism], emptied of their religious meanings and filled them instead with new, secular definitions, informed by alternative traditions from premodernity: they declared their independence from the tradition in terms taken from the tradition."[3] Therefore, the question which arises if Biale is correct even within the margin of error is, from what tradition did many of these secular Jewish thinkers receive their impetus and thought? Biale's response is Moshe ben Maimon, the rabbi who developed a God who "can only be worshipped by philosophers" because He "is virtually a God that does not exist."[4]

However, and despite the fact that I agree with Biale to a certain extent, this is a blanket and powerful statement to make without some measurable level of evaluation and consideration. Leo Strauss makes the argument that Maimonides's writings, especially *Guide of the Perplexed*, was both a philosophical work and something more, something secretive and hidden. He writes that the *Guide* contains both a philosophical section and a non-philosophical section that is "exoteric" in nature.[5] Therefore, a brief examination of medieval Jewish philosophy is in order to determine if Biale's premise is correct or if the observations of Biale, Strauss, and Arbel are overlapping or unique coincidences. Norbert Samuelson sets out or defines the concept of Jewish philosophy in the medieval period by combining the idea of theology and philosophy into a mutual definition based upon the ideas of Torah (however compassed of both Scripture and the talmudic literature) and philosophical thought that "was either Neoplatonic or atomistic or Aristotelian in origin."[6] The supposed goal of the Jewish medieval philosopher was to compare/contrast and present the greater case for the Torah if there

2. Biale, "Not in the Heavens," 344.
3. Biale, "Not in the Heavens," 344.
4. Biale, "Not in the Heavens," 347–48.
5. Green, *Leo Strauss on Maimonides*, 616–18.
6. Samuelson, "Medieval Jewish Philosophy," 262 and Shatz, "Biblical and Rabbinic Background," 16.

was conflict between the two.⁷ David Shatz agrees in principle with Samuelson's definition but notes that medieval Jewish philosophy shared as much in common with the philosophic thoughts of other cultures as they did with the works of Scripture themselves.⁸

I argue that this melding of religion and philosophy, especially within the Maimonidean Jewish sphere, created a dynamic that was ripe not only for the sense of the elitism that I have already discussed in the rationale for his creation of the *Guide of the Perplexed* but also furthers the mentality that only truly developed minds could understand the deeper messages of Scriptures that Rambam presented.⁹ Therefore, the question that will continue to be answered throughout this section to the end of the book is, what does this Neoplatonic Maimonidean *via negativa* God offer to the people?

Steven Katz, who writes an overarching historical narrative of Neoplatonism from Philo to the medieval period, acknowledges this difficulty even if ultimately attempting to defend the logically illogical that such *via negativa* arguments become "devoid of content" because ultimately there is nothing that has meaning.¹⁰ This sense of a Maimonidean rabbinic Judaism being devoid of content not only in the medieval period but also in the modern ages can be realized when one simply reads the lengthy words of a Reform Jewish rabbi who finds solace in the words of Rambam that justify his invalidation of Scripture as anything but sacrosanct and pure:

> Maimonides implored his generation to study physics as well as metaphysics if they would truly know God. When asked what he would say about the Torah account of Creation if science were one day to prove that the universe was infinite in time and therefore could have had no beginning, he responded that in that event he would be necessary to understand the Torah differently! He asserted also that every expression in the literature of Judaism which is inconsistent with reason must be interpreted as a figure of speech.¹¹

---

7. Samuelson, "Medieval Jewish Philosophy," 262.
8. Shatz, "Biblical and Rabbinic Background," 17–19.
9. Freudenthal, "Biological Limitations of Man's Intellectual Perfection," 137, 139, 143. I would define Freudenthal as labeling Maimonides not simply as an elitist but also an oligarchist in many ways for he argues that the Cairo rabbi believed that "men are unequal with respect to their intellectual potential is a matter of biology" (139).
10. Katz, "Utterance and Ineffability in Jewish Neoplatonism," 279–80, 282.
11. Gittelsohn, "No Retreat from Reason," 188–89, 192–93. It should be noted that this article is over 40 years old. How much more has the descent from a general acknowledgement of scriptural affirmation has the Reform Jewish denomination gone since then?

This transition from a concept of a *via negativa* God to outright rejection of absolute truths did not occur within a Jewish vacuum. There were Jewish philosophic individuals in the intervening centuries as has been hinted at previously and in the beginning words of this section that bridged the gap from the twelfth century to today—from Spinoza to Mendelssohn to Derrida to mention only three—who illustrate the detrimental impact that Maimonidean thought has played on not simply Jewish philosophy but also on the Jewish soul.

One of the first major Jewish scholars up for discussion is Baruch Spinoza (1632–1676). A man who has been given perhaps unfairly the label of being "the first secular Jew."[12] However, the question which must truly be considered here is whether the *via negativa* concepts perpetuated by Rambam facilitated Spinoza's ability to ultimately reject God's presence on an even greater level than the Cairo rabbi could even have imagined or anticipated. Biale believes so and ultimately argues that while the two philosophers were diametrically opposed on one level, they were "dialectical twins" on another.[13] Does Biale have a point or an agenda? And if Biale has a point, the next question is then "what then hath Rambam wrought?"

As I briefly consider this question from Biale regarding Spinoza, I am confronted not only with two diametrically opposite opinions but also whether Spinoza deserves the term Jewish heretic or simply misguided searching individual. Steven Nadler offers a list of Spinoza's possible Jewish sins—questioning the providence of God, the perpetuity of the Torah's obligation upon man, and wondering whether the soul continues to exist after death.[14] The first and third "sins" would be considered as errors even within a Christian milieu; however, it is the second error that deserves special attention as it is applies to the question at hand.

Warren Zev Harvey, an Orthodox rabbi, will find many overlaps between Rambam and Spinoza on the nature of good and evil even if there are nuances in specific considerations on the issues. The similarities relate to word choices, the question of intellectual truth as being disconnected from imagination, and that Adam's greatest sin was "his abandonment of rational

---

12. Sonsino and Syme, *Finding God*, 78–80; Angel, *Maimonides, Spinoza and Us*, 12–18; and Biale, "Not in the Heavens," 348.

13. Biale, "Not in the Heavens," 349. See also Guttman, *Philosophies of Judaism*, 301–23 (esp. 302). Guttman writes a key statement that should be considered in the overall argument as it relates to the diametrically opposed or dialectical twins argument: "Of course, Jewish philosophers such as Maimonides, Gersonides, and Crescas, who exerted a strong and continuing influence on Spinoza, are quite distant from the latter's pantheism." Guttman would, I believe, argues for a both/and conclusion to the argument.

14. Nadler, "Baruch Spinoza."

knowledge." The differences while slight in one respect are significant in that they differ on how they define evil and the fact that Spinoza sees in Jesus something that Rambam refuses to acknowledge—a potential for "exalted knowledge."[15] However, James Diamond sees nothing in common between the two Jewish philosophers. Diamond will argue from biblical interpretation—in which Spinoza had a quasi-literal exegetical approach to his critique of Maimonidean Aristotelian philosophy—that the two had nothing in common except Jewish heritage.[16]

Therefore, who is correct about Maimonides's influence on Spinoza's negation and/or naturalization of God—Biale, Harvey, or Diamond? The probable answer is a composition of all three. Biale is approaching the question from the bias of a Jewish scholar who teaches at a state university. Harvey is an Orthodox rabbi who tries to balance Orthodoxy in a modern world. Diamond is a prolific writer on Maimonides who appears to be protective of the legacy of the rabbi. However, and given that Spinoza is known for his naturalism, the tiebreaker most likely comes from an unexpected source—a naturalist theologian. Frederick Ferré defines his version of the term as "the theoretical effort of religious persons to consider the universal bearing of the God they worship on the world at large."[17] Ferré argues that this concept, which is also Spinozian, is something that the Cairo rabbi could affirm because it approaches the Creator of the universe from "universal or pervasive properties of things."[18] Therefore, Biale's statement of dialectical twins is an overstatement; however, I argue on a simplistic level that Spinoza could not have developed a naturalistic concept of God that becomes the natural theology we see today without the first inklings of it coming from the mind of Maimonides.

If Spinoza was the first secular Jew to Biale, Moses Mendelssohn (1729–1786) was in many respects the first modern Jew, as he provided to the Enlightenment an approach to reading the Bible that resembled the personification of Jewish rationalism.[19] Mendelssohn's place as one of the members of the German Jewish Enlightenment is secured because of his belief that "Judaism [is a] religion founded upon reason alone" but who also believed on the eternality of the soul.[20] However, less well-known is that he

15. Harvey, "Maimonides and Spinoza," 131–46.
16. Diamond, "Maimonides, Spinoza and Buber Read the Hebrew Bible," 320–36.
17. Ferré, "Natural Theology and Positive Predication," 113.
18. Ferré, "Natural Theology and Positive Predication," 120.
19. Biale, "Not in the Heavens," 352. A different perspective of Mendelssohn's story but also one that acknowledges the German Jewish scholar's focus on reason and rationalism can be found in Guttman's *Philosophies of Judaism*, 330–44.
20. Dahlstrom, "Moses Mendelssohn."

studied with the Maimonidean scholar Israel Samoscz and wrote a commentary of Maimonides's *Treatise on Logic*.[21] Therefore, James H. Lehmann has legitimacy in making the claim that Mendelssohn was "the bridge between Maimonides and the *Haskalah* [movement]."[22]

Lehmann notes that the logic and rationality of Maimonides's approach to religion and faith was the primary appeal for Mendelssohn; however, the rigidness of Rambam's requirement for Jewish people to follow the Thirteen Principles of faith and for non-Jews to affirm the Noahide principles were an unnecessary drawback in Mendelssohn's appeal for an egalitarian world.[23] Therefore, we find within the teachings of Mendelssohn a rational conundrum for one whom Lehmann describes as wanting to always treat the Cairo rabbi with "certain reverence."[24] This would explain why the *Haskalah* movement as a whole "pictured Mendelssohn as the New Maimonides" and his biographer adapted the name Rambeman to model this new representation.[25] Mendelssohn and Maimonides might not have been symbiotic on all Jewish practices and concepts; however, the concepts of reason espoused by Rambam found a natural home in the German Jewish Enlightenment mind of Moses Mendelssohn. This home will find root and flowering in Reform Judaism and its natural offshoots will be explored further and later.

If Spinoza was the first secular Jew and Mendelssohn was the first modern and rational Jew, Jacques Derrida (1930–2004), the "father of Deconstructionism," could be called the first ambiguously, paradoxical, and resistant Jew.[26] A Sephardic Jew who experienced a certain level of Nazi oppression from the Vichy government that controlled the French colony of Algeria,[27] this modern philosopher might seem out of place in my argument of Maimonides and philosophers, given that there are continual questions as it relates to his Judaism, his possible Christianity, the question as to whether he even had a belief in God, and the fact there is no discernible

---

21. Dahlstrom, "Moses Mendelssohn."

22. Lehmann, "Maimonides, Mendelssohn and the Me'afim," 88. Lehmann also provides a great but succinct definition of the *Haskalah* movement: "The Berlin *Haskalah* was the first of a number of Jewish movements in Central and Eastern Europe which sought to adapt the political and cultural situation of the Jews to the modern world of Enlightenment" (p87).

23. Lehmann, "Maimonides, Mendelssohn and the Me'afim," 90–92.

24. Lehmann, "Maimonides, Mendelssohn and the Me'afim," 92.

25. Lehmann, "Maimonides, Mendelssohn and the Me'afim," 101.

26. Shakespeare, "Thinking about *Fire*," 242; Geraci, "Jacques Derrida and Abraham's Heritage," 249; and Lawlor, "Jacques Derrida."

27. Lawlor, "Jacques Derrida."

evidence of a viable Maimonidean connection.[28] However, I argue that Derrida's confusion, isolation, and ultimately the philosophic question he raises over the value of speech and silence are the ultimate manifestation of Jewish Maimonideanism even if Rambam's name is never mentioned.

Steven Shakespeare writes of Derrida's two key religious concepts that are integral to making my subtle point. The first is that the modern philosopher's Judaism is one based on rabbinic thought from the Talmud—"a tradition of reading and interpreting the Torah in the absence of any direct manifestation of God." The second is that Derrida is not a "pure atheist" but one who sees God in deistic terms as retreating from the world "into an inaccessible otherness."[29] It should be acknowledged that Shakespeare sees these two notations as coming from a kabbalistic concept which Maimonides would have rejected; however, both of these concepts ring resoundingly of thoughts coming from the Cairo rabbi. However, it should be the words of Derrida himself who settles the matter at hand. He explains in an interview with John Caputo, Kevin Hart, and Yvonne Sherwood his concept of prayer and other issues:

> When I pray, I am thinking about negative theology, about the unnamable, the possibility that I might be totally deceived about my belief, and so on. It is a very skeptical—I don't like this word, "skeptical," but it will have to do—prayer. And yet this "skepticism" is part of the prayer. Instead of "skepticism," I could talk of *epoché*, meaning by that the suspension of certainty, not of belief. This suspension of certainty is part of prayer ... But I can't tell if I am praying to someone invisible, to the transcendent one, or if I am praying to those others in myself that I want to address out of love and for the protection of their lives.[30]

However, and uniquely, this same negation-filled description of prayer is also compounded by Derrida's anthropomorphic visualizations of how God might appear as He hears the scholar's prayers.[31] This conundrum continues as he acknowledges that within his deconstructive prologue, "God could not be the omnipresent first cause;" however, his Jewish tradition demands that he acknowledge that the name of God "is the empty place, beyond any name."[32] His own deconstructionism creates a sense of bipolar identity

---

28. Dault, "Rosenzweig and Derrida at Yom Kippur," 99–103.
29. Shakespeare, "Thinking about *Fire*," 243, 245.
30. Caputo et al., "Epoché and Faith," 30–31.
31. Caputo et al., "Epoché and Faith," 30–31.
32. Caputo et al., "Epoché and Faith," 37.

within himself. Names are important; however, they are not.[33] The importance of the words of prayer are important; however, silence and speech are not. He identifies with Jesus and the incarnation; however, he struggles with the concept of God's sovereignty.[34] Again, I argue that Derrida exemplifies the end result of Maimonidean theology and philosophy which offers a *via negativa* God but no ultimate answers on which one can define either God or—as one of my old seminary professors used to argue—the answers to "Life's Ultimate Questions." From Spinoza to Mendelssohn to Derrida, and countless others that we could have examined, the philosophy of Maimonides impacted Jewish thought concerning God and philosophy in negative ways from his death in 1204 until today.

UNDERSTANDING OF GOD IN GENERAL

Rambam's *via negativa* perception of the Holy One has impacted and continues to impact modern Judaism in two specific ways and means:

1. God's presence in lives on a personal level and
2. the ability to communicate with God in prayer. For if one does not understand that one can know God personally, how can one worship him as God?

Deirdre Carabine seeks to defend the Cairo rabbi by arguing that ultimately *via negativa* can "be a springboard into the search for unity with the transcendent;" however, she also acknowledges that without cautionary points established it can also be a rapid decline into *negation negationis* if it remains strictly religiously intellectual and perfunctory in its practice.[35] Rabbi Mark Solomon describes this modern dichotomy with the Sephardic rabbi and his *via negativa* [and the corresponding silence of God that by necessity comes with it] in the most honest and refreshing of ways when he states: "The Western Church, with its fondness for theological systems and definitions, have never been particularly comfortable with this, and Jews

---

33. Botwinick, *Skepticism, Belief, and the Modern*, 29. Botwinick is a self-proclaimed agnostic in his book; therefore, one should argue that he has an agenda. However, he writes a most intriguing statement in his book as he examines the deistic motif and influence of Maimonides's *via negativa* on future philosophers: "What Maimonides does to the word "God" (invokes a context in relation to which the meaning of the word becomes destabilized) Derrida applies to all words in natural and artificial languages. In key respects, the Maimonidean tradition of skepticism culminates in Derrida."

34. Caputo et al., "Epoché and Faith," 42.

35. Carabine, *Unknown God*, 323. Carabine utilizes a statement from *Guide of the Perplexed*, part 1, chapter 58, as her justification point.

revere Maimonides far more than they understand, or even agree with him" (emphasis added).[36] Therefore, I argue that this is exactly what Rambam has established with his *via negativa*, especially given his disdain for God's place in human history and the possibility of miracles being a way that God speaks to man and man speaks to God.[37]

One of the great comforts of the Christian walk is the knowledge that God is there with us on each step of this life's journey. The poem by Mary Stevenson Zangare, "Footprints in the Sand," has been reproduced on wallprints, cards, and everything imaginable that could be sold in Christian bookstores since it was first written in the late 1930s.[38] Christians believe that we can know God through our relationship with Messiah Jesus and the presence of the Holy Spirit in our lives. When life hits a dark night of the soul, we can rest assured that we are not alone. However, the Jewish psychologist and philosopher Erich Fromm (1900–1980)[39] raises a very important question as it relates to Maimonidean theology—"How can there be a 'science of God' when there is nothing one can say or think about God?"[40] Can the Jewish people of today, therefore, have a dynamic and intimate present feeling of God if they are too focused on intimating God's actions "and not of God Himself" alone?[41] In a desperate desire to preserve rabbinic traditions and experiences, have the rabbis of today, under the continuing influence of Rambam, created a God so intangible that he becomes scientific to the point of non-existence and/or agnosticism? Many Jewish scholars argue

36. Solomon, "Praise of Silence," 95.

37. Spero, "Maimonides and the Sense of History," 128, 130, 134. I have already mentioned Maimonides's disdain for the miraculous; however, Spero states it more clearly when he writes two interesting pieces of information: "In short, God as the consummate pedagogue works *around* the principle of man's freedom. In designing the Torah and guiding history, God seeks to achieve His goals by adapting the means to fit man's range of responses" (emphasis of around was not added but was in the original text) and "At the same time he rejected apocalyptic and supernatural elements and instead ruled in accordance with those talmudic rabbis whose views were purely naturalistic."

38. A brief history of the poem by Mary Stevenson Zangare is available at: http://footprints-inthe-sand.com/index.php?page=Main.php.

39. New World Encyclopedia Contributors, "Erich Fromm." Two additional items should also be noted:

1. Fromm came from an Orthodox German Jewish family and
2. he was a talmudic scholar until he abandoned Judaism at the age of 26.

40. Fromm, *You Shall Be As Gods*, 11.

41. Kellner, *Maimonides on Human Perfection*, 43–44. Interestingly, Kellner notes that Rambam does not discuss the very personal and intimate command of God from Lev 19:2b—"You shall be holy, for I the LORD your God am holy," in his halakhic works but only in his philosophical works.

to the contrary and present a "safeguard concepts" defense;[42] however, can one have a relationship with someone that one cannot feel or experience?

Shubert Spero raises further questions that he seeks to answer based on the Maimonidean principles of *via negativa*: "[H]ow [can] the Torah presume to legislate love [Dt 6:5] . . . how can one learn to love someone like God who cannot be seen?"[43] However, I argue that Spero is unsuccessful in his questions and arguments, as the questions continue to be asked across the spectrum of Jewish thought. For example, a similar question was raised by the Jewish mystic, Zionist and first Ashkenazi Rabbi of Jerusalem, Abraham Isaac Kook (1865–1935), who longed and fought for a return of the Jewish people to Israel as a means to forestall the religious apathy that he saw approaching in their minds and hearts.[44] Lawrence Kaplan notes that while Rav Ko'ok saw Rambam as a giant in the work of halakhic scholarship, he also saw that man became distant from God when there was no ability to access Him through relationship.[45] The twentieth-century Jerusalem rabbi sought to find a way to combine "man's desire for God's closeness" (i.e., affirmation) with "the spiritual movement of man's purification of that desire" (i.e., negation).[46] However, the question that I ask and Spero asked in his 1983 article is basically, is such a combination possible? Can one become close and distant at the same time? If so, what kind of a relationship would one have with a family member much less with the Creator of the universe?

Spero and Kaplan both note that Maimonides's answer to such a question was built upon a logic that I argue would make the fictional members of the Vulcan race from Star Trek proud—we can grow to have an awareness of this emotion of love towards God once we have sufficiently developed our cognitive abilities of contemplation, knowledge, logic, and rationalization.[47] However, even Spero raises the question—"But does this necessarily lead to love? Does the recognition of wisdom in someone imply that I will love that person?"[48] This is the crux of the problem for modern Judaism—can the

---

42. Spero, "Is the God of Maimonides Truly Unknowable?," 78. Spero presents this argument of safeguarding as a place from which both "Biblical *and* Rabbinic experiences [that] could be poured" (emphasis added). This utilization of both concepts is key for understanding Spero's argument.

43. Spero, "Maimonides and Our Love for God," 321.

44. Robinson, *Essential Judaism*, 393–95.

45. Kaplan, "Love of God in Maimonides and Rav Kook," 227–28. The term "Rav" is another word for Rabbi. Other substitutes often seen are Rebbe or Reb. These substitutes are often seen in the more Orthodox and Eastern European cultures.

46. Kaplan, "Love of God in Maimonides and Rav Kook," 228.

47. Spero, "Maimonides and Our Love for God," 322–23 and Kaplan, "Love of God in Maimonides and Rav Kook," 230.

48. Spero, "Maimonides and Our Love for God," 323.

matrix that Maimonides established in the twelfth century allow for a relational construct with God that permits spiritual intimacy and relationship? Or was Rambam's intrinsic desire to build a wall against even the possibility of Jesus of Nazareth being the Messiah, much less God the Son as incarnate God, so paramount that the edifice between the Jewish people and God called *via negativa* was more important?

Spero, albeit not in the terms or from the perspective that I share, struggles with the same issues; however, he seeks to find an alternative approach for the twentieth and further centuries that I believe is unsuccessful for he continues his reliance on Maimonidean thought. Spero acknowledges the love of God towards humanity and wants the world to experience the pleasure of that love; however, the possibility that one could perceive of Jesus as being the full extension of that love as expressed in John 3:16 sadly is never considered by Spero.[49] Spero's solution are found with these words: "Man need only open himself to a *disinterested contemplation* of these values of moral rightness or, perhaps, holiness in the Torah and to an aesthetic appreciation of nature and it will result in love for the God who is Himself these values growing into a passionate longing to draw closer to Him" (emphasis added).[50] Therefore, despite his earlier criticism of Rambam, Spero returns to the logically illogical approach of the Cairo rabbi. If one wants to have spiritual intimacy, then one must acquire knowledge and think about it long enough and then it might happen. Consequently, if it does not happen, logic states it is the fault of the individual. No wonder Erich Fromm who grew up as an Orthodox Jew but ultimately abandoned it for a life of psychological thought writes the following: "I can understand what the Bible or genuinely religious persons mean when they talk about God, but I do not share their thought concept; I believe that the concept 'God' was conditioned by the presence of a socio-political structure in which tribal chiefs or kings have supreme power."[51] Sadly, Fromm was conditioned first by his Orthodox Jewish faith and then by Freudian psychology to not believe in spiritual intimacy. How many other Jewish people lost their hope to know God because of similar experiences?

As a matter of personal knowledge growth in my work in Jewish evangelism, I attend sessions at the Jewish Community Center to develop my awareness of Jewish thought and belief. A few years ago, I attended a session I roughly remember entitled "How to Pray as a Jew." The Orthodox rabbi explained the history of how these ritual prayers were created,

---

49. Spero, "Maimonides and Our Love for God," 327.
50. Spero, "Maimonides and Our Love for God," 330.
51. Fromm, *You Shall Be As God*, 1 and Sonsino and Syme, *Finding God*, 118–19.

incidentally all post-AD 70, and how the prayers gained their place in the Siddur (Jewish prayer book). A woman in the audience asked the rabbi the question I wanted to ask—"Can we ever just talk to God on our own?" The rabbi discouraged such spontaneous prayers as it might result in saying the "wrong" things and angering Hashem (God). His advice was in many ways Maimonidean because it was simply to stick to the Siddur because it had been tested and tried over centuries—the words might be rote but they would not make God angry at you.[52] I left the session grieving for the rabbi and all the people in attendance for I knew, from my perspective as an evangelical Christian, the greatest moments of my prayer life truly reflected the groanings of Rom 8:26.

However, it is not simply the concept of personalized prayers that is discouraged on a grand scale, but also the idea of personal prayers are not encouraged. Maimonides himself wrote in the *Mishneh Torah*: "Communal prayer is always heard by God. The Holy One Blessed be He never rejects the prayers of the many, even if there are sinners among them. Therefore, a person should always participate with a congregation and never pray alone whenever he can pray with a congregation."[53] And while Ehud Benor would argue that this communal approach to prayer was Maimonides's *modus operandi* vehicle of expressing "an intellectual love for God,"[54] Steven Schwarzschild would offer another Maimonidean approach—silence.

In a 1961 article for *Judaism: a Quarterly Journal*, Schwarzschild incorporates not only Maimonides as his model but also Jewish mystics to argue that silence is the best approach to take before the Sovereign God. His rationale for this approach could perhaps best be summarized by his own words but I will bullet-point it in this way:

1. Does God have time to bother?

2. Not praying shows how truly pious you are because it shows the level of your faith.

3. Your life cannot be really that bad if you have strength to pray.

4. Maimonides says the best way to praise God is to be silent (Ps 65:2).[55]

Ultimately, Schwarzschild does grant that people must pray because we are after all human; however, his advice is not what I consider helpful either:

52. This argument is repeated in a scholarly form as well. Hyman, "Maimonides on Religious Language," 190; Benor, "Petition and Contemplation," 63; and Reif, "Maimonides on the Prayers," 79.

53. Maimonides, *Mishneh Torah*, book 2, chapter 8, sec. 1.

54. Benor, "Petition and Contemplation," 59.

55. Schwarzschild, "Speech and Silence Before God," 196, 198—99, 201.

Pray other people's prayers. You will appropriate them to yourself by using them and pouring your own personality into them. Do not wait until you "feel like" praying or until you know how to pray. You never will. And even if we could occasionally speak without having to use the thoughts and words of others, how shabby and sentimentally self-indulgent such worship turns invariably turns out to be![56]

I postulate that this approach, of "preferred silence" but if necessary follow the mandated prayers advocated by Schwarzschild, is one of the primary causes as to why we find that 45 percent among American Jewry today seldom or never pray.[57]

Therefore, if one reads Solomon Goldman attempt to explain Maimonides's rationale for *via negativa*, one is ultimately led to the reality that what Rambam wrought is the loss of what Goldman calls "pushing thought to the limit, and of attempting in words or symbols that to which there is no longer anything corresponding in our imagination" in his twentieth-century "negative science."[58] For while Goldman might not completely agree with my analysis of his argument, my question is: can one have truly prayed if one cannot imagine or conceive that there is someone there to hear our prayers? Or would one bother to pray if, as Rabbi Harold Kushner argues, that the miraculous element of God is not possible and finding the presence of God is a matter of simply "doing the right things" as much as praying to find Him in our lives?[59] Many Jewish people have decided in the *negativa*.

---

56. Schwarzschild, "Speech and Silence Before God," 204.

57. Pew Research Center, "U. S. Public Becoming Less Religious." This survey was of American religious beliefs as a whole; however, a subsection of the survey did include Jewish Americans.

58. Goldman, *Jew and the Universe*, 99–101 (esp. 101). Simon Rawidowicz writes that "Maimonides' theory of God is the central pillar of his philosophical system. All the other sections of his system are either rooted in his theory of God or indissolubly connected with it" (Rawidowicz, *Studies in Jewish Thought*, 269). However, I argue that he has ultimately created a God so disconnected from any sense of personal reality that he has truly created an "un-God" beyond any semblance of recognition.

59. Kushner, *Who Needs God*, 204 and Sonsino, *Many Faces of God*, 188. Rabbi Kushner would argue in his personal work that he needs God in his life but based upon this work and previous efforts by the rabbi, the God of Kushner is not an all-powerful sovereign of the universe.

UNDERSTANDING OF THE PERSON OF MESSIAH

There is not a monolithic belief structure among all fifteen million Jewish people living in the world today but most of them, at least those who hold to a belief in some form of God, will state they hold to some form of Maimonides's twelfth principle regarding the messiah. For example, Mayim Bialik, actress on *The Big Bang Theory* and holder of a PhD in neuroscience, states this about her Modern Orthodox belief about the messiah and the messianic age: "The concept of a messiah is a general . . . notion that we are partners in making the world better, in moving the world forward. The Messiah is progress, participation, suiting up and showing up for life."[60] An interesting definition from one who holds to the label of "Modern Orthodox" but, as we will discover, common among most of the world's Jewry today. Therefore, a relevant question is whether the idea of a person of messiah is even relevant to the vast majority of Jewish people today? Yes, there is a contingent of faithful, ultra-Orthodox Jewish people working feverishly to rebuild the temple in Jerusalem but does the rest of the world's Jewry even care?

Joseph Saracheck in his chapter on Maimonides and his messianic teachings writes this about the Cairo rabbi:

> Upon the Jews of his own and subsequent days he has exerted a magnetic power. He is reverenced and admired as the protagonist of his race . . . , he codified Biblical and Talmudic laws on the basis of their underlying motives and common characteristics. He also rationalized the ceremonial disciplinary phases of Judaism as well as its theology.[61]

Indeed, this is quite lofty praise for a Sephardic rabbi who traveled from Spain across Northern Africa during the apex years of the Middle Ages. However, it is ironic that while his chapter begins with such praise, Sarachek ends his chapter by noting that Rambam's positions on eternal life would "today" (in 1932) perhaps "be regarded as untraditional and even heretical."[62]

However, this is the enigma that Maimonides presents for modern Jewry. How does one respond to his categorical statements, especially as it relates to the identity, purpose, and person of the messiah? Maimonidean defenders claim that one cannot continue to be a "good Jew" if one abandons

---

60. Berman et al., "What Does the Concept of Messiah Mean Today?"
61. Sarachek, *Doctrine of the Messiah in Medieval Jewish Literature*, 126.
62. Sarachek, *Doctrine of the Messiah in Medieval Jewish Literature*, 161.

the Rambam's definition of who can and cannot be messiah.⁶³ Reform Rabbi David Wolpe of Sinai Temple in Los Angeles affirms a messianic belief but one with a definite Maimonidean twist:

> Today the Messiah must represent an ideal of peace whose fulfillment lies in our own hands. The age of magic formulas or mitzvot flipping the eschatological switch is past. The nobility in the messianic vision is to live so that when the Messiah comes, we will no longer need him. That may prove beyond our powers, in which case, quite literally, God help us.⁶⁴

Rabbi Phillip Sigal belonged to the Conservative Jewish denomination; but he also struggled with the person and purpose of the messiah. He acknowledges that apocryphal literature which pre-dates Jesus presents a messianic figure quite different than Rambam's figure—including the concept of a preexistent figure and a divine messiah. While Rabbi Sigal would never acknowledge the truth of Messiah Jesus, he would accede that:

> When one takes into consideration the long-continuing tradition of a pre-existent Messiah which requires incarnation at the appropriate time, and the various pre-Christian strands that point to an idea of divine conception and the Isaac allusions it might be considered reasonable to hypothecate that this, as in other facets of Christology expressed in the New Testament, we are dealing with elements of Judaic theology and not with original post-separation Christian concepts or Hellenistic philosophical encrustations.⁶⁵

Therefore, Maimonides's definition is not as status quo in a historical and/or theological sense within Judaism as presumed; however, many choose Rambam's status quo of *via negativa* God over Messiah Jesus.

Today in Israel, there exists another tension about the messiah. During a recent trip to the land, I had the privilege of being driven from Tel Aviv to Jerusalem by Moshe the taxi driver. His family arrived in the land in the 1920s from Eastern Poland/Russia as they were original twentieth-century Zionists. His grandfather settled the land, his father fought in the 1948 War for Independence, and his children have served in the Israeli Defense Forces (IDF). Only what appears to be either a slight case of polio or cerebral palsy

---

63. Schwarzschild, "Messianic Doctrine in Contemporary Jewish Thought," 139. Interestingly, Schwarzschild goes against modern Jewish exegesis of Isaiah 53 and allows for a messianic interpretation; however, he treads very lightly over the passage itself (248–49).

64. Berman et al, "What Does the Concept of Messiah Mean Today?"

65. Sigal, "Further Reflections on the 'Begotten' Messiah," 221–33 (esp. 231).

prevented Moshe from taking his place in the IDF; however, he remains a staunch Zionist and defender of the land. For many Sabres (native Israelis), their effort to rebuild the land, to defend it, and to bring a nation back from the dead is messianic in its most basic and modern form.[66] Therefore, many Zionists have created for themselves a messianic state without a messianic belief system. Moshe does not need a personal messiah because his family in his family created the only messiah they need, Israel.

Therefore, I will close this section with a series of questions about the individual definitions of messiah revealed in this section: Are they violators of the biblical definition of messianism? Yes. Are they also violators of the Maimonidean precepts, as the purpose of the *Mishneh Torah* was to serve as a form of a constitution for when the people returned to the Holy Land? Yes. Would many Zionists hold to Rambam's Thirteen Principles of faith? Not at all. These answers along with what has been presented earlier sadly represent the state of messiah in the twenty-first century not only for Israeli Jews but also for worldwide Jewry.

UNDERSTANDING OF GOD AND THE PERFECTION OF SCRIPTURE

Growing up, the first song I remember learning was "The B-I-B-L-E." I still have my baby dedication Bible sitting on a bookshelf in my home alongside my first baby shoes. One of the rules in my childhood home that I still find myself observing is to never accidentally put a drink on top of a Bible lest it spill, for while the book itself was not holy, the words inside represent the Word of God to humanity. Therefore, I remember in shock and horror another seminar at the Dallas JCC when an Orthodox rabbi picked up a copy of the Hebrew Scriptures and described those same words I cherish as worthless and unintelligible without someone who had proper training instructing the masses as to the meaning of the words. He then threw the Tanakh on the floor almost in disdain while he went on to pontificate about the value of the Talmud and other Jewish works. Yes, the rabbi was seeking to elicit a response from his audience; however, do not the teachings of Rambam as we have already examined encourage such an attitude, such a reaction, such a consideration?

Many Christians have read Chaim Potok's *The Chosen* or have seen the movie version starring Robby Benson (20th Century Fox, 1982). Potok dug deeper into the psyche of Orthodox Jewish life in such works as *Davita's Harp* and *My Name is Asher Lev*; but it is the life and spiritual angst of David

---

66. Luz, *Wrestling with an Angel*, 103–4.

Lurie found *In the Beginning* that one finds the penultimate example of the conflict between Scripture and Talmud and between father and son present. David wants to explore in his rabbinical studies the fertile ground of textual criticism of the Tanakh while his father wants him to "stick with the Talmud" like all good rabbinical students do. This internal conflict manifests itself even today in other ways, as only 11 percent of American Jewry believe that the Torah is the literal Word of God while only roughly 35 percent consider Judaism as vital to their daily lives.[67] The father of modern Judaism has seemingly lost its searching child to other endeavors if vitality of Maimonidean halakah is lost when 57 percent of American Jewry will admit freely to eating pork.[68]

Another modern juxtaposition related to the Scripture with Maimonidean ties is the question of trustworthiness of the biblical story itself. Aside from the statistic given regarding only 11 percent of American Jewry believing the Torah is God's Word, what did Maimonides bring to the spiritual table when he sought to meld the Mosaic account of creation with the Aristotelian approach? In other words, can *ex nihilo* and Greek philosophy coexist?[69]

Orthodox Rabbi Harvey would fight against anyone who would claim that Rambam denied the Mosaic account of creation; however, he would accede that he would rebut the "vulgar notion(s) [or accounts] of creation."[70] However, one must ask what are these "vulgar notion(s)" which brought out such a distaste for the Cairo rabbi? Ze'ev Levy would explain them as the anthropomorphic and/or simplistic notions found in Scripture that were placed there in essence to satisfy the simple or uncomplicated minds.[71] Interestingly, Levy will argue that such simplistic notions allow also for both contradictions, perhaps intentionally or unintentionally, and the presence

---

67. Pew Research Center, "U. S. Public Becoming Less Religious," 58.

68. Pew Research Center, "U. S. Public Becoming Less Religious," 88. See also, for a more academic perspective on Maimonidean halakah, Epstein, "Distinctiveness of Maimonides' Halakhah," 66 and Blidstein, "Oral Law as Institution," 167, 176. Epstein writes that Maimonides's stress on halakah was about "moralization and perfection," two issues which are not at the mental forefront of the vast majority of Jewish minds.

69. Husik, "Anonymous Mediaeval Christian Critic of Maimonides," 160. Husik writes: "Maimonides, as we know, was troubled by the fact that a literal understanding of the Scriptures seemed incompatible with the results derived from a study of the philosophy in vogue at the time, i.e., the philosophy of Aristotle." Husik argues that Rambam's approach was to not follow the literal but to rationalize so that philosophy would carry the day.

70. Harvey, "Third Approach," 293.

71. Levy, "Ultimate Reality and Meaning," 166.

of a possible Godhead to be seen in the Tanakh.[72] Evangelical Christians would agree with Levy on his second proposition but disagree with him on his first argument; nevertheless, such arguments coming from a Jewish scholar is shocking.

Therefore, one can see that at the core of Maimonidean philosophy regarding creation of man, Rambam might have upheld the view of *ex nihilo* but only on the most philosophic of strands. One is allowed to question whether Maimonides saw the people of Adam and Eve as real or philosophical symbols of what happens when one allows passion to become master of one's mind.[73] As one reads Andrew Gluck's own philosophical analysis of the subject, one can conclude that Maimonides would have agreed with Gluck's assessment: "Though the Bible is authoritative, it can always be interpreted allegorically when it conflicts with reason as when it refers to God as being corporeal."[74]

However, and as I have asked earlier in this chapter, what has Rambam wrought in the modern Jewish age with this approach? While an apologist for Maimonides, Goodman still acknowledges that it is a modern reading of Scriptures that describes things about God that "could not be true of Him," things that "are incompatible" with Him, and things that are incoherent and unrecognizable to His nature.[75] The remainder of the section in his work involves Goodman attempting to explain how Maimonides's *via negativa* resolves the inconsistencies of Scripture; nevertheless, the presentation of the possibility that the Word of God is inconsistent and impossible to understand is present throughout medieval and modern Jewish thought. This inconsistency creates a vacuum filled by a type of Jewish higher form criticism that rejects the very essence of the Torah itself.[76] It is not simply the David Luries of fiction but also the religious platform regarding the faith of the Union for Reform Judaism today that we can find such vacuous thoughts of higher criticism:

> Reform Judaism maintains faith in the Covenant between God and Israel as expressed over the generations in the teachings of an *ever-evolving Torah and tradition*. Stirred by the mandate of *tikkun olam*, Reform Judaism seeks to be the living expression of those teachings. It welcomes all who seek Jewish connection to pursue a life of meaning as inspired by the Divine and

---

72. Levy, "Ultimate Reality and Meaning" 167–68.
73. Berman, "Maimonides on the Fall of Man," 8.
74. Gluck, "Maimonides' Arguments for Creation Ex Nihilo," 221–54 (esp. 250).
75. Goodman, *Rambam*, 54.
76. Levenson, "Eighth Principle of Judaism," 205–25.

proclaimed in the truths grasped by Jewish teachers throughout time.[77]

This concept of an "ever-evolving Torah and tradition" has allowed for a Jewish world that is spinning out of control as there is no scriptural anchor on which to hold. There is no anchor I argue because Maimonides would not allow for a literal reading of the text because such a reading might draw the people to the truth of Messiah Jesus—a drawing and a reading he could not allow.

UNDERSTANDING OF GOD IN LIGHT OF THE HOLOCAUST (SUFFERING AND EVIL)

His name is Josef Hausner. I met him on January 11, 2000. He was the first Holocaust survivor I ever met face-to-face. Since then I have become friends with five other survivors—William, Rosalie, Agnes, Vera, and Jack—all of whom have a large piece of my heart, but it all begins and ends for me in many ways with Josef. He was a lonely man living in a luxurious Manhattan apartment but who had watched his mother shot before his eyes as they boarded for a train ride to humanity's version of hell. He was a lost man who was confronted with an empty synagogue when he returned from Poland in 1945 as his wife and children were nothing but ashes now. He became an agnostic ex-rabbi who had given up on God because no one from his synagogue returned from the camps. However, he liked me and would occasionally visit the Manhattan women's Bible study led by the idealistic Texas Jewish missionary who fought desperately for Josef's soul until his dying day on January 17, 2002. To this day, I do not know but have a heartbreaking sense of where Josef's soul resides in eternity even though his body resides on Mount Scopus in Jerusalem.

I write of Josef's story today because many Christians and churches are unaware of the long history of anti-Semitism and virulent hatred directed toward the Jewish people throughout history that has only been summarily discussed in the earliest pages of this book. I was once again reminded of this reality as I walked through the streets of Maimonides's Cordoba when I came upon one of the most disturbing crosses of my life, representing a depraved period of Christian anti-Jewish bigotry. The cross known as *La Cruz del Rastro* represents the massacre of Jewish *Conversos* and traditional Jews in 1473 who were slaughtered during Easter Week. Several crosses,

---

77. Faith Statement of the Union for Reform Judaism (emphasis added): http://www.urj.org/what-we-believe/what-reform-judaism.

with the last one in 1927, have been erected since to commemorate the event.[78] Perhaps it was the heat of July in Spain, but I was overwhelmed by this event, Chaucer's bigotry in *Canterbury Tales*, Shakespeare's caricature of Shylock in *Merchant of Venice,* and all the other events throughout "good Christian history."[79]

However, it is not only Christians like myself who struggle with the reality of evil, suffering, and the penultimate moment of the Holocaust, but also, obviously, the Jewish people themselves. Daniel Cohn-Sherbok examined the writings of eight leading Jewish scholars in a 1989 work entitled *Holocaust Theology* about the theological meaning of the Holocaust, including the purpose of evil and suffering, and discovered that each scholar rationalized a different meaning and purpose to the period. No scholar could answer the core questions in a satisfactory manner—Where was God? Why did it happen? Was there a purpose to it all? From where did all this evil come?[80]

The question of the origination of evil is relevant in both Jewish and Christian circles. Did God create evil as it appears to imply in Isa 45:7—"The One forming light and creating darkness, Causing well-being and creating calamity; I am the Lord who does all these"? Harry Blumberg states that Maimonides fought against such an interpretation because while God did create matter, it is matter that allows itself to be "the cause of all corruption and evil."[81] Therefore, man, because we are a subject of matter, were corrupt in the mind of Rambam when we became obsessed with the things of good and evil and not the higher ideals of truth and falsehood.[82] Consequently, it could be argued that the Cairo rabbi would argue that humanity is the creator of his own evil—an idea that would hold merit within some Christian thought. However, the difference lies in two areas:

1. the concept that miracles can still occur within Christendom and
2. the categorization of evil that Maimonides affirmed.

78. More information on *La Cruz del Rastro* and the massacre itself is available online at: http://www.redjuderias.org/google/google_maps_print/cordoba-en.html.

79. Weissberger, "Motherhood and Ritual Murder," 7.

80. Cohn-Sherbok, *Holocaust Theology*. Cohn-Sherbok has since revised his original work under the title *God and the Holocaust* and written a new and expansive work under the title *Holocaust Theology: A Reader*. While I have not read the new work, I found something raw and visceral about the original work. From the bitter pain of Elie Wiesel to the disdain for God by other writers, the loss and confusion that one could read on the page was palatable and gut-wrenching.

81. Blumberg, "Theories of Evil in Medieval Jewish Philosophy," 153.

82. Harvey, "Maimonides and Spinoza," 133 and Berman, "Maimonides on the Fall of Man," 8.

Theodicy is in essence a study of the theology of suffering and evil in the world. Alvin Reines describes Maimonides's theodicy as "his vindication of the justice and goodness of God as the creator or ground of a universe in which there appears to be injustice and other evils."[83] The problem that many in the Jewish community and in the greater world at large would have with a cursory reading of Reines's definition, and the assumption that he accurately reads Rambam correctly, is the word "appears." The pogroms of nineteenth-century Russia, the Crusades, and the barbarous selections which led to the human ashes found in the Auschwitz gas chambers did not give the inference of appearance but actually happened and they were unjust and evil. Indeed, the teachings of Rambam are taught in synagogues today and the rabbis teach that biblical miracles are not to be understood as either literal or real. In fact, Howard Kreisel emphatically states that the Cairo rabbi would argue that if they had occurred that they "were [simply] a product of the Deity's impersonal governance of mankind."[84] It is no wonder then that I once heard an older Jewish man respond with "He was taking a nap," when asked the immortal question, "Where was God during the Holocaust years?"

However, it is his categorization of evil that seems out of reality in this modern world. Evil is the "lack of perfection," "the absence of wisdom" and can be resolved with enough education and training in the Torah.[85] One also questions, as will be illustrated shortly, how the Jewish people today—especially in light of what they experienced since Rambam's day—can still hold to this particular Maimonidean teaching on evil and sin. For as Rabbi Norman Saul Goldman illustrates, Rambam held to the view that sin is a disease "of the soul" rather than being "an ontological characteristic" (i.e., people are not born evil or with what we call in Christian circles "Original Sin").[86]

However, ultimately it is what Blumberg writes about Maimonides's view concerning man's selfishness of his own pain that might possibly explain why and how Jewish people are turning away from modern Judaism and often toward nothing at all:

> Such people are of the opinion that evil and suffering in this life far exceed the good things. The reason for this error is that such people think only of themselves as occupying important places in the universe and are blind to the fact that they are very insignificant and infinitesimal in comparison with the rest of

83. Reines, "Maimonides' Concepts of Providence and Theodicy," 169.
84. Kreisel, "Miracles in Medieval Jewish Philosophy," 114.
85. Goldman, "Maimonides on the Pathology of Evil," 10.
86. Goldman, "Maimonides on the Pathology of Evil," 8.

the universe, ... If man suffers and evil befalls him, it is due to imperfections arising out of his matter, and man alone is the cause of his own misfortunes.[87]

Therefore under this Maimonidean structure and stricture, the call by David Blumenthal for Judaism to create a "theology of protest" by which survivors can confront or "address God, face to Face, presence to Presence" would never be considered and healing would never begin.[88] While the concept of considering God as abusive or blaming Him in light of the Holocaust might and should be considered extreme, Blumenthal utilizes this approach as a means to reconnect and not disconnect the person to a relationship with God.[89]

Consequently, Christianity indeed can offer the greatest hope to this burden that has become unnecessarily cumbersome. The image of Jesus on the cross corresponds to suffering on the grandest of scales. Chaim Potok as an Orthodox Jew understood this reality in his work *My Name is Asher Lev* and we must share this hope (as will be expanded upon in the final chapter). For my heart continues to break as I ponder these words from the second- and third-generation descendants of survivors (note the despondency of so many of the rabbis):

- Rabbi Moshe Waldoks—"Ultimately the Shoah has become a projection of our own inclinations and political tendencies. The fact, however, is that the Shoah has no intrinsic meaning."
- Rabbi Dov Lipman—"Only God could ensure this remarkable turnaround from my ancestors' downtrodden trek to their slaughter to my upstanding march to that very same spot declaring that the Jewish people are alive and well."
- Rabbi Michael Marmur—"We are witnesses to God and humanity, and that call to witness is not predicated on assurances of reward in this world or the next."
- Aliza Olmert—"The secular social contract was shaped by the fathers of secular Zionism, with the kibbutz and the youth movements providing inspiration. We lived by a code of positive and negative mitzvoth that was broadcast from the centers of that secular Zionist ethos."
- Joseph Berger—"Ultimately, after wrestling with these supreme questions I can't give a cogent explanation as to why I pray to a God whose

87. Blumberg, "Theories of Evil in Medieval Jewish Philosophy," 157.
88. Blumenthal, *Facing the Abusing God*, 257–59.
89. Blumenthal, *Facing the Abusing God*, 257.

I existence I would not try to argue for or whose management I often question."

- Peter Singer—"The Holocaust gives us sufficient reason to reject the possibility of the existence of God, or at least of a God worthy of our prayers and worship."
- Rabbi Mordechai Liebling (Reconstructionist)—"Since childhood I have been unable to believe in an omnipotent, omniscient God. No such God could exist and allow this to happen."
- Chaim Reiss—"One should never criticize or look down on anyone who went through the Shoah and lost faith in God."[90]

CHAPTER SUMMATION

"What Hath Maimonides Wrought?" This is the summary statement of this chapter. His impact in the Jewish philosophic realm trickled downward from Spinoza's questions to Derrida's silence. Rambam's views of God, Scripture, and Messiah have left the Jewish people with a vacuum of belief that is either being left empty or being filled with alternative religious concepts that are only temporary solutions to an eternal question. Yet one could almost say that it is the void of hope that Maimonides's concept of God left for the Jewish people during their darkest hours, whether that hopelessness was in the forest surrounding the killing field today known as Babi Yar or in the ashes left in the ovens at Auschwitz that cannot be explained away. When the Jewish people needed a sense of hope most, Rambam's teachings in the *Guide of the Perplexed* and his Thirteen Principles meant little. Indeed, "What Hath Maimonides Wrought?"

---

90. Rosensaft, *God, Faith & Identity from the Ashes*, 9, 17, 18, 26, 31, 36, 50, 56.

7

Modern Judaism's Understanding of Specific Christian Doctrines in Light of Maimonides and His Yahweh

IN MY ALMOST TWENTY years as a Jewish missionary and evangelist, I have come to two inevitable conclusions:

1. Jewish people as a collective whole cannot differentiate the nuances and differences in Christian denominations and

2. despite two thousand years of church history, the intricacies of major church doctrines are a confusing maze for many if not most Jewish people.

This chapter, though it may be the shortest of the eight chapters in this book, will attempt to provide not only examples of both conclusions that Jewish people have about Christian doctrines but also illustrate how Maimonidean (modern) Judaism has suffered by not realizing that a true Christian is not in competition with Judaism but is simply the final fulfillment of biblical Judaism.[1] Therefore, and in many regards, I consider it the most important chapter of the entire book.

---

1. Novak, "End of the Law," 35. Novak writes: "Indeed, the case can be made that much Jewish self-understanding can be seen as the Jewish attempt to further distinguish Judaism from Christianity, especially in the face of repeated Christian attempts to absorb Judaism into itself by claiming Christianity to be fulfillment of Judaism."

THE DOCTRINE OF THE INCARNATION

A few years ago, I was returning from a trip to Israel when I was pulled aside for special screening. The young woman who had just finished her two years in the Israeli Defense Force (IDF) and had now been assigned to Ben Gurion Airport was lovely, friendly, and, typical of most young native Israelis, an agnostic. After a five-minute inspection of my suitcase and determining that I was not a threat, she nevertheless still had to remain with me until I was released to my gate. We began to discuss (intentionally on my part) my relationship with Messiah Jesus and she became fascinated to learn that not all Christians were Catholic, because she was under the impression that this was some sort of a requirement. She also was shocked to discover that not all Christians pray to Mary. While not going into my opinion of the aberrant concept known as *Theotokos*, I explained that I viewed Mary as a wonderful woman who, though chosen to be the mother of God the Son, was still a sinner in need of Messiah as we all are. She was amazed as this was the first time this view was ever explained to her—and she lives only miles from Bethlehem and Jerusalem.

However, such concepts as the incarnation and the deity of Jesus are difficult concepts for many Christians to truly grasp as well. Therefore, it should come as no surprise that Jesus's Jewish brothers and sisters, especially given the misinformation coming from rabbinic Judaism, would truly struggle with the idea of incarnation.[2] Michael Wyschogrod in one of the most transparent Jewish admissions of the struggle, points to two historical causes for this tension among his own people:

1. the continuing fear remaining from the pre-Babylonian captivity days of becoming polytheistic and
2. the drumbeat influence of Maimonidean teachings. Additionally, Wyschogrod admits that Rambam's influence has hampered the debate regarding incarnational issues in Judaism today.[3]

This issue of the incarnation is crucial for Jewish people today because it is not simply the question of whether Jesus could be Messiah but whether or not Jesus could be God Himself.[4]

---

2. Rashkover, "Christian Doctrine of the Incarnation," 254. See also Shapiro, "Possible Deus Homo," 358–65. Shapiro allows for no possibility for an incarnational interpretation of Hebrew Scripture texts and immediately goes to rabbinic views.

3. Wyschogrod, "Jewish Perspective on the Incarnation," 199–202.

4. Wyschogrod, "Incarnation," 208.

The Jewish scholar Randi Rashkover attempts to explain the concept of a Jewish incarnation by utilizing the active Jewish engagement with the Torah as the fulfillment of an incarnational reality; however, she also allows for Jesus to be the incarnational reality for Christians.[5] In other words, she attempts as my grandparents would have said to have her cake and eat it as well in the framework of a dual covenantalist. As a non-believing Jewish scholar, Elliot Wolfson offers an intriguing counter-point to Rashkover's argument as he acknowledges the existence of theophanies (as they are known in Christian circles) in the Hebrew Scriptures as well as recognition of those events in rabbinic traditions.[6] Therefore, the concept of a non *via negativa* God is not impossible with Judaism but allowable.[7] Therefore, while Christianity is not anthropomorphic in formulation, it is interesting that Wolfson sees such a possibility in existence.

However, such a compromise of incarnational reality on the part of both Rashkover and Wolfson compromises truth on both sides of the covenantal aisles. As an evangelical Christian, I have the uncompromising truth of John 14:6 and Acts 4:12 as well as missional commands of Isaiah for the Jewish people to be a light to the nations. How is this eternally possible for anyone if there are two incarnational realities? Ultimately, what Dr. Rashkover does not yet recognize is that she has stumbled upon the truth of the incarnation. Jesus is the incarnate God and He is the living embodiment of the Torah as well. John 1:1 tells us this basic truth—"In the beginning was the Word, and the Word was with God, and the Word was God In the beginning was the Word, and the Word was with God, and the Word was God."

Such a truthful stumbling by the Jewish people is still possible today as it was for one of the most prominent Jewish scholars of the second century—Simeon Ben Zoma. According to Samson Levey, the *Babylonian*

---

5. Rashkover, "Christian Doctrine on the Incarnation," 255–61.

6. Wolfson, "Judaism and Incarnation," 239–54. See also Hamori, "Divine Embodiments in the Hebrew Bible," 161–83. Hamori takes the basic argument of Wolfson and elevates to a higher educational level. She acknowledges the theophanies present in the Hebrew Scriptures and considers the relevance that these moments have for the incarnational discussion. She attempts to not take sides in the issue but acknowledges that it "invites a vitality in choosing to leave open to God all possibilities."

7. Sommer, *Bodies of God and the World of Ancient Israel*, 135–43. It should be noted that Sommer has what appears to be a kinship with Wellhausen and his thought that I cannot affirm; however, this section of his work is interesting and enlightening. What is especially intriguing is his affirmation that many Jewish scholars must admit that Maimonidean Judaism is a "strained nature of hermeneutic thought" and that to follow to the nth degree Rambam would require "the creation of a new religion whose earliest sacred document would be found in the tenth century C.E. philosophical writings of Maimonides' predecessor, Saadia Gaon." I would agree with Sommer to an extent but state Rambam would want the document to begin with the *Mishneh Torah* alone.

Talmud changed their lofty status of Ben Zoma from being a genius to either insane or a heretic. By all accounts, this change occurred over his allusions to the possibility of a virgin giving birth and statements that one could assume are Trinitarian to nature. While references to Simeon Ben Zoma are still found in the Talmud, they are found almost in quiet whispers because many do not want to believe someone like Simeon could believe in the incarnational truth of Messiah Jesus but by all accounts he did. And it is still possible for Jewish people to believe as well.[8]

THE DOCTRINE OF THE RESURRECTION

One of the most unique and affirming books defending the resurrection of Jesus of Nazareth was written by Rabbi Pinchas Lapide, a Jewish scholar who did not believe in the Messiahship of Jesus. In one way, he followed the Maimonidean argument that Jesus's presence would eventually bring the gentiles to a complete awareness of the Jewish God; however, in another way he argued that Jesus was uniquely the Messiah for the non-Jewish people of the world. Interestingly, what he refused to deny was that Jesus of Nazareth rose from the dead and that His resurrection was a Jewish event occurring in a Jewish timeframe to a Jewish audience.[9] Lapide believed in the resurrection without reservation but unfortunately he died without believing in the Messiahship of Jesus.

The question of Jesus's resurrection for Maimonides in the medieval period and even today for Jewish scholars is not quite so simple as it was for Rabbi Lapide. As has already been noted, Maimonides desired that Jesus's bones be "ground to dust" so it is obvious that he countenanced no possibility of Jewish resurrection for the prophet from Nazareth.[10] Other medieval Jewish scholars appear to largely avoid the subject of the resurrection of Jesus, as they sought to focus on why Jesus could not be the Messiah because he did not bring about the earthly messianic kingdom that Maimonides and other scholars so longed to see.[11] However, what was interesting in an article by McMichael is that medieval Christian scholars sought to bring the subject back to resurrection and the Jewish scholars appeared to want to ignore it altogether.[12] The arguments appeared to be as the old cliché describe it as "two ships passing in the night" and today they seem to still be passing.

8. Levey, "Best Kept Secret of the Rabbinic Tradition," 454–69.
9. Lapide, *Resurrection of Jesus*, 45–46, 140–46.
10. Maimonides, *Epistles of Maimonides*, 98.
11. McMichael, "Resurrection of Jesus," 1–18.
12. McMichael, "Resurrection of Jesus" 1–18.

The argument keeps arising but neither side seems to focus on the core issue—did Jesus arise or not? Indeed, when I bring the subject of Dr. Lapide's argument and book up to other rabbis, they quickly seek to deflect to other issues. It is as if the question of whether the greatest miracle of all time occurred or not is forbidden to discuss in "mixed company." The topic of the resurrection appears to be the elephant in the room of Jewish homes.

One cannot blame Maimonides solely for this silence as there have been Jewish critics of the Maimonidean view of naturalism and rationalism as it relates to the miraculous since Rambam's death;[13] however, the question of the Messiah arising from the dead and bringing the kingdom in an "already but not yet" concept is not conceivable as a topic for discussion. It is as if such a discussion opens up a fearful wound or vacuum that Lapide's book dared to consider but is not be touched by many.

THE DOCTRINES RELATED TO FORGIVENESS, MERCY, AND GRACE

One of the more consternating actions that I can take towards those anti-missionaries that often love to spew some of the most vile accusations against me is to extend words of forgiveness, mercy, and grace towards them. They simply do not understand how I can pray for them, forgive them, and love them, especially after they said and attempted to do some horrible things to me. When I attempt to explain to them that I do these actions because of the forgiveness, mercy, and grace that I have been granted by Messiah Jesus, they are simply befuddled as this is outside of the confines of rabbinic Judaism they understand.[14]

Perhaps this misunderstanding is caused by a literal reading of an "eye for an eye" or because of the perceived need to "defend their territory" against the perceived threat of Jewish evangelism. Indeed, Jewish missions is considered a survival threat by many, as they argue we are seeking to finish what Hitler began. However, I would also argue it is because of a misunderstanding created by what it means for the righteous to live by faith in Hab 2:4 and how it should be defined.

---

13. Ravitzky, "Anthropological Theory of Miracles," 231–72.

14. I struggled to explain this thought process until the following article appeared in my email inbox— Forman, "Chief Rabbi." The article cites a rabbinic teaching *BT Berakhot* 58a which states: "If a man comes to kill you, rise early and kill him first." I have been told that Jewish evangelism is a form of murder; therefore, what is done to me is justifiable.

Rabbi Kellner argues that Paul develops the argument in Rom 1:16–17 because Habakkuk was illustrating that we can never be righteous enough for salvation except through the grace of God and that it is our faith in the forgiveness and mercy of Messiah that we can have hope. The rabbi is absolutely correct in his understanding of the Pauline argument.[15] However, the Maimonidean and modern Jewish belief is tied to the allegorical 613 commandments and the Thirteen Principles of belief.[16] One is "redeemed" not by forgiveness, mercy, or grace by recognizing one's inability to be good enough but by seeking and/or striving to obey laws that are impossible to achieve. It is impossible to obey today not only because many of the Maimonidean 613 commandments relate to temple observance but also because of the "fence" that I mentioned earlier has been added as a safety measure against accidental disobedience.

Isa 64:6 (verse 5 in the Jewish Publication Bible) states—"For all of us have become like one who is unclean, And all our righteous deeds are like a filthy garment; And all of us wither like a leaf, And our iniquities, like the wind, take us away." This is not a verse that is commonly read or commented on in rabbinic Jewish circles today because it confronts a very hard truth— no one can achieve the Maimonidean call for perfection that is required to achieve acceptance by God. In fact, I once asked a rabbi about this verse and he was unfamiliar with it and asked me if it was in the Christian Bible. This verse reminds both Christian and Jew that forgiveness, mercy, and grace are needed and are possible only through one individual; however, the Jewish people are unaware in large numbers of this possibility.

THE DOCTRINE OF SALVATION AND ETERNAL LIFE

On my last trip to Israel, I drove from Jerusalem to meet with an Orthodox Jewish woman living in northern Israel. Today, we have a friendship that is based on honesty and transparency. She states that she is "unconvertible" and she knows that my fervent prayer is that she will one day become a believer in Messiah Jesus. In fact, one of my last statements before I left her place was that she would one day love (i.e., have a relationship with) Jesus as I do. To this day, we are still friends despite our spiritual differences regarding Jesus and our understanding as it relates to salvation and eternal life. However, the key to understanding the difference between my Israeli friend and me is not simply whether or not she believes in Jesus or not but also

---

15. Kellner, "How Ought a Jew," 270–71.
16. Kellner, "How Ought a Jew," 272–74.

what she understands about the concept relating to salvation, redemption, and eternal life.

The Jewish scholar David Hartman offers two models of Jewish redemption or salvation from the teachings of two medieval scholars. One is obviously Maimonides and the other is the more mystically-minded Nahmanides. The Nahmanides model is based on the God-involved premise of the exodus motif in which God is involved in freeing the slaves from bondage; the Maimonides model is based on the erudite focus of Sinai in which a deistic God of the universe offers the Torah and the people are to live up to the expectations he establishes.[17] Nahmanides considers the example of Jer 31 of God offering to engrave a new covenant on the heart of man as an illustration of preemptive and active engagement of God in the lives of humanity. However, neither the medieval scholar nor Hartman engage in the possibility that this Jer 31 illustration could be prophetically illustrative of Messiah Jesus.[18] Instead, Hartman seeks to meld the two scholars in the form of a common ground of understanding, and ultimately ends up missing the point for Jewish people then and today as it relates to salvation and redemption. Hartman seeks to have his Nahmanides feelings of God and Maimonides legalistic observance of Torah, but how can the twain ever meet?

Additionally, many in the ecumenical community today seek to follow Hartman's approach by having a Christian God of compassion and a Jewish Adonai of Torah? Maureena Fritz, who seeks to redefine the incarnation in such a way that strips it of any meaning whatsoever for either Judaism or Christianity, does so in such a way that it defines the redemption of humanity in a way that limits God's role to what man allows Him to do.[19] Incidentally, Fritz is a Roman-Catholic; however, she takes her rationale for this approach from Jewish scholarship—from Rabbi Akiba to Rabbi Eliezer to midrashes to kabbalah.[20]

Therefore, this opens up a twofold question:

1. what is the path to salvation for the Jewish people today and
2. does Judaism truly understand the Christian means of redemption?

There is no salvation through the sacrifices of the temple given that it was destroyed in AD 70. Additionally, Maimonides, who argued for the necessity of the renewal of the sacrificial system when the temple was eventually

---

17. Hartman, "Sinai and Exodus," 373–87 (esp. 383).
18. Hartman, "Sinai and Exodus," 376–77.
19. Fritz, "Midrash," 703–14.
20. Fritz, "Midrash," 703–14.

restored during the Third Temple Period, believed sacrifices served as "sin-offerings" and were to be used as symbolic procedures for the securing of "atonement."[21] However, many modern Jewish people today recoil from the thought of reinstituting a sacrificial system as anathema and anti-PETA. Therefore, the question which naturally arises among many people—what about today? How do Jewish people receive atonement and/or redemption today?

Rabbi Kellner, who has been cited extensively in this book, takes this question one step further and points out that Maimonides argues that his Thirteen Principles are the bottom line philosophies for which a Jewish soul must believe in order to attain a place in the "World to Come."[22] Apparently, Rambam determined within himself the right to establish a dogmatic creed above and beyond the Torah (Levitical Law) which today many Jewish people follow. Others choose not to follow either because they do not believe in an afterlife or they have created a way of their own devices; nevertheless, redemption, salvation, and eternity have become in many cases a device of their own making for the Jewish people today.

To answer the second question, one often hears from a Jewish person that we as Christians only have to state that Jesus is the Messiah. Jehuda Melber in attempting to explain Hermann Cohen's Jewish systematic theology separates the Trinity into a duality and argues that we must believe in both God and Jesus as if they were separate divine individuals.[23] Neither statement is accurate; however, many Christians and churches sadly could not do much better.

Therefore, a final question arises for me and one that I have asked more than one rabbi—if Jesus is not the Messiah for the gentiles and salvation is not possible through Him for me, why are you not telling me how to go to heaven via Judaism? Rabbi Bentzion Kravitz of Jews for Judaism cited to me one night at the Dallas JCC the historical dangers of Jewish proselytism of Christians as one reason;[24] however, he became befuddled when I asked him if he did not love me enough to risk persecution for my eternal soul? The growing push, as has been discussed earlier, of Noahidism is an approach; however, the question is still a thorn in the flesh for many Jewish people. If Judaism is the truth—why is it so exclusive? Eugene Korn

---

21. Hendel, "Maimonides' Attitude Towards Sacrifices," 164.
22. Kellner, "Could Maimonides Get into Rambam's Heaven?," 231–42.
23. Melber, *Judaism*, 420.
24. Wacholder, "Attitudes Towards Proselytizing in the Classical Halakah," 15 and Frydman-Kohl, "Covenant, Conversion and Chosenness," 79.

traces the history of many Jewish people who sought to find a way around Maimonidean thought and ultimately rejected it and/or rewrote it for a modern age.[25]

However, ultimately I would like to turn the argument around to us in the Christian church. If John 14:6 is truly exclusive and yet we as Christians have failed to share the exclusively inclusive truth of Messiah Jesus with his blood lineage, then we must ask ourselves, why? Perhaps it is because we are just as guilty as the Jewish people of not completely understanding our path of salvation.

CHAPTER SUMMATION

This chapter has sought to examine four general but specific Christian doctrines—the incarnation, resurrection, forgiveness/mercy/grace, and salvation from the perspective of eternal life. What I have attempted to illustrate through each of these of these sections is that Maimonidean thought has created a morass, a confusion, and ultimately a veritable quagmire of thoughts and opinions that the Jewish cliché, "two Jews, three opinions," is not just an adage but a fact. Rambam's rationalism and desire for reason created a separation as it relates to the issues of praying to God, identifying the Messiah, or believing one is even possible in the twenty-first century.

Therefore, and with all of these Jewish concerns established, the Jewish people are also naturally confused regarding core Christian doctrines and teachings. One primary example among all that are discussed in this chapter is the issue of the incarnation. Given that they do not have a strong biblical basis and foundation, the possibility of a pre-incarnate appearance of Jesus in the Tanakh is still taboo even though modern Orthodox scholar Michael Wyschogrod is willing to consider discussing it.[26] Other core Christian doctrines such as the idea of "turning the other cheek" and "not returning evil for evil" that I classified as forgiveness/mercy/grace were also highlighted in this chapter in perhaps more of an anecdotal fashion; however, I believe I illustrated how these have been misunderstood by some within the Jewish faith as something that they are not rather than what they truly represent. Additionally, I am not alone in my argument. Michael Marmur, utilizing the personal writings of Rabbi Abraham Joshua Heschel, argues that the rabbi marched with Martin Luther King across the bridge at Selma and

---

25. Korn, "Gentiles, the World to Come, and Judaism," 265–87.

26. Held, "Promise and Peril of Jewish Barthianism," 321 and Soloveichik, "God's First Love," 43–48.

expressed discomfort with the rigid rationalism and lack of empathy of the Cairo rabbi.[27]

Ultimately, however, it is the core issue of salvation that resides as the great stumbling block between Christianity and Judaism. A stumbling block which I believe I have argued throughout this book that lies not simply with one verse in 1 Corinthians but truly at the feet of a twelfth-century Sephardic Jewish philosopher. His desire was to create an anti-Christian apologetic, a Jewish barrier of his own design if I might argue, because of his desire to create a *via negativa* God that separated the relatives of Jesus and the reality of Messiah Jesus.[28] It is time for the consideration to end and for it now to be confronted.

---

27. Marmur, "Heschel's Two Maimonides," 230–54. See also Sonsino, *Many Faces of God*, 43–44.

28. Krakowski, "What Must a Jew Believe," 91–98. Krakowski does not consider the possibility of anything but a Maimonidean perspective when he writes the following: "Contra [Menachem] Kellner, all medieval authorities accept that Judaism requires belief in specific doctrines ('faith that'), because absent acceptance of the defining principles, the faith one 'believes in' *is not Judaism*" (emphasis added).

8

Development of an Apologetic Approach for Evangelism among the Jewish People in Light of Maimonides's Yahweh

BEGINNING THIS FINAL CHAPTER that has stretched literally across two millennia, I believe it is important to bring the focus back to the main question. My original question was whether a Sephardic rabbi who was forced from his Spanish home as a child required and encouraged the Jewish people to abandon the possibility of a personal, intimate relationship with the God of Judaism because of a fear that it also would lead them to a personal relationship with the Jewish carpenter known as Jesus of Nazareth (aka the Messiah). I have sought to show through a historical narrative of Christian history, a pilgrimage of Moshe ben Maimon's own life and writings, and the subsequent consequences of the Cairo rabbi's teachings on modern Judaism that the answer is yes.

However, in my own journey of Rambam's teachings and life, I have also discovered that Maimonides's thoughts and precepts conflicted with not only the rabbinic Judaism he formulated but also with his own views about God and Judaism itself. For how could he say that "All Israel have a share in the World to Come" at the conclusion of his Thirteen Principles of faith,[1] while at the same time threaten any who opposed his teachings with this statement: "A person who separates himself from the congregation of

---

1. Maimonides, *Pirkei Avot*, 155. The exact placement of this statement is in his introduction to the tenth chapter of the Sanhedrin tractate, *Pereq Heleq*.

Apologetic Approach for Evangelism among the Jewish People 161

Israel and does not fulfill mitzvot together with them, does not take part in their hardships, or join in their [communal] fasts, but rather goes on his own individual path as if he is from another nation and not [Israel], does not have a portion in the world to come?"[2] How could he argue for Aristotelian rationalism while at the same time arguing for the purity of Jewish faith? How could he argue that one could know God while at the same time advocating a God that is so remote and distant that relatively modern Jewish philosophers such as Spinoza, Mendelssohn, and Derrida (to name only three) could advocate a form of his *via negativa* even though they themselves could be classified as holding to a marginally deistic form of theism?

This is why I approach this last chapter with both trepidation and hopefulness. 800 years of Maimonidean influence on the Jewish people has left a mark of religious marginalization to the God of Israel that must be breached; however, it cannot be opened casually or even in the traditional means that many Jewish-Christian mission organizations have tried over the last decades. It must be considered in light of the sway and power that Rambam continues to have on rabbinic Judaism and it must be considered carefully as we the Christian church are not only asking Jewish people to consider something that is considered taboo but also in many ways anathema when we ask them to believe in Jesus the Jewish (and gentile) Messiah.

Therefore, this chapter will consider as a beginning point three specific aspects in developing an apologetic approach for evangelism among the Jewish people:

1. the return of biblical Judaism via a minimum of three theological aspects—the possibility of the incarnation, the reality of miracles, and the nature of redemption;

2. a comparison of Maimonidean thought as opposed to the truth of Jesus's teachings; and

3. the restoration of the concept of community to Christian thought as a means to draw Jewish people home.

Each of these three areas will be explained in greater detail in this chapter as well as their relationship to the rabbi from Cairo who died over 800 years ago but whose legacy is ever present in the teachings of rabbis who still lead synagogues today.

---

2. Maimonides, *Mishneh Torah*, book 1, chapter 3, sec. 11.

RETURN MINIMALLY THREE ASPECTS OF BIBLICAL JUDAISM TO THE JEWISH PEOPLE

One of the primary focuses that I have sought to stress in this book is that we should recognize the difference between biblical and rabbinic Judaism. The biblical Judaism of the Torah, the writings, and the prophets is what Messiah Jesus affirmed in Luke 24:44—"Now He said to them, 'These are My words which I spoke to you while I was still with you, that all things which are written about Me in the Law of Moses and the Prophets and the Psalms must be fulfilled,'" is not the same as the rabbinic Judaism that is practiced today. I detailed the formation of rabbinic Judaism that was authorized by Rabbi Judah the Prince in an earlier chapter, but I maintain that it reached its zenith and/or greatest reality through the writings and teachings of the Sephardic rabbi living in Egyptian exile, Moshe ben Maimon.

The Canadian Jewish scholar James Diamond would affirm my premise while granting that the legacy of Rambam has weathered some rocky periods since his death in 1204. Phrases such as "the positions he took on matters crucial to Jewish existence and the practice of Judaism seminally influence the evolution of Jewish thought, worship, and observance ever afterward" and "[h]e augmented (or, some might say, encumbered) Judaism with a new fundamental credo, which quickly became sacrosanct," and his works "achieved a canonical status in Judaism" are statements that can be found in just the first two pages of his work *Maimonides and the Shaping of the Jewish Canon*.[3] However, it is Diamond's observation that Rambam was masterful at "reappropriat[ing] . . . a biblical verse or rabbinic adage [to] leave a new textual legacy for the ongoing development of Jewish thought" that most adequately illustrates his ability to co-opt biblical texts to eliminate the possibility of a personal God and the truth of Jesus's Messiahship.[4]

This ability, or what I would more truly describe as a legacy, explains how even to this day, the mere discussion of possible diversion from his path will lead to charges of heresy in some circles of Orthodox Judaism.[5] The fear of being labeled a heretic can truly be traced back not only to the warnings in the *Mishneh Torah* but also in some of his lesser-known writings such as

---

3. Diamond, *Maimonides and the Shaping of the Jewish Canon*, 1, 2 (the third statement was found in a footnote). Diamond utilizes as an introductory quote a statement from Isaac Husik's 1941 *A History of Mediaeval Jewish Philosophy* that is worthy of note even if it is utilized as a secondary source: "In the post-Maimonidean age all philosophical thinking is in the nature of a commentary on Maimonides whether avowedly or not."

4. Diamond, *Maimonides and the Shaping of the Jewish Canon*, 5.

5. Krakowski, "What Must a Jew Believe," 91–98.

his "Treatise on the Unity of God." In this treatise, Rambam writes about the characteristics of true prophets; however, the implicit warning that he gave to the people ought to be grasped as well:

> And he should instruct the people to serve the Lord, may He be praised, and [to believe in] His unity and to *reject Divine plurality*. He must, in general, command [the people to do] good, which leads to the ultimate success, and warning them against doing evil, which would prevent it. *We are obligated to accept [such a prophet] at all times* since his teachings do not contradict any of the fundamental principles of the Torah of Moses our teacher, of blessed memory, *and these are thirteen fundamental principles that we have mentioned.*[6]

Though Josef Wohlmuth attempts to make an intriguing argument about the differences between Jewish thought and Christian theology,[7] I again contend that today's Judaism is not and can never be the biblical Judaism that was given to Moses and the other prophets, including Amos the sheepherder and the husband of a harlot Hosea , as it was realized and fulfilled (Matt 5:17–20) by Jesus of Nazareth. Therefore, it is implicit upon this section to examine three aspects of biblical Judaism that we can return to the Jewish people that might also allow us to offer them a personal, intimate relationship with God through Messiah Jesus.

Theophanies and the Incarnation

It is disingenuous for S. Daniel Breslauer to write in one section of *A Dictionary of the Jewish-Christian Dialogue* the following statement: "Christians, on the other hand, often fail to realize that Jews do have access to a close, intimate relationship with God,"[8] when Marc Angel writes in a separate section:

> While Judaism is based on revelation, there has been a tendency to play down the role of personal revelations. There is a fear that individuals may espouse absurd opinions or engage in improper

---

6. Rosner, *Existence of God and Unity of God*, 68 (emphasis added).

7. Wohlmuth, "Twentieth-Century Jewish Thought," 389–409. Wohlmuth's primary argument is that Christianity is dependent upon Judaism (which it is) for its existence; however, he as well confuses biblical and rabbinic Judaism. Consequently, his entire argument falls on this basic premise. Additionally, he incorporates the arguments of Derrida into his overall scope which is unusual because very few modern writers have except perhaps myself.

8. Breslauer, "God, Jewish View," 82.

behavior—claiming that they do so at God's command. Since revelation to an individual can never be proven objectively, much confusion and evil can occur by giving credence to everyone who claims to have had a special revelation.[9]

Whose is the real truth within rabbinic Judaism today—Breslauer or Angel? Can one have a personal, intimate relationship with God or is a Jewish person restricted from advocating or proclaiming personal experiences out of fear that their proclamations will be construed as histrionic at best or evil at worst? Barry Holtz, who does not believe in Jesus but wants to believe in God, struggles with this very question. He even asks, is he allowed to believe in the God of the Torah that was present and real, Jeremiah's God that was present but difficult, the Maimonidean God that was rational but present in the negative sense, or no God at all since even this perspective is allowed in modern Judaism?[10] One can note that nowhere in this listing by Holtz is the option of the God the Father, Son, and Holy Spirit because the Jewish people have taught that it is an impossibility for Judaism. However, my question is simply, is it?

In John 1:1, Christians find the most overt statements of the truth of the incarnation and one that has been stated repeatedly throughout this book—"In the beginning was the Word, and the Word was with God, and the Word was God." Christians, especially evangelical Christians, affirm that "Word" in this verse represents the person of Jesus because the Gospel of John is the theological foundation of Jesus's Messiahship and deification claims.[11] In many respects, Christianity and many Jewish people have assumed that Judaism has no answer to this incarnational doctrine. However, Jacob Neusner, one of the great talmudic and Jewish scholars of modern times, has sought to circumnavigate the concept of Christianity's unique claim and find a form of Jewish incarnational theology through the form of the Torah, and for the Torah to literally become the "sage on the stage." Neusner went back into the annals of rabbinic history and found the concept within the Jerusalem Talmud (c. AD 400) whereby "the process by which the sage came to be represented as the living Torah" (i.e., the Word became flesh and dwelt among man).[12] What I found interesting is that while Neusner did note Jesus in his articles, he avoided two observations:

9. Angel, "Revelation, Jewish View," 167–68.

10. Holtz, *Finding Our Way*, 64–109 (esp. 71–79).

11. Jocz, "Invisibility of God and the Incarnation," 179. It should be noted that Jocz was a Jewish believer in Jesus.

12. Neusner, "Is the God of Judaism Incarnate?," 213–38 (esp. 214) and Neusner, "Story-Telling and the Incarnation of God," 197–228.

1. the almost 400-year gap between John 1:1 and the Jerusalem Talmud and
2. why Maimonides never mentions this concept especially since he preferred the Jerusalem Talmud, as has been mentioned previously in this work.

Incidentally, Michael Fishbane deals with the reality with what he calls "divine appearance" or "biblical anthropomorphisms" as it relates not only to Ezek 1:26 and Dan 8:16 but also the midrashic texts that predate Rambam.[13] Fishbane notes that these verses and texts are ones that the Cairo rabbi dealt with in his studies but the nature of these verses create an obvious interpretative conundrum within both faith communities for who is the voice and who is the form of the man?[14] A theophanic manifestation of the Messiah would be the answer of many evangelical Christians, but modern Judaism dares not to go in this direction.

Therefore, we can see that the concept of the incarnation, as well as theophanies, was not a foreign concept to Judaism either in pre-Maimonidean thought or in ultra-Orthodox Jewish thought today. While not allowing for a belief in Jesus among its adherents, the Hasidic (aka Haredi) community today will affirm that their leadership can become tzaddiks (holy men or righteous leaders). Shaul Magid acknowledges that such a position "when detached but not wholly severed from its historical and theological roots in Christianity—the one-time mysterious embodiment of God in Jesus of Nazareth (John 1:45, 46), is not antithetical to Judaism."[15] Magid's article is summarized in this rather lengthy but important quotation:

> Incarnational thinking in Judaism must point to a broader notion that the boundaries between the human and the divine are permeable and the absolute distinction separating the human and the divine (an idea that is fundamental to halakha) cannot survive that permeability. That is, while there may be a distinction between *being* God and being *with* God or a residence *for* God, the latter two are sufficient aspects of incarnational thinking. Or, being God is not a necessary condition to speak of incarnation as opposed to indwelling, although is surely is in John and Christianity more generally.[16]

13. Fishbane, "Some Forms of Divine Appearance," 261–70.
14. Fishbane, "Some Forms of Divine Appearance," 262–64.
15. Magid, "Ethics Disentangled from the Law Incarnation," 37.
16. Magid, "Ethics Disentangled from the Law Incarnation," 37. I believe a brief content footnote is deserved here. I once visited the ohel (gravesite) of Menachem Schneerson—the seventh rabbi of the Lubavitch Jews in Jamaica, Queens, New York.

In other words, a strand of Hasidic Judaism would argue that anyone could become incarnational with God if they are simply holy (aka righteous) enough. Obviously, this is not a belief that could withstand biblical scrutiny; however, it illustrates the point that Judaism is not opposed to the idea of God becoming man—only Maimonidean (rabbinic) Judaism.

Therefore, is a theophanic and incarnational God a possibility in biblical Judaism? The messianic Jewish scholar Jacob Jocz affirms the possibility but with this important caveat—"the complex theophany can only be understood from the characteristic biblical concept of revelation which implies an encounter with God, but at a distance, and only by mediation. What hinders man from approaching is not His invisibility but His holiness."[17] Jocz goes on to argue that biblical Judaism (or what he called the "ancient Synagogue") still harbored a hope to come *"panim el panim"* with God via the Shekinah glory of God (Ps 92:6; Is 6:2).[18] As a Jewish believer in Jesus, Jocz offers no quarter or equivocation on this most difficult of concepts. He is steadfast and argues the same for the church of the incarnate Jesus. Therefore, he emphasizes repeatedly a lesson that we can still learn from him, which is that we should not to attempt to explain the incarnation from a sense or a desire for dialogue that requires compromise but from a sense of strength—"God became man; man did not become God."[19] This is not an anthropomorphic concept as many within modern Judaism will argue; instead, it is a recognition that "if religion is to mean anything to human devotees, the supreme focus of their worship must not be beyond representation as supremely worthy . . ."[20] We must know God by name. We must recognize who He is when we worship Him. We must have a closeness to

---

I can only describe his grave as a shrine, a mecca, and a pilgrimage for the Lubavitch. Many of his followers still believe he is in the messiah—even though he died in 1994—and will go to his graveside on the anniversary of his death to see if this will be the year he rises from the dead. Others take his message around the world and are better missionaries than Christians.

17. Jocz, "Invisibility of God and the Incarnation," 180.

18. Jocz, "Invisibility of God and the Incarnation," 181.

19. Jocz, "Invisibility of God and the Incarnation," 186. Jocz would have great difficulties stomaching the approaches to interfaith dialogue that come from such examples as the following: Goshen-Gottstein, "Judaism and Incarnational Theologies," 219–33; Davies, "Outside the Incarnation," 132–39; and Gamberini, "Incarnation at the Crossroad," 99–112. I abhor these approaches as well. They water down the truth of Jesus for the sake of discussion; thereby, negating the possibility of any real truth being shared.

20. Ferré and Ferré, "In Praise of Anthropomorphism," 211. The title of the article is misleading as the point of the article is actually to defend Aquinas's *via negativa* over and against Maimonides's. The article wanted to illustrate that only a God that was accessible, even if He was understood ultimately in the negative, was worthy of worship. See also Jordan, "Names of God and the Being of Names," 161–90.

Him. We must know that we can love Him. This is biblical Judaism first. This is also the Christian faith because Jesus was and is Jewish.[21]

The Possibility and Reality of Miracles (especially the Resurrection)

When I was a doctoral student at Liberty University's School of Divinity, it would be expected that I would utilize the resurrection and miracle scholarship offered by Gary Habermas. However, and I have spoken to Dr. Habermas about this issue, the question of the miraculous and resurrection studies within modern Judaism is a completely different apologetic concern than the one he fights with such skeptics as Bart Ehrman. The issue of the miraculous—especially the possibility of a man rising from the dead of His own volition which thereby allows Jewish and all humanity to also one day live forever—is one that must be approached from at least a two-pronged rationale. The first question is did Jesus rise from the grave and is this a miracle that is relevant to biblical Judaism? The second question is does the miracle reality of Jesus's resurrection truly impact a Jewish person's eternity?

Therefore, and with only a few exceptions, the references I will use in this section will come via Jewish scholarship. Pinchas Lapide, who was mentioned earlier, would make even the most ardent Christian defenders of the resurrection proud with his summary justification of Jesus's resurrection. He considers Jesus's resurrection not only wholly rational but also an example of what could only be called an "authentic Jewish experience."[22] Additionally, Lapide defends the 1 Cor 15 account of the resurrection as the "oldest faith statement" within Christianity and shows that it provides a plethora of Judaic illustrations that only serve as validation for its truthfulness:

1. Vocabulary was not Pauline in style or form (i.e., written to and for the typical gentile audience that received his epistles)
2. Hebrew Scripture style of the "parallelism" found within the framework
3. "Aramaic and Mishnaic Hebrew way of narration"
4. Nature of not mentioning God's name in the passage "in accordance with the Jewish fear of the name"
5. Utilization of Cephas and not Peter

21. Henrix, "Son of God Became Human as a Jew," 114–43. It should be noted that I had problems with various aspects of this chapter, including that it was a bit ecumenical for my taste. However, there are nuggets of merit that can be fine-tuned and nuanced for evangelical purposes within the pages—even though that would more than likely not be the author's intent.

22. Lapide, *Resurrection of Jesus*, 95, 117.

6. Using the phrase "in accordance with the scriptures . . . corresponds with the faithfulness of the early church to the Hebrew Bible"

7. Usage of the twelve allows Lapide to cast doubt on Judas's suicide (which I diverge from the scholar at this point)

8. The repetition of the concept that Jesus died, buried, was raised, and appeared is consistent with other narratives.[23]

This is because the witnesses of the resurrection were Jewish and saw themselves as practicing a form of fulfilled Judaism, and they died as Jewish believers in Jesus.[24] There was no sense of contradiction of believing in the resurrection of the dead and being Jewish, as they lived in first-century Israel and not in the twenty-first-century Jewish world. Lapide again expresses it well when he writes: "The unavoidable conclusion that forces itself on us from these facts is that the Easter event, in whatever way one wants to understand it, was primarily and chiefly a Jewish experience."[25] Yes, Lapide hoped in a modified form of Maimonidean thought that gentiles would eventually come to Judaism through faith in Jesus;[26] however, it is important to recognize that the presence of a resurrection thought was not uncommon in Jesus's time but it was anticipated, expected, and present throughout the teachings of the Hebrew Scriptures as Lapide illustrates in his work—a work that should and must be utilized as a beginning place for discussion point with Jewish searchers.[27] This was the point that Peter in Acts 2 made during the Jewish Festival of Shavuot (aka Pentecost), and the argument that Alister McGrath refers to as "historical apologetics."[28] McGrath illustrated that the Jewish people had been anticipating and expecting the coming of the Messiah because the teachings were present in the Tanakh. Peter also showed that by necessity, because of the teachings of the Hebrew Scriptures, the Messiah had to die, be buried, rise again, and appear to His disciples

---

23. Lapide, *Resurrection of Jesus*, 98–99.

24. Stylianopoulos, "New Testament Issues in Jewish-Christian Relations," 588. Stylianopoulous's article is from an interfaith dialogue perspective; however, his statement about the ethnicity of the first-century church was elegantly phrased and deserved to be confirmed as such.

25. Lapide, *Resurrection of Jesus*, 45–46.

26. Lapide, *Resurrection of Jesus*, 92.

27. Lapide, *Resurrection of Jesus*, 46–65. Lapide provides a summary listing of biblical and talmudic passages that support his position of the miracle of the resurrection from the story of Enoch and Elijah to Honi the Circle Drawer and Rabbi Sera.

28. McGrath, *Mere Apologetics*, 59–63. It should be noted that this note of "historical apologetics" is McGrath's specific approach to sharing the gospel to the Jewish people.

before His ascension. This was the fulfillment of Scripture—their Torah, writings, and prophets. It still is today, despite the confusion that modern (rabbinic) Judaism presents to the people.

The teachings of today's Judaism on the Reform side is summarized, and somewhat hyperbolized, with this statement: "Reform Judaism denies the doctrine of resurrection and has expunged it from its liturgy, saying it is a foreign import. Moderate Reform and Conservative Judaism sometimes identify resurrection with immortality of the soul (an idea that can be traced to Maimonides)."[29] It is summarized because even Jon Levenson admits that the modern world and much of modern Jewry itself assumes that Jews are only focused on "this–worldly and uninterested in, or even positively skeptical about, the return from death and the World-to-Come."[30] It is hyperbolized because it needs to be pointed out that this radical skepticism is oversimplified even within the Reform movement, for there is a history of a general resurrection concept.[31] Additionally, there is also a movement within some of the liberal wings of Judaism towards wanting to believe that there is something more than "dust to dust" after this life is over.[32] Neil Gillman writes of this movement:

> [T]he principle arguments for the recent reaffirmation of the doctrine of bodily resurrection are both theological and anthropological. The theological argument suggests that God, in order to be really God, must be stronger than death. If death wins out, then death is God and we should worship death—which is inconceivable.[33]

Another component that impacted the changing milieu of resurrection thought is the horrific psychological impression that the Holocaust had upon the minds and souls of the Jewish people. An impression that impacted the need to believe that the photos of the bodies of the victims at Bergen-Belsen, Dachau, and elsewhere being swept into pits had a future and a purpose.[34]

29. Breslauer, "Eschatology, Jewish View," 55.
30. Levenson, *Resurrection and the Restoration of Israel*, 1–2.
31. The Pittsburgh Platform (1885) is considered as one of the founding documents for American Reform Judaism. The seventh principle of the document affirms "that the soul of men is immortal" even while denying "bodily resurrection," heaven, and hell as they were "ideas not rooted in Judaism." Isaacs and Olitzky, *Critical Documents of Jewish History*, 59. It should be noted that Levenson's usage of a portion of this principle of the Pittsburgh Platform directed me towards a full reading of the principle itself.
32. Gillman, *Doing Jewish Theology*, 68–86 (esp. 69, 73).
33. Gillman, *Doing Jewish Theology*, 73.
34. Gillman, *Doing Jewish Theology*, 86.

Therefore, the allegorization of potential resurrection passages in the Hebrew Scriptures that one finds in Levenson's *Resurrection and the Restoration of Israel* would offer no comfort or hope to a world Jewry that is beset by death, destruction, and terrorist attacks.[35] The hope of a miracle should not be considered as ceased or reduced to mere allegory as Isaacs argues.[36] For truly the greatest miracle and hope for humanity of all time was not simply cited by Paul in 1 Cor 15:55 but first promised in Hos 13:14: "Shall I ransom them from the power of Sheol? Shall I redeem them from death? O Death, where are your thorns? O Sheol, where is your sting? Compassion will be hidden from My sight."

Redemption, Righteousness, and Salvation

My pastor, in a recent sermon illustration, utilized a statement from former New York City mayor Michael Bloomberg that exemplifies the standard Jewish understanding of what it takes to achieve a place in heaven, even if they doubt its existence. The former mayor's quote: "I am telling you if there is a God, when I get to heaven I'm not stopping to be interviewed. I am heading straight in. I have earned my place in heaven. It's not even close."[37] This statement illustrates a sense of semi-agnosticism, a heightened sense of self, and a grandiose vision of what it takes to move from Gracie Mansion to a heavenly one and is also, from my perspective as an evangelical Christian, lamentably tragic. Therefore, and while some individuals engaged in the interfaith dialogue process might try to present the argument

---

35. Levenson, *Resurrection and the Restoration of Israel*, 23–34, 123–32. These are the two primary chapters I read in the book; however, as I glanced through the rest of the book, I was startled to read that Levenson focused on attempting to allegorize all potential resurrection passages and/or turn to rabbinic scholarship to find alternative solutions to the dilemma whether one lives again after death. The passage dealing with the Torah itself includes the following two statements worthy of attention:

1. "In biblical thinking, it is possible to continue even after death, and without either resurrection or immortality in the sense of survival as a bodiless soul" (30) and
2. "but we do hope to show that the rabbis' expectation of resurrection has far more continuities with their biblical predecessors than has heretofore been recognized" (34).

The passage of Elisha raising the son of the woman of Shunem in 2 Kgs 4, according to Levenson, relates more to the question of infertility than resurrection and is more of a legacy than a miracle. He also believes that the child of 2 Kgs 4 will "die a second and irreversible death."

36. Isaacs, *Miracles*, 67, 69–70.

37. Peters, "Bloomberg Plans a $50 Million Challenge to the N.R.A."

Apologetic Approach for Evangelism among the Jewish People 171

that modern Jewry does not engage in the works—only salvation motif,[38] the presumption among the Jewish people is that if they do enough good works (*mitzvot*) and perform enough acts of charity (*tzedakah*) they will achieve the necessary points on the eternal scale to earn their place in the World to Come.

This presumption was made dramatically real to me via a three-way discussion I had with a rabbi (Hanan) I have previously mentioned and one of his followers. Rabbi Hanan had been invited by a mainline denominational pastor to present his perspective on Jesus. The pastor is accustomed to me appearing at these events and even enjoys the exchange that occurs when I engage the rabbi in a discussion. Rabbi Hanan made the observation that while Christians are dependent upon someone else (Jesus) to redeem them from their sins, Judaism teaches that redemption is possible through personal righteousness. This is when I brought up the point of personal righteousness being akin to filthy rags (Is 64:6) and he was left grasping for answers. One of his followers who was attempting to assist the rabbi jumped into the discussion and argued that Christians have it easy as Jesus taught nothing but "Judaism Light." I then asked the rabbi's disciple if he had ever actually read the Sermon on the Mount which calls Jesus's followers to a higher standard than biblical Torah and a standard that is impossible to live by but is made achievable through Messiah Jesus's fulfillment of the Torah and our belief in Him. Ultimately, both Rabbi Hanan and his disciple were left speechless and the Christian church pastor was left smiling because I was able to say what even he could not due to the restrictions placed upon him by his organizational governance.

However, the truths that I shared with Rabbi Hanan and the others in attendance was not my perspective. I was only utilizing the truths of biblical Judaism which is the realization and fulfillment of Christianity. For while some argue that modern Judaism is a completed form of redemption (vis-à-vis the argument of Franz Rosenzweig),[39] the repeated custom of seek-

---

38. Breslauer, "Salvation, Jewish View," 182. However, it is interesting to note that Breslauer contradicts himself in this article when he states the following argument regarding works or what he refers to as self-sacrifice: "Some people attain in one moment of self-sacrifice what it takes others a lifetime to achieve" (181). He attempts to present one face to the Christian audience for dialogue while acknowledging that there is a high degree of works involved in modern Judaism for he also writes, "The Jew does not *earn* either salvation or redemption, but Jewish deeds are understood as the *preparation* for each" (182). At least Gillman, *Doing Jewish Theology*, is honest enough as he attempts to unravel the Jewish mystery of eschatology and kabbalah to write that redemption is "human, through the resources, the commandments, are God's gift to us" (62).

39. Wohlmuth, "Twentieth-Century Jewish Thought," 391, 393. It should also be noted that Maimonides's own belief that sacrifices would be reinstituted when his

ing God's forgiveness on Yom Kippur and one rabbi's admission to me that modern Judaism is practicing a "Plan B" type of Jewish practice because sacrifices are no longer practiced, belies this argument. Additionally, the progressive wing of Judaism has abandoned the concept of a redemptive type of messianic hope and are seeking to redeem themselves, as if this was even possible (Is 64:6).[40] I postulate that the progressive wing of Judaism, or what I would more accurately call the deistic, secular, or agnostic wing, has determined that if Maimonides is correct and God, if He exists at all because after all He only is a "non-corporeal agent . . . cannot suffer a tangible sensible harm," "cannot suffer harm or injury of any sort" and would not need to hear or extend forgiveness.[41] Therefore, for these Progressive Jewish souls, seeking redemption or salvation is an exercise in futility.

However, this sense of futility in humanity is exactly what McGrath describes in his work *What Was God Doing on the Cross?* He wrote, "We *feel* alienated from God because we are alienated from God. We *feel* ourselves to be guilty in his sight because we are *guilty* in his sight."[42] Incidentally, this expression of lament is almost identical to the 1894 *Union Prayer Book for Jewish Worship* wording that was used for almost one hundred years in the Reform Yom Kippur Eve services:

> We feel, O God, that our sins and transgressions are many and that we need Thy pardoning grace. For shouldst Thou strictly mark all our failings, O Lord, who would be able to stand to stand before Thee? . . . When we are oppressed with a sense of our unworthiness, we are comforted by the assurances given unto us in Thy word, that the sacrifice Thou desirest is a meek and contrite spirit, and that they who confess their sins and forsake them shall find mercy and pardon, and *be again accepted by Thee*.[43]

I acknowledge that not all Jewish people today are of the Reform and/or secular strain, for Rabbi Hanan in the example of this section would consider

---

version of the messiah appeared contradicts Rosenzweig and Wohlmuth's position.

40. Jacobi, "'In Its Time I Will Hasten It,'" 115, 118.

41. Verbin, "Can God Forgive Our Trespasses?," 185–87, 189. It should be noted that Verbin recognizes the audacity of his argument and he attempts to soften this concept with alternative philosophies and philosophers. However, what I found most intriguing was his closing paragraph in which he concludes that prayer is helpful whether it is God who exercises forgiveness or not (198).

42. McGrath, *What Was God Doing on the Cross?*, 91.

43. The Central Conference of America Rabbis, *The Union Prayer Book for Jewish Worship: Part II*, 87 (emphasis added). This is from my personal copy of *The Union Prayer Book* and one of my most prized possessions that I found almost by accident at a used bookstore.

himself Orthodox. However, what all Jewish people share in common is a confusion of what it means to be redeemed, saved, and to be found truly righteous by God. On one hand, many are aware of the "Plan B" nature of modern Judaism. On the other hand, many like Michael Bloomberg are seeking to earn their own righteousness. Others have simply given up because of their deistic sense of God's distance and inaccessibility. However, we in the Christian church can help the Jewish people discover the biblical Judaism that illustrates that indeed God does want a meek and contrite spirit (Ps 51:17) because it is only he who can restore to us the joy of His salvation (51:12). For as McGrath states, "Our relationship to God is changed by the cross, as is our experience of God."[44] This is as well a Yom Kippur concept that is fully realized in Heb 6:19–20—"This hope we have as an anchor of the soul, a *hope* both sure and steadfast and one which enters within the veil, where Jesus has entered as a forerunner for us, having become a high priest forever according to the order of Melchizedek."

REMIND MODERN JEWISH PEOPLE OF MAIMONIDEAN THOUGHT VS JESUS'S TEACHINGS

In Matt 11:28–30, Jesus's words offer the promise of rest and comfort— "Come to Me, all who are weary and heavy-laden, and I will give you rest. Take My yoke upon you and learn from Me, for I am gentle and humble in heart, and you will find rest for your souls. For My yoke is easy and My burden is light." Conversely, Rambam offered a series of conflicting and confusing instructions to individuals who were confronted with the option of martyrdom or self-preservation. For while he offered comfort to the Moroccan and Yemeni Jews, Maimonides's guide for when and how a Jewish soul should choose to give up his life was anything but restful:

> If a *kuthi* (unbeliever) will arise and force a Jew to break one of the commandments of the Torah on the pain of death, he should break the commandment and not be killed, for it is said of the commandments, if a man abide by them he shall live . . . When does this apply? When all the commandments are at stake, excepting idol worshiping, adultery, and murder. Where these three prohibitions are concerned, if a Jew is told, break one of them or else you will be killed, it is best he should permit himself to be killed and not transgress . . . If the Jew is alone and not in the presence of ten other Jews [*minyan*], then he should

---

44. McGrath, *What Was God Doing on the Cross?*, 89.

> transgress and not be killed. But if he is ordered to commit the sin in the presence of ten Jews, he should rather allow himself to be killed and not transgress, even when the intention is merely to force him to transgress one of the other commandments (i.e., not one of the other enumerated above).[45]

Yes, it can be offered that Jesus did promise his followers opposition and persecution; however, He also offered them peace and ultimate victory with Him (John 14–16). The rabbi from Cairo, in the section above, offered none of the above and only offered biblical misperceptions and contradictory teachings that confused the Jewish people then and even now.[46] Therefore, this section of chapter 5 will seek to differentiate three areas of thought and teaching about which Jesus and Rambam disagreed: misogyny, discrimination, and theodicy. I advance the proposition that when modern and world Jewry truly understand Jesus's position on these issues, they will be drawn to Jesus of Nazareth and away from the rabbinic Judaism promulgated today and that began with Moshe ben Maimon.

Misogyny

In his work *Davita's Harp*, Chaim Potok relates the story of young Davita who considers the Orthodoxy of her stepfather while also longing for a closer relationship with him, and the talmudic rationale of why her mother chooses not to pray. The following is the exchange between herself and her mother:

> I realized, as we sat together week after week in the little synagogue in Sea Gate, that she never prayed. One Shabbos during

---

45. Maimonides, "Laws of Martyrdom," 77–78. Please note that Katz took his translation from portions of the *Mishneh Torah*.

46. Teicher, "Christian Theology and the Jewish Opposition," 69, 72; Kellner, "On Reading Rambam," 225–33; and Statman, "Negative Theology," 58–70 (esp. 58–61). Teicher's point in his argument is that while the Christian church did burn Maimonidean works in the thirteenth century, it was often at the encouragement of Jewish leadership (72). Kellner's article in the *Hakirah* journal is part and parcel of an ongoing debate between himself and other Orthodox scholars as to whether Maimonides should be lionized or recognized as human. However, it is Statman's article that is of particular interest because of the first sentence in the article. He writes: "The purpose of this paper is to show that in its negative theology, modern Orthodoxy has gone far beyond anything we find in classical Jewish thought, and that its version of this theology threatens to empty the commandments of meaning." And while Statman will not go to the point of complete separation from Maimonidean thought, he does admit that if one follows the Shlomo Pines version of Rambam's thought one will end up with an agnostic/deistic concept of God (61).

the service I quietly asked her about that. "A woman is not required to pray," she said. "What do you mean?" All around us women were praying. "A woman may pray if she wishes. But she is not required to pray. *That's the law.* Ask your father. I don't wish to pray. I prefer to read the Bible instead." The women's section in that little synagogue was even more confining than the one in the yeshiva synagogue. A heavy muslin curtain had been drawn across the last few rows from wall to wall, *forming a space that resembled a large cage.* We could hear the service and see nothing. I found no holes or tears in that curtain. My new father was leading the service. I enjoyed hearing his deep baritone voice *and wished I could see him*.[47]

As I consider this story from Potok, my memory also goes back in time to when I lived in New York City and attended a meeting of the Jewish Orthodox Feminist Alliance (JOFA). I listened carefully to the women expressing a new form of discontent at being placed being a behind metaphorical curtain that hampered any sort of relationship with God. As I rode home on the F train that Sunday afternoon, I told a friend riding with me that it was all I could do not to jump on a chair and begin singing "Jesus Loves Me (You)" to them as this was the real message they needed to hear. However, and before Jewish women can hear this truth, they must first move beyond the traditional rabbinic message that tells them something that is a completely different reality.

Halbertal notes that Rambam followed the rabbinic, Islamic, and Aristotelian attitudes towards women and this is made evident in the positions he expressed in the *Mishneh Torah* regarding what could only be called in today's vernacular spousal abuse.[48] This misogynistic attitude extended to the idea of women not being educated in the Talmud, even though the Torah was grudgingly permissible, and allowed for excessive freedom of movement.[49] The *Mishneh Torah* Book One: Knowledge reveals the extent of this misogyny:

47. Potok, *Davita's Harp*, 315 (emphasis added).

48. Halbertal, *Maimonides*, 35–36. A plethora of examples was given by Halbertal that I could use in the *Mishneh Torah*; however, the one that I have chosen to include is from book 4, chapter 21, sec. 10: "Whenever a woman refrains from performing any of the tasks that she is obligated to perform, she may be compelled to do so, even with a rod." It should also be noted that while I have traditionally sought to utilize Twersky's translation, this translation is from the following online source: http://www.chabad.org/library/article_cdo/aid/952895/jewish/Ishut-Chapter-Twenty-One.htm. See also Kraemer, *Maimonides*, 343–46.

49. Baskin, "Jewish Women in the Middle Ages," 103, 107; Meiselman, *Jewish Woman in Jewish Law*, 34; and Kraemer, *Maimonides*, 340–41.

> Even though she will receive a reward, the Sages commanded that a person should not teach his daughter Torah, because most women cannot concentrate their attention on study, and thus transform the words of Torah into idle matters because of their lack of understanding. [Thus,] our Sages declared: "Whoever teaches his daughter Torah is like one who teaches her tales and parables." This applies to the Oral Law. [With regard to] the Written Law: at the outset, one should not teach one's daughter. However, if one teaches her, it is not considered as if she was taught idle things.[50]

Therefore, and while there is a growing rebellion among Jewish women against the perceived and real disenfranchisement in rabbinic Judaism, the sense that the founders did not care about the spirituality of the women of Judaism is ever present.[51] Consequently, there is a place and opportunity within the sphere of Jewish evangelism to illustrate that Jesus's teachings and a proper understanding of Christian teachings opens the door to women—a door that allows women to enter and occupy the same space in worship and praise to God as men.

This can begin intentionally by illustrating that Jesus encouraged women to learn (Luke 10:38–42) and he permitted them to be the first to witness His resurrection (John 20). The idea of women as witnesses within rabbinic Judaism is fraught with confusion and contradictory opinions, even within the purview of Rambam.[52] Additionally, and despite the misogynistic dispersions to the contrary, Paul opened the door to women to have roles in worship that would have been unheard of in the synagogue then and even today.[53] Brian Dodd notes that Paul commended such women as Phoebe, Aquilla, the daughters of Philip, and additional ones throughout his epistles.[54] For in Messiah Jesus, there is neither male nor female because we are all one in Him. This is a message that needs to be shared today for as I was leaving Israel on my last trip, the construction began on the egalitarian

---

50. The source for this translation of the *Mishneh Torah*, book 1, chapter 1, sec. 13 also came from an online source: http://www.chabad.org/library/article_cdo/aid/910973/jewish/Talmud-Torah-Chapter-One.htm. Please note that I was directed to this quotation by Meiselman's *Jewish Woman in Jewish Law*.

51. Adler, "Jew Who Wasn't There," 12–18. Adler does a good job of casting dispersions on a wide range of rabbinic Jewish scholarships and not simply Rambam. This is a fair assessment; however, she does not exclude Maimonides from her analysis.

52. Meiselman, *Jewish Woman in Jewish Law*, 73–80.

53. Dodd, *Problem with Paul*, 19–36.

54. Dodd, *Problem with Paul*, 22–29. It should be noted that Dodd seeks to make Junia/Junius a female in this work. A step that I am not willing to make; however, the book itself is invaluable in dispelling stereotypical myths about Paul.

prayer section at the Western Wall but sadly it has never been finished due to Orthodox opposition. Sadly, they also do not know that this occurred almost two millennia ago when Jesus cried out "It is Finished," but it is time that they finally hear the truth that "Jesus Loves Them" not despite the fact they are women but because they are women.

Discrimination

The term "social justice" is a common watchword in today's world. This concept is especially true in the Jewish world based upon almost twenty years as a missionary because one cannot attend, read, or hear about a bar/bat mitzvah ceremony without being exposed to their "Tikkun Olam Project." The phrase *Tikkun Olam* is Hebrew for "repair/heal the world" and the idea of a bar/bat mitzvah project that seeks to heal the world revolves around doing something to make the world a better place. Therefore, and despite Christianity's less than stellar past and occasional present, an avenue of apologetic evangelism within the Jewish community would be to illustrate the truth of Jesus's teaching regarding equality among all people as opposed to what the rabbi from Cairo advocated. For Rambam's teachings would indeed be surprising to many in the Jewish community who fight so strenuously for social justice without realizing that the greatest proponent of what we might call today biblical social justice is Jesus of Nazareth, who came to draw all people to Himself (John 12:32).

This section could focus on a multiplicity of areas related to the area of discrimination; however, I will briefly focus on two specific areas: religion and slavery. For as has already been mentioned but is worthy of repetition, Rambam's idealistic hope was to one day require either conversion to Judaism and/or adherence to Noahide convictions:

> Moreover, Moses our Teacher was commanded by God to compel all human beings to accept the commandments enjoined upon the descendants of Noah. Anyone who does not accept them is put to death. He who does accept them is invariably styled a resident alien. He must declare his acceptance in the presence of three associates. Anyone who has declared his intention to be circumcised and fails to do so within twelve months is treated like a heathen infidel.[55]

This hope was not based upon Isa 51:4 of bringing justice to the nations but more along the lines of bringing vengeance upon the gentiles for sinful

---

55. Maimonides, *Mishneh Torah*, book 14, chapter 8, 10.

actions, similar to what happened to Shechem in Gen 34.[56] In contradistinction, and sadly throughout history as illustrated in chapter 1, the Christian church failed to live out this truth for the Great Commission which was not about discrimination, vengeance, or bloodshed. Jesus's message was and still is about this living truth in John 10:10—"The thief comes only to steal and kill and destroy; I came that they may have life, and have it abundantly."

For while there are consequences for not receiving this offer of religious life, the consequences are not to be meted out by the human followers of God the Son (which has been the sin of Christianity for two millennia) but only by God the Father himself. Paul the apostle understood this reality when he wrote his heart cry in Rom 9:3—"For I could wish that I myself were accursed, separated from Christ for the sake of my brethren, my kinsmen according to the flesh, . . ." This is the message of Jesus's teachings that needs to be shared with the Jewish people as opposed to the religious discrimination that is hidden within the layers of Maimonidean Judaism.

The second form of discrimination is Rambam's attitude toward the lesser classes, particularly towards those who would be considered slaves. And while the argument could be made that the Cairo rabbi lived in a different place and time, it should be pointed out that his teachings regarding women are still upheld in many ultra-Orthodox settings; therefore, these should be considered as well. Meiselman notes, even while seeking to defend and rationalize the issue, that slaves were considered in the same position as women in regards to fulfillment of all Torah obligations, even if the male slave was seeking to convert, and was not allowed to be a witness because even a free non-Jew male was not allowed to stand before a tribunal.[57] However, it is Rambam's own words that indict him and which would cause socially justice-minded Jewish minded individuals to cringe:

> When a Jew has relations with a Canaanite maid-servant—even if she is his own maid-servant—the offspring is considered a Canaanite slave with regard to all matters. And one may use him for service forever as any other slave . . . It is permissible to have a Canaanite slave perform excruciating labor. Although this is the law, the attribute of piety and the way of wisdom is for a person to be merciful and to pursue justice, not to make his slaves carry a heavy yoke, nor cause them distress. He should allow them to partake of all the food and drink he serves.[58]

56. Halbertal, *Maimonides*, 251–53.

57. Meiselman, *Jewish Woman in Jewish Law*, 51–52, 75–76. Meiselman in his defense of the law of witnessing notes that "only a completed obligated Jew can testify" (76).

58. Maimonides, *Mishneh Torah*, book 12, chapter 9, secs. 1, 8. The original source

Obviously, the charge will rightfully be brought against Christianity that we have also erred on this issue. My own Baptist denomination in 1845 was founded upon a platform and from a rationale of slavery; however, we have renounced and continue to seek to address the incorrect biblical eisegesis by which we were founded, repent of our sinful past, and seek reconciliation with our African-American Christian family.[59] This point/counterpoint is an excellent issue by which we can show the Jewish people that Christianity can be on the forefront of biblical/social justice issues and that we care about the issue of discrimination because as Gal. 3:28 states, "There is neither Jew nor Greek, there is neither slave nor free man, there is neither male nor female; for you are all one in Christ Jesus."

Theodicy

No one likes the word suffering. No one except the most masochistic in society enjoys even the concept of suffering. However, the reality is that suffering is a part of life. Sadly, the Jewish people as a collective whole have experienced an inordinate amount of suffering over the last two millennia, and, as I have highlighted in chapter 2, during the first millennia or so often at the hands of those who called themselves Christians. I have also written and presented in academic and ministry settings about the subject of Christian anti-Semitism to often astounded audiences who were unaware of our tragic past.[60]

Obviously, Christian guilt as it relates to our apathy and inaction during the Holocaust years has often overwhelmed us. However, it should not preclude us from having an evangelistic message even though the temptation and pressure to do so is ever present.[61] Actually, I contend that it should

---

for section 8 came from Halbertal, *Maimonides*, 272. I found the statement for section 1 along with 8 at the following online translation: http://www.chabad.org/library/article_cdo/aid/1363819/jewish/Avadim–Chapter–Nine.htm.

59. "Resolution on Racial Reconciliation," http://www.sbc.net/resolutions/899. See also Dodd, *Problem with Paul*, 81–110, which provides an excellent counterpoint on the issue of slavery in the Greco-Roman world as compared to slavery of the Civil War period.

60. One prime example where I have presented on the subject in an academic milieu is at the 2010 International Society of Christian Apologetics meeting in Fort Worth, Texas. The topic was entitled, "An Apologetic Response on How to Share the Gospel of Messiah Jesus in Light of the Holocaust." Additionally, my first master's thesis (MAComm) was related to the issue of literature written during a time of suffering (1933–1945) and their perception of God and His presence.

61. It should be noted that I am on guard against allowing this subsection from becoming a boondoggle; therefore, I am providing a list of three journal articles and

motivate us to be more engaged in Jewish evangelism, more passionate in sharing the gospel with the Jewish people, and more proactive as we have already failed more than once.

For as mentioned previously, the Jewish people as a collective unit are struggling with the issue of theodicy and suffering and the place of God behind it all, especially as it relates to the Holocaust/Shoah. It has been stated that "[o]ver the last seventy years, no Jewish ideology, of either the left or the right, has emerged that has not relied on the Shoah as to its basis and justification."[62] I affirm this statement, for even Sherbok-Cohn's *Holocaust Theology* compendium illustrates that no two modern Jewish scholars can agree on one reason for Jewish suffering:

1. Bernard Maza: The Jewish people brought the Shoah upon themselves.
2. Ignaz Maybaum: The Holocaust serves as proof that the Jewish people are the Suffering Servant of Isaiah.
3. Emil Fackenheim: We must not allow Hitler to win—*Am Yisrael Chai!*
4. Eliezer Berkovits: The Shoah was a test of the Jewish witness to the world.
5. Arthur A. Cohen: The Holocaust was man's fault because God was incapable of stopping what happened.
6. Richard Rubenstein: God died in the ovens of Auschwitz.
7. Elie Wiesel: How can one hate God on one hand and worship Him as God on the other hand—yet we must?
8. Marc Ellis: Israel must not move from victim to victimizer.[63]

---

one book that seek to discourage Jewish evangelism due to Holocaust pressures. This is by no means an extensive list and I could provide a far more thorough list; however, I contend that this is sufficient to prove the argument: Fleck, "Jesus in the Post-Holocaust Jewish-Christian Dialogue," 904–6; Osborn, "Christian Blasphemy," 339–63; Schoon, "Christian and Jews after the Shoah," 299–314; and Eckstein, *What Christians Should Know*, 287–99. Fleck's article should surprise no one since it comes from the Unitarian Universalist perspective. Osborn's article is, for lack of a better word, tricky because one must read it carefully to understand the nuance of his argument; however, the premise behind it is simply to leave the Jewish people alone. Schoon's chapter appeals to both the guilt reflex of Christendom as well as to historical precedence as it illustrates the European denominational renunciation of evangelism among the Jewish people. Eckstein's book should surprise no one since he is a Jewish non-believer in Jesus. However, what should surprise people is the publisher and two of the endorsers of the book—Paige Patterson and Bailey Smith (former presidents of the Southern Baptist Convention) and leaders of the "Conservative Resurgence" in the 1970s and 1980s.

62. Rosensaft, *God, Faith & Identity from the Ashes*, 9.

63. This is a summary of both my analysis of the book as well as Cohn-Sherbok's

However, we should not be surprised as this conundrum of opinions, voices, and conflict can be traced back to Rambam himself. Joseph Turner points out that "Maimonides' position concerning the problem of evil is based upon the Aristotelian understanding" of the issue because "suffering . . . contains deep educational import."[64] On an intellectual level, this is an understandable and arguable position. However, this is not a response that meets an individual's need at the moment of suffering and pain. This is not a response that comforts during the dark night of one's soul.

Therefore, Christianity vis-à-vis Jewish evangelism has the opportunity to provide a voice through the teachings of Jesus to meet the Jewish people who are still struggling. However, we must ourselves confront three intellectual and spiritual questions that I posed at the International Society of Christian Apologetics in 2010:

1. How do we illustrate Jesus's love after two millennia of antipathy?
2. How do we model compassion amid the ashes of Auschwitz?
3. How do we share Jesus after the Shoah?[65]

Jocz's response summarizes the answer far better than I ever could when he writes: "The secret of the Christian faith is not Christ's 'genius' but his love. This is the underlying motif of much of the New Testament . . . What Jesus does for men and women, Jew or Gentile, is to give them new freedom to love God and to love each other."[66] This is, in essence, the answer to the Jewish question regarding theodicy—the core answer to suffering was when Jesus's love for the world kept him on the cross for the sins of humanity. He suffered for our sufferings. He died so that we might live. He endured sin's temptation for a moment so that we could escape sin for eternity (Heb 4:14–16). This is the ultimate essence of "incarnational theology" that we in the Christian church must share with the Jewish people; however, we often forget this message ourselves.

---

critique of the scholars. Cohn-Sherbok, *Holocaust Theology*, 25–27, 39–42, 52–55, 65–67, 77–79, 89–91, 101–3, 116–118.

64. Turner, "Philosophical and Midrashic Thinking," 70–71.

65. Downey, "An Apologetic Response on How to Share the Gospel." I have tweaked the wording of the questions for conciseness.

66. Jocz, *Jewish People and Jesus Christ after Auschwitz*, 167.

RESTORE THE CONCEPT OF COMMUNITY (KEHILLA) TO THE CHRISTIAN EKKLESIA

Many Christians and churches will speak of the word "community" as a central component of our spiritual walk and mutual accountability to each other; however, I contend that the idea of community often only extends to Baptist potluck suppers and "community groups" that meet once a week. The idea of "community" or the word *kehilla* in Hebrew takes on a life of its own in the Jewish world that can best be described through the words of C. Bezalel Sherman who wrote of the Jewish community in the early 1960s. This definition while perhaps appearing dated reveals a startling reality for those of us who exist outside of the Jewish world:

> The Jewish community is frequently held responsible for the behavior of the individual Jew, but the individual Jew is not allowed to shed his Jewish group label if he no longer cares to stay in the Jewish community. This creates a gap between him and his non-Jewish neighbors while introducing an element of compulsion into his association with fellow-Jews. In this sense, we may speak of membership in the Jewish community as not being altogether a matter of voluntary choice.[67]

This is a stark, painful, and awkward definition. However, does Sherman's definition from more than a generation ago read that much differently than the one provided in 2009 by Misha Galperin and Erica Brown? "It is the mutual voice of Jewish responsibility that most closely resembles being members of an extended family with all of the joys, anxieties, frustrations, idiosyncrasies, and responsibilities that membership in a family brings."[68] Both definitions bring their own sense of stresses and obligations that are infinitely hard to break, especially if one is told that to leave Judaism is to leave your ethnicity, your heritage, and your family.[69] However, the words of Rambam are even more harsh to a Jewish person who considers leaving the *kehilla*:

> A person who separates himself from the community [may be placed in this category] even though he has not transgressed any sins. A person who separates himself from the congregation of Israel and does not fulfill mitzvot together with them, does not take part in their hardships, or join in their [communal] fasts, but rather goes on his own individual path as if he is from

---

67. Sherman, "American Jewish Community," 55.
68. Brown and Galperin, *Case for Jewish Peoplehood*, 15.
69. Eckstein, *What Christians Should Know about Jews and Judaism*, 294–95.

another nation and not [Israel], does not have a portion in the world to come.[70]

Therefore, it is imperative that the evangelistic community in the Christian world discover a way to return in full measure to the *kehilla/ekklesia* model of Acts 2—which was in fact comprised of Jewish believers—if we ever hope to develop a functional model of Jewish evangelism and reverse the confusion regarding incarnational theology which is the fully fleshed concept of community. While writing in regards to evangelical theology proper, David Clark best expressed this concept that I hope to expand upon in these final pages of this work when he wrote: "Theological truth, properly expressed, forms spiritual community and fashions godly persons who worship God, love each other, and serve the world—to the glory of the triune Creator."[71] If this closing section can develop such a model, we have begun to develop a standard that will close the argument against Rambam's *via negativa* apologetic that negates the possibility of the incarnation and Tri-Unity of the Godhead. It will also close the distance and allow the Jewish people to know that a relationship with God is possible not only with the Father but also with the Son Messiah Jesus and the Holy Spirit.

Importance of this Concept

In the good and happier times before my *Texas Jewish Post* friend, that I mentioned previously "unfriended" me, she shared with me one of the most honest and tragic reasons for not believing in Jesus as Messiah: "I cannot believe in Jesus. Do you know what it would do to my standing in the community? Do you know what it would cost me?" Indeed, John Donne, while not writing of the Jewish world, could not have expressed it more eloquently or more aptly as it relates to the emotional, spiritual, and sociological ties that the Jewish world has on a Jewish person when he wrote:

> No man is an island,
> Entire of itself,

---

70. Maimonides, *Mishneh Torah*, book 1, chapter 3, sec. 11. The following is from the online translation: http://www.chabad.org/library/article_cdo/aid/911896/jewish/Teshuvah-Chapter-Three.htm. Two items should be noted. The first is that the Twersky translation was limited in some places and I had to go to some outside translations once I went outside of chapter 3. The second is that I utilized this and the Galperin/Brown quotation in a presentation I did at the Lausanne Consultation for Jewish Evangelism Conference in Jerusalem, Israel, in August 2015. This is an issue that is of great concern to me and one that I have considered for quite some time.

71. Clark, *To Know and Love God*, 418.

> Every man is a piece of the continent,
> A part of the main.
> If a clod be washed away by the sea,
> Europe is the less.

For my dear friend, the call of community is more valuable and more important, even if it is most transient, than the call of eternal life with Messiah Jesus. However, we in the Christian community should not be surprised by this truth at this point in this book. The general misunderstanding of life after death created by rabbinic (Maimonidean) Judaism manifested this reality. It was created by the confusion about the possibility of a close, personal relationship with God because of the *via negativa* teachings by Rambam that have been transmitted over time by the rabbis in the synagogue. It was developed by the strong pull of the community to "stay Jewish" even if the pull of the synagogue has lost its power. Therefore, this section will illustrate the importance of the Christian church to restore the concept of community as a means of building an apologetic approach evangelism to the Jewish people.

However, the first question many will ask is, what does this idea of community look like? I propose that this is the wrong question to ask as it is putting the cart before the horse. By following this practice, and not truly understanding the importance of the word community, we will make many of the same mistakes that we have made in the past and continue to make in the present.

Reform Rabbi Alvin J. Reines developed a construct entitled the "Polydoxy Principle." Polydoxy according to Reines is "that every person possesses an inherent right to ultimate self-authority over her or his psyche and body" and has the ability "to determine the religious or philosophic beliefs she or he will accept, the observances she or he will keep, and the morality she or he will follow."[72] The ultimate purpose behind Reines's idealistic polydoxy was to create a universal community in which anything was permissible and/or allowable; thereby, negating any specific belief system.[73] However, such a concept in my opinion creates a religious anarchical system

---

72. Reines, "Polydox Confederation," 84. Reines passed away in 2004; however, the work of the Polydox Institute (http://polydoxinstitute.org/index.htm) continues and they state the following interesting maxim: "Dr. Reines was a medieval scholar and is considered to be the person who broke the ancient code of Maimonides." Obviously, others would disagree with such a blatant statement; however, Reines was a student of Rambam and also held the view that his *via negativa* was such that God was not accessible in any regards (i.e., "absolute transcendence") in the "human experience." See also Reines, "Maimonides' True Belief Concerning God."

73. Reines, "Polydox Confederation," 84–88.

Apologetic Approach for Evangelism among the Jewish People 185

in which there is no community but only chaos. Additionally, Eugene Korn acknowledges that despite the calls for dialogue, the Jewish leadership is suspicious of this possibility for success for two reasons:

1. the historical backstory that is filled with less than positive outcomes and
2. the hesitancy of rabbinic Judaism with "sharing the covenant" with Christianity.[74]

The second mistake being made today is that some in the messianic Jewish community will argue that it is time for both a post-missionary period between Christianity and the Jewish people, even though as I showed on page one that only approximately 3 percent know Jesus as Messiah, and a separation is needed between the gentile and Jewish believing communities.[75] The primary problem with this approach is that it relies on multiple stereotypes and biblical errors:

1. that all in the Christian church uphold the doctrine of supersessionism;
2. that all Jewish believers want or need to maintain a Torah-observant lifestyle;
3. that all those outside of the faith community of Messiah Jesus perceive of missions/evangelism as a pejorative word;
4. that the Jewish community will accept them if "they look and behave more Jewish;"
5. that all Christians expect Jewish believers to abandon their heritage; and
6. that a dividing wall between Jew and gentile was even biblical.[76]

Mark Kinzer's reasons are built upon a sandy foundation of allegories and suppositions that create divisions and greater suspicions between all believers in Jesus at a time when the call for unity must be greater now than ever. The idea of "two corporate subcommunities" or "two distinct communal entities"[77] is at its core unbiblical as Eph 2:11–16 reminds all of us (specifi-

---

74. Korn, "Covenantal Possibilities in a Post-Polemical Age." The purpose of Korn's article is to discover means and methods around the obstacles as he is a pursuer of dialogue; however, I appreciated his transparency in acknowledging the issues.

75. Kinzer, *Postmissionary Messianic Judaism*, 12–16.

76. Kinzer, *Postmissionary Messianic Judaism*, 12–16, 43, 151, 263.

77. Kinzer, *Postmissionary Messianic Judaism*, 152, 160. Kinzer believes further that "if the Jewish branch of the ekklesia maintains solidarity with the Jewish people as a whole, then the Gentile ekklesia is thereby brought into meaningful relationship with

cally verse 14): "For He Himself is our peace, who made both *groups into one* and broke down the barrier of the dividing wall." However, and what is of greatest concern to the issue of evangelism, is the apparent closet universalism that he displays when he argues for community at the cost of open evangelism—"the Jewish ekklesia bears witness to the One already present in Israel's midst. It does not need to make him present; it only needs to point other Jews to his intimate proximity" as "the Jewish ekklesia [needs to] bear(s) witness discreetly, sensitively, and with restraint."[78] This is not community and the Jewish people would not recognize it as an option. This is an abandonment of the commission that is set before us by Messiah Jesus in Matt 28. Therefore, an alternative approach that allows a Jewish individual to recognize Jesus as Messiah and recognize that a close, personal relationship with God is possible, regardless of what Maimonidean (rabbinic) Judaism has taught him, needs to be considered and established.

Possible Model—Dietrich Bonhoeffer's Finkenwalde

I was invited to make a presentation at the tenth International Conference at the Lausanne Consultation on Jewish Evangelism, Jerusalem, Israel, August 16–21, 2015, on the topic "A Fear of Loss of Community as a Hindrance to the Gospel in Jewish Evangelism."[79] In the general overview of what I will unpack in greater detail here, I pointed out that while Christian churches do struggle with understanding the Jewish mindset and emotional struggles about the issue of making a decision for Jesus, it would be foolhardy to separate churches from the evangelistic operation. We who are on the mission field and those who are sitting in the pews need each other for this Jewish evangelism endeavor if we hope to be successful, and perhaps the model was established during the early but increasingly dark days of Hitler's Third Reich by Dietrich Bonhoeffer, who died from the gallows of Flossenbürg on April 8, 1945.[80]

"all Israel" (152). I argue that this does not sound significantly different than Rambam's rationale than Jesus was brought into the world to bring gentiles to Judaism.

78. Kinzer, *Postmissionary Messianic Judaism*, 304–5.

79. For full access to the PowerPoint presentation, go to: http://www.lcje.net/IndexofPapers2015.html. I also presented a modified form of this for two of Dr. Tim Sigler's classes at Moody Bible Institute, Chicago, Illinois, October 2015.

80. Metaxas, *Bonhoeffer*, 527–32 and Devine, *Bonhoeffer Speaks Today*, 36–37. I am not naïve enough to believe that Bonhoeffer would be welcome in many sections of my own Southern Baptist Convention; however, I would argue that his progression from Liberal to Barthian Neo-Orthodox should make him welcome most anywhere in the evangelical world.

Apologetic Approach for Evangelism among the Jewish People

While Bonhoeffer has been revitalized, recast, and recognized again as the European evangelical I believe him to be following the success of Metaxas's biography, I have always been a tremendous admirer of the German pastor. His writings and teachings are well-known but his efforts to save German Jewish believers (Operation 7) during the most dangerous years of the Holocaust are not.[81] However, there are still those within the liberal Christian theological spectrum and Jewish world that have conflicting emotions about the German pastor. William Jay Peck castigates Bonhoeffer for both advocating the church's responsibility to share the gospel to the Jewish people and while maintaining a quasi-deicide position regarding the Jews.[82] Writing from the perspective of a Jewish man, Stanley Rosenbaum offers no quarter but views the German pastor as one who did not do enough to stop Hitler then and whose writing today encourages Jewish evangelism; therefore, he is a menace that should be rebuked.[83]

Interestingly, Peck and Rosenbaum are both right because Bonhoeffer did believe in Jewish evangelism; however, the focus of this section will examine another area of his work that I believe will help in the work of missions to the Jews today—his *Finkenwalde* approach. Finkenwalde is a location in Germany where Bonhoeffer and others of the Confessing Church established a seminary for men and women, but it is much more in my opinion of an idealistic concept community than a geographical location. Sadly, and ultimately, the seminary at Finkenwalde lasted only a few months before it was closed by the Gestapo in 1937;[84] however, the lessons and structure of the *Finkenwalde* ideal can assist us today in Jewish evangelism.

For it was an ideal, a concept, a vision of what community could be; however, it should not be confused for a utopian commune.[85] Bonhoeffer defined the concept of Christian community as:

> Christianity means community through Jesus Christ and in Jesus Christ. No Christian community is more or less than this. Whether it be a brief, single encounter or the daily fellowship

---

81. Willis, "Bonhoeffer and Barth on Jewish Suffering," 600 and Metaxas, *Bonhoeffer*, 388–89, 423, 441. Ironically, it was the actions of Operation 7 that caused the original arrest warrant. It was only after the failure of Valkyrie and the July 1944 assassination attempt on Hitler's life that the other subversive activities became known.

82. Peck, "From Cain to the Death Camps," 158–76. Obviously, I wish as well that his statement regarding the idea that the Jewish people had nailed Jesus to the cross had not occurred; however, this does not negate the rest of what Bonhoeffer did vis-à-vis Operation 7, the Barmen Declaration, and his other activities.

83. Rosenbaum, "Dietrich Bonhoeffer," 301–7.

84. Metaxas, *Bonhoeffer*, 297–99 and Devine, *Bonhoeffer Speaks Today*, 83–85.

85. Metaxas, *Bonhoeffer*, 266 and Devine, *Bonhoeffer Speaks Today*, 83–85.

of years, Christian community is only this. It means, first, that a Christian needs others because of Jesus Christ. It means, second, that a Christian comes to others only through Jesus Christ. It means, third, that in Jesus Christ, we have been chosen from eternity, accepted in time, and united for eternity.[86]

I postulate that Bonhoeffer's view of the word mirrors in many ways the definitions provided earlier by the Jewish scholars Sherman, Galperin, and Brown; however, there is also added the key component of *the* Someone in which to believe. Bonhoeffer again in *Life Together* writes:

> The more genuine and the deeper our community becomes, the more will everything between us recede, the more clearly and purely will Jesus Christ and his work become the one and only thing that is vital between us. We have one another through Christ, but through Christ we do have one another, wholly, and for all eternity.[87]

Through this approach, we as the Christian church are answering the ultimate question that many Jewish searchers have as they consider the person of Jesus—"Who will be there for me?"[88] Martinson writes of Bonhoeffer's ethos that "God is here, not as eternal nonobjectivity but graspable in his Word within the church."[89] This is key not only in the sense of community that we are building in this section but also in rebutting the premise of Maimonides's Yahweh premise—can a believer in Jesus have a close, personal relationship with God because of the truth of incarnation theology? Bonhoeffer answers the question not only for the gentile but also for the seeking Jewish heart when he wrote: "Silence is the simple stillness of the individual under the Word of God. We are silent before hearing the Word because our thoughts are already directed to the Word, as a child is quiet when he enters his father's room."[90]

Additionally, *Finkenwalde* established a system of daily prayers and Bible readings that are very similar to the midrashic system established by rabbinic Judaism.[91] Such a model would enable the new Jewish be-

---

86. Bonhoeffer, *Life Together*, 21.

87. Bonhoeffer, *Life Together*, 26.

88. Martinson, "Spiritual but Not Religious," 335. It should be noted that the primary aim of Martinson's article and his usage of Bonhoeffer as a principle example is to the generic postmodern generation; however, I contend that the question is especially relevant not only to the Jewish people as a generic whole but also especially to Jewish post–moderns. Therefore, the usage of this article is both relevant and invaluable.

89. Martinson, "Spiritual but Not Religious," 336.

90. Bonhoeffer, *Life Together*, 79.

91. Bonhoeffer, *Life Together*, 51–52, 61–66.

liever to transition to the Christian community without following a Kinzer post–missionary model that is truly no model at all and thereby would encourage true discipleship. Therefore, the community created at Finkenwalde by Bonhoeffer in the 1930s can ultimately be a prototype for a model that we can create today for Jewish seekers and new believers within the sphere of the greater Christian church. If developed carefully and cautiously, it will answer the question of community loss as well as resolving the problem of God-relationship that Jewish people are seeking to resolve. For as Bonhoeffer writes again in *Life Together*, "Christian brotherhood is not an ideal which we must realize, it is rather a reality created by God in Christ in which we may participate,"[92] which is truly the heart of Acts 2:42–47 and a heart of the Christian community which we appear to have forgotten in the twenty-first-century church.

CHAPTER AND BOOK SUMMATION

As this chapter concludes, I have reached the end of this book. As I consider this chapter not only singly but also within the whole structure of the work itself, I would like to make the following recommendations to my fellow Jewish evangelists as well as to the overarching world of missiology and the Christian church:

1. I believe additional studies in the area of Jewish sociology are necessary and have largely been overlooked by Jewish mission organizations for far too long. We ask Jewish people to abandon their community, their sociological undergirding, and their historical heritage, but fail to offer them the same in return. This must change if we want to change the percentage of Jewish believers in the near and long-term future. I believe this is also true in each and every people group that we as the Christian world seek to reach—biblical sociology is an unresearched field in missiology and this needs to end.

2. For far too long, Jewish evangelism and mission organizations have been afraid to confront the heresies which exist within rabbinic Judaism out of fear of offending Jewish seekers and the establishment. This needs to change as the Jewish people are themselves offended by the misogyny, discrimination, and lack of answers regarding theodicy within Maimonidean Judaism, and Christianity has the answers if we will only deliver the truth of Messiah Jesus.

---

92. Bonhoeffer, *Life Together*, 30.

3. The Christian faith is Judaism realized as Matt 5:17–20 reveals to us. Jesus did not come to begin a new religion. He came to fulfill the truths of Judaism and not abolish the Tanakh as He is the Word. There can be debatable questions as to the role of the Trinity in the Hebrew Scriptures; however, the hope of the incarnation (Isa 9:6), the possibility of miracles and resurrection of the dead, and salvation are ever present despite Rambam's protestation to the contrary. We should embrace these truths and illustrate them to the Jewish people, for truly we know the Scriptures of the Tanakh far better than the average Jewish person and often times even better than a talmudically-trained rabbi.

However, and before I write my concluding thoughts on Rambam, I would like to make a major recommendation for the Christian academic community as it applies to this twelfth-century Jewish philosopher—a Jewish scholar who I believe forever changed the face of rabbinic Judaism. Aside from a smattering of articles and musings from the theological mainstream and liberal end of the spectrum, the study of Maimonides has been left to the Jewish academic community. This abandonment has been to the detriment of the evangelical academic world not only because this indicates an alarming lack of awareness that Jesus utilized rabbinic patterns in his teachings but also that the disciples did as well in their later epistles (i.e., 1 Pet 3:15 and the *Pirkei Avot*). Maimonides does not and should not be the primary voice for modern Judaism and we in the Christian community should point out the better options.

Ultimately, Moshe ben Maimon established a Judaism that was by his design and for his purpose a counter-apologetic to the Christian faith. For if Jesus of Nazareth was the Messiah then the teachings of the previous one thousand years prior to his birth would have been for naught. However, what Rambam wrought was a teaching that created another thousand years of lost Jewish souls that know nothing of the Messiah and nothing of God the Father. For Rambam was either wrong or he lied when he stated in the *Mishneh Torah* that

> The Sages and prophets did not long for the days of the Messiah that Israel might exercise dominion over the heath, or be exalted by the nations, or that it might eat and drink and rejoice. Their aspiration was that Israel be free to devote itself to the Law and its wisdom, with no one to oppress or disturb it, and thus be worthy of life in the world to come.[93]

---

93. Maimonides, *Mishneh Torah*, book 14, chapter 12, sec. 4.

However, the Talmud itself states that the prophets foretold of only the days of the Messiah;[94] while, the Hebrew Scriptures tell us that the Messiah's name will be Immanuel or "God with us" (Is 7:14). This is the essence of incarnational theology. This is the essence of showing that God longs to have a close and personal relationship with the people. This is the essence of illustrating that Maimonides's Yahweh is no Yahweh at all.

---

94. *BT* Sanhedrin 99a.

Bibliography

Abelson, J. "Maimonides on the Jewish Creed." *The Jewish Quarterly Review* 19.1 (1906) 24–58.
Adams, Marilyn McCord. *Horrendous Evils and the Goodness of God*. Ithaca, NY: Cornell University Press, 1999.
Adler, Rachel. "The Jew Who Wasn't There: Halakhah and the Jewish Woman." In *On Being a Jewish Feminist: A Reader*, edited by Susannah Heschel, 12–18. New York: Shocken, 1995.
Albl, Martin. "The Image of the Jews in Ps.–Gregory of Nyssa's Testimonies against the Jews." *Vigilae Christianae* 62.2 (2007) 161–86.
Altmann, Alexander. "Maimonides' Attitude toward Jewish Mysticism." In *Studies in Jewish Thought: An Anthology of German Jewish Scholarship*, edited by Alfred Jospe, 200–219. Detroit: Wayne State University Press, 1981.
———. "Maimonides and Thomas Aquinas: Natural or Divine Prophecy?" *AJS Review* 3 (1978) 1–19.
Amirav, Hagit. "The Christian Appropriation of the Jewish Scriptures: Allegory, Pauline Exegesis, and the Negotiation of Religious Identities." *Annali di Storia dell'Esegesi* 28.2 (2011) 39–55.
Angel, Marc D. *Maimonides: Essential Teachings on Jewish Faith and Ethics: The Book of Knowledge and the Thirteen Principles of Faith, Annotated and Explained*. Woodstock, VT: Jewish Lights, 2012.
———. *Maimonides, Spinoza and Us: Toward an Intellectually Vibrant Judaism*. Woodstock, VT: Jewish Lights, 2009.
———. "Revelation, Jewish View." In *A Dictionary of the Jewish-Christian Dialogue: Expanded Edition*, edited by Leon Klenicki and Geoffrey Wigoder, 166–68. Mahwah, NJ: Paulist, 1984.
Anonymous. "The Narrative of the Old Persecutions, or Mainz Anonymous." *The Jews and the Crusaders: The Hebrew Chronicles of the First and Second Crusades*, edited and translated by Shlomo Eidelberg, 95–115. Hoboken, NJ: KTAV, 1996.
Aquinas, Thomas. *Summa Theologica*. http://www.ccel.org/ccel/aquinas/summa.
Arbel, Ilil. *Maimonides: A Spiritual Biography*. New York: Crossroad, 2001.
Augustine. *The City of God* 18:46. In *Nicene and Post-Nicene Fathers of the Christian Church: St. Augustine's City of God and Christian Doctrine*, vol. 2, edited by Philip Schaff. Edinburgh: T. & T. Clark, n.d. http://www.ccel.org/ccel/schaff/npnf102.iv.XVIII.46.html.

———. *The Confessions: The Works of Saint Augustine: A Translation for the 21st Century*, part I, vol. 1. Edited by John E. Rotelle and translated by Maria Boulding. Hyde Park, NY: New City, 1997.

———. "In Answer to the Jews (Adversus Judaeos)." In *The Fathers of the Church: A New Translation: Saint Augustine: Treaties on Marriage and Other Subjects*, edited by Roy J. Deferrari and translated by Marie Ligouri, 387–416. New York: Fathers of the Church, 1955.

———. Letters XXVIII and LXXI, in *Nicene and Post-Nicene Fathers*, vol. 1. Edited by Philip Schaff. Edinburgh: T. & T. Clark, n.d. http://www.ccel.org/ccel/schaff/npnf101.vii.1.XXVIII.html and http://www.ccel.org/ccel/schaff/npnf101.vii.1.LXXI.html.

———. "Reply to Faustus, the Manichean." In *Disputation and Dialogue: Readings in the Jewish-Christian Encounter*. Edited by F. E. Talmadge, 28–32. New York: KTAV, 1975.

———. "Sermon 56." In *Essential Sermons, The Works of Saint Augustine: A Translation for the 21st Century*, edited by Boniface Ramsey and translated by Edmund Hill, 84–94. Hyde Park, NY: New City, 2007.

Bachrach, Bernard S. "The Jewish Community of the Later Roman Empire as Seen in the *Codex Theodosianus*." In *'To See Ourselves as Others See Us': Christians, Jews, 'Others' in Late Antiquity*, edited by Jacob Neusner and Ernest S. Frerichs, 399–421. Chico, CA: Scholars, 1985.

Bale, Anthony. "Christian Anti-Semitism and Intermedial Experience in Late Medieval England." In *Religions of the Book: Christian Perceptions, 1400–1600*, edited by Matthew Dimmick and Andrew Hadfield, 23–44. New York: Palgrave Macmillian, 2008.

Barnard, L. W. "The Early Roman Church, Judaism, and Early Christianity." *Anglican Theological Review* 49.4 (1967) 371–84.

Barnett, Ovrut D. "Edward I and the Expulsion of the Jews." *The Jewish Quarterly Review* 67.4 (1977) 224–35.

Baskin, Judith R. "Jewish Women in the Middle Ages." In *Jewish Women in Historical Perspective*, edited by Judith R. Baskin, 101–27. Detroit: Wayne State University Press, 1998.

Basser, Herbert W. "Allusions to Christian and Gnostic Practises in Talmudic Tradition." *Journal for the Study of Judaism in the Persian, Hellenistic and Roman Period* 12.1 (July 1981) 87–105.

Bates, Carrie L. "Gender Ontology and Women in Ministry in the Early Church." *Priscilla Papers* 25.2 (2011) 6–15.

Bates, Matthew. "Justin Martyr's Logocentric Hermeneutical Transformation of Isaiah's Vision of the Nations." *Journal of Theological Studies*, 60 (2009) 538–55.

Bercot, David W. *A Dictionary of Early Christian Beliefs: A Reference Guide to More than 700 Topics Discussed by the Early Church Fathers*. Peabody, MA: Hendrickson, 2005.

Ben Ezra, Daniel Stökl. "'Christians' Observing 'Jewish' Festivals of Autumn." In *The Image of the Judaeo-Christians in Ancient Jewish and Christian Literature*, edited by Peter J. Tomson and Doris Lambers-Petry, 53–73. Wissenschaftliche Untersuchungen zum Neuen Testament Series 158. Tübingen: Mohr-Siebeck, 2003.

Benisch, A. *Two Lectures on the Life and Writings of Maimonides*. London: Wertheim, Aldine Chambers, Paternoster Row, 1847.

Benjamin, Rick. "Augustine on Cain and Abel." In *Eve's Children: The Biblical Stories Retold and Interpreted in Jewish and Christian Tradition*, edited by Gerard P. Luttikhulzen, 129–42. Leiden: Brill Academic Publishers, 2003.

Benor, Ehud. "Meaning and Reference in Maimonides' Negative Theology." *Harvard Theological Review* 88.3 (1995) 339–60.

———. "Petition and Contemplation in Maimonides' Conception of Prayer." *Religion* 24.1 (1994) 59–66.

Ben-Sasson, Menahem. "Maimonides in Egypt." *Maimonidean Studies* 2 (1991) 3–30.

Berger, David. "Christian Heresy and Jewish Polemic in the Twelfth and Thirteenth Centuries." *Harvard Theological Review* 68 (1975) 287–303.

———. "Mission to the Jews and Jewish-Christian Contacts in the Polemical Literature of the High Middle Ages." *American Historical Review* 91.3 (1986) 576–91.

Berger, Pamela. "The Roots of Anti-Semitism in Medieval Visual Imagery: An Overview." *Religion and the Arts* 4.1 (2000) 4–42.

Berkovits, Eliezer. "The Two-Fold Tetragrammaton of the Thirteen Attributes." In *The Leo Jung Jubilee Volume; Essays in His Honor of the Occasion of His 70th Birthday*, edited by Menahem M. Kasher et al., 45–52. New York: Jewish Center, 1962.

Berman, Daphna, et al. "What Does the Concept of Messiah Mean Today? (Interviews)." *Moment Magazine* (March-April 2012). http://www.momentmag.com/what-does-the-concept-of-the-messiah-mean-today/.

Berman, Lawrence V. "The Ethical Views of Maimonides within the Context of Islamicate Civilization." In *Perspectives on Maimonides: Philosophical and Historical Studies*, edited by Joel L. Kraemer, 13–32. Littman Library of Jewish Civilization. Oxford: Oxford University Press, 1991.

———. "Maimonides on the Fall of Man." *AJS Review* 5 (1980) 1–15.

Biale, David. "Not in the Heavens: The Premodern Roots of Jewish Secularism." *Religion Compass* 2.3 (2008) 340–64.

Binder, Stéphanie E. "Jewish-Christian Contacts in the Second and Third Centuries C.E.? The Case of Carthage; Tertullian and the Mishnah's View on Idolatry." In *Studies in Rabbinic Judaism and Early Christianity: Text and Context*, edited by Dan Jaffé, 187–230. Leiden: Brill, 2010.

Birnbaum, Ruth. "Maimonides, Then and Now." *Judaism: A Quarterly Journal* 54 (2005) 66–78.

Blau, Yitzchak. "Flexibility with a Firm Foundation: On Maintaining Jewish Dogma (Review Essay)." *The Torah u-Madda Journal* 12 (2004) 179–91.

Bleich, J. David. "Divine Unity in Maimonides, the Tosafists and Me'iri." In *Neoplatonism and Jewish Thought*, edited by Lenn E. Goodman, 237–54. Albany, NY: State University of New York, 1992.

Blidstein, Gerald J. "Oral Law as Institution in Maimonides." In *The Thought of Moses Maimonides: Philosophical and Legal Studies*, edited by Ira Robinson et al., 167–82. Lewiston, NY: Edwin Mellen, 1990.

Blumberg, Harry. "Theories of Evil in Medieval Jewish Philosophy." *Hebrew Union College Annual* 43 (1972) 149–68.

Blumenthal, David R. *Facing the Abusing God: A Theology of Protest*. Louisville, KY: Westminster/John Knox, 1993.

———. "Maimonides on Angel Names." In *Hellenica et Judaica: Hommage Á Valentin Nikiprowetzky*, edited by A. Caquot et al., 357–69. Leuven-Paris: Peeters, 1986.

———. "Maimonides' Intellectual Mysticism and the Superiority of the Prophecy of Moses." In *Approaches to Judaism in Medieval Times*, edited by David R. Blumenthal, 27–51. Chico, CA: Scholars, 1984.

———. "Maimonides: Prayer, Worship, and Mysticism." In *Approaches to Judaism in Medieval Times*, edited by David R. Blumenthal, 1–16. Atlanta: Scholars, 1988.

———. "Religion and the Religious Intellectuals: The Case of Judaism in Medieval Times." In *Take Judaism, For Example: Studies for the Comparison of Religion*, edited by Jacob Neusner, 117–42. Chicago: University of Chicago Press, 1983.

Boethius. "God Is Timeless." In *Philosophy of Religion: Selected Readings*, edited by Michael Peterson, et al., 136–39. New York: Oxford University Press, 2001.

Bohak, Gideon. "Magical Means for Handling *Minim* in Rabbinic Literature." In *The Image of the Judaeo-Christians in Ancient Jewish and Christian Literature*, edited by Peter J. Tomson and Doris Lambers-Petry, 267–79. Wissenschaftliche Untersuchungen zum Neuen Testament Series 158. Tübingen: Mohr-Siebeck, 2003.

Bokser, Ben Zion. *The Legacy of Maimonides*. New York: Philosophical Library, 1950.

———. "Religious Polemics in Biblical and Talmudic Exegesis." *Journal of Ecumenical Studies* 16.4 (1979) 705–26.

Bonhoeffer, Dietrich. *Life Together: The Classic Exploration of Faith in Community*. Translated by John W. Doberstein. New York: HarperOne, 1954.

Botwinick, Aryeh. "Maimonides' Messianic Age." *Judaism: A Quarterly Journal* 33.4 (1984) 418–25.

———. *Skepticism, Belief, and the Modern: Maimonides to Nietzsche*. Ithaca: Cornell University Press, 1997.

Boulding, Maria. "Introduction." In *The Confessions: The Works of Saint Augustine: A Translation for the 21st Century*, part I, vol. 1, edited by John E. Rotelle and translated by Maria Boulding, 9–33. Hyde Park, NY: New City, 2002.

Bourgel, Jonathan. "The Jewish-Christians' Move from Jerusalem as a Pragmatic Choice." In *Studies in Rabbinic Judaism and Early Christianity: Text and Context*, edited by Dan Jaffé, 107–38. Boston: Brill, 2010.

Boušek, Daniel. "Polemics in the Age of Religious Persecution: Maimonides' Attitude toward Islam." *Asian and African Studies* 20 (2011) 46–85.

Breslauer, S. Daniel. "Eschatology, Jewish View." In *A Dictionary of the Jewish-Christian Dialogue: Expanded Edition*, edited by Leon Klenicki and Geoffrey Wigoder, 52–55. Mahwah, NJ: Paulist, 1984.

———. "God, Jewish View." In *A Dictionary of the Jewish-Christian Dialogue: Expanded Edition*, edited by Leon Klenicki and Geoffrey Wigoder, 79–82. Mahwah, NJ: Paulist, 1984.

———. "Salvation, Jewish View. In *A Dictionary of the Jewish-Christian Dialogue: Expanded Edition*, edited by Leon Klenicki and Geoffrey Wigoder, 180–84. Mahwah, NJ: Paulist, 1984.

Broadie, Alexander. "Maimonides and Aquinas on the Names of God." *Religious Studies on the Names of God* 23.2 (June 1987).

Brody, Robert. "Maimonides' Attitude towards the Halakhic Innovations of the Geonim." In *Thought of Moses Maimonides*, edited by Ira Robinson et al., 183–208. Lewiston, NY: Edwin Mellen, 1990.

Brown, Erica, and Misha Galperin. *The Case for Jewish People: Can We Be One?* Woodstock, VT: Jewish Lights, 2009.
Brown, Reva Berman, and Sean McCartney. "Living in Limbo: The Experience of Jewish Converts in Medieval England." In *Christianizing Peoples and Converting Individuals*, edited by Guyda Armstrong and Ian N. Wood, 169–91. Turnhout: Brepois, 2000.
Brown, Peter. *Augustine of Hippo: A Biography*. Berkeley, CA: University of California Press, 2000.
Brown, Schuyler. "The Matthean Community and the Gentile Mission." *Novum Testamentum* 12.3 (1980) 193–221.
Buchanan, George Wesley. "Worship, Feasts and Ceremonies in the Early Jewish-Christian Church." *New Testament Studies* 26 (1980) 279–97.
Buijs, Joseph A. "Attributes of Action in Maimonides." *Vivarium* 27.2 (1989) 85–102.
———. "Comments on Maimonides' Negative Theology." *The New Scholasticism* 49 (1975) 87–93.
———. "Is the Negative Theology of Maimonides Intelligible?" In *Torah and Wisdom: Studies in Jewish Philosophy: Kabbalah, and Halacha: Essays in Honor of Arthur Hyman*, edited by Ruth Link-Salinger Hyman, 9–17. New York: Shengold, 1992.
———. "A Maimonidean Critique of Thomistic Analogy." *Journal of the History of Philosophy* 41.4 (2003) 449–70.
———. "The Negative Theology of Maimonides and Aquinas." *The Review of Metaphysics* 41.4 (1988) 723–38.
Burkitt, F. C. *The Religion of the Manichees: Donnellan Lectures for 1924*. Cambridge, UK: Cambridge University Press, 1924.
Burrell, David. "Naming the Names of God: Muslims, Jews, Christians." *Theology Today* 47.1 (1990) 22–29.
Braine, David. "Negative Theology." In *Routledge Encyclopedia of Philosophy* 6, edited by Edward Craig, 759–62. London: Routledge, 1998.
Caputo, John D., et al. "Epoché and Faith: An Interview with Jacques Derrida." In *Derrida and Religion: Other Testaments*, edited by Yvonne Sherwood and Kevin Hart, 27–50. London: Routledge, 2004.
Carabine, Deirdre. *The Unknown God: Negative Theology in the Platonic Tradition: Plato to Eriugena*. Louvain Theological and Pastoral Monographs 19. Louvain: Peeters, n.d.
Carmichael, Joel. *The Satanizing of the Jews: Origin and Development of Mystical Anti-Semitism*. New York: Fromm, 1992.
Carroll, James. *Constantine's Sword: The Church and the Jews*. Boston: Houghton-Mifflin, 2001.
Chazan, Robert. "Medieval Anti-Semitism." In *History and Hate: The Dimensions of Anti-Semitism*, edited by David Berger, 49–65. Philadelphia: Jewish Publication Society, 1986.
Chernick, Michael. "Some Talmudic Responses to Christianity, Third and Fourth Centuries." *Journal of Ecumenical Studies* 17.3 (1980) 393–406.
"The Chronicle of Solomon bar Simson." In *The Jews and the Crusaders: The Hebrew Chronicles of the First and Second Crusades*, 20–72. Translated and edited by Shlomo Eidelberg. Hoboken, NJ: KTAV, 1996.
Clark, David K. *To Know and Love God: Foundations for Evangelical Theology—Method for Theology*. Edited by John S. Feinberg. Wheaton, IL: Crossway, 2003.

Cohen, Arthur. *The Teachings of Maimonides*. New York: KTAV, 1927 (1968).
Cohen, Jeffrey Jerome. "The Flow of Blood in Medieval Norwich." *Speculum* 79.1 (2004) 26–65.
———. "Robert Chazan's 'Medieval Anti-Semitism': A Note on the Impact of Theology." In *History and Hate: The Dimensions of Anti-Semitism*, edited by David Berger, 67–72. Philadelphia: Jewish Publication Society, 1986.
Cohen, Jeremy *Living Letters of the Law: Ideas of the Jew in Medieval Christianity.* Berkeley, CA: University of California Press, 1999.
Cohen, Joseph P. "Figurative Language, Philosophy, Religious Belief in Maimonides' Guide of the Perplexed." In *Studies in Jewish Philosophy: Collected Essays of the Academy for Jewish Philosophy, 1980–1985*, edited by Norbert Max Samuelson, 367–96. Lanham, MD: University Press of America, 1987.
Cohen, Mark R. "Maimonides' Egypt." In *Moses Maimonides and His Time*, edited by Eric L. Ormsby, 21–34. Washington, DC: Catholic University Press of America, 1989.
———. *Under Crescent and Cross: the Jews in the Middle Ages*. Princeton, NJ: Princeton University Press, 1994.
Cohen, Martin A. "The Sephardic Phenomenon: A Reappraisal." *American Jewish Archives* 44.1 (1992) 1–79.
Cohen, Shaye J. D. "The Significance of Yavneh: Pharisees, Rabbis, and the End of Jewish Sectarianism." *Hebrew Union College Annual* 55 (1984) 27–53.
Cohn-Sherbok, Dan. *Holocaust Theology*. London: Lamp, 1989.
———. *The Paradox of Anti-Semitism*. London: Continuum, 2006.
Dahlstrom, Daniel. "Moses Mendelssohn." *The Stanford Encyclopedia of Philosophy*, edited by Edward N. Zalta. http://plato.stanford.edu/archives/sum2015/entries/mendelssohn.
Dault, David. "Rosenzweig and Derrida at Yom Kippur." In *Derrida and Religion: Other Testaments*, edited by Yvonne Sherwood and Kevin Hart, 97–109. London: Routledge, 2004.
Davidson, Herbert A. "The First Two Positive Commandments in Maimonides' List of the 613 Believed to Have Been Given to Moses at Sinai." In *Creation and Re-Creation in Jewish Thought: Festschrift in Honor of Joseph Dan on the Occasion of His Seventieth Birthday*, edited by Rachel Elior and Peter Schäfer, 113–45. Tübingen: Mohr Siebeck, 2005.
Davies, Daniel. "Outside the Incarnation: An Approach to Christian Doctrine in Interfaith Encounters." *Modern Theology* 30.1 (2014) 132–39.
Davies, Paul E. "Early Christian Attitudes toward Judaism and the Jews." *Journal of Bible and Religion* 13.2 (1945) 72–82.
Davila, James R. "Of Methodology, Monotheism and Metatron: Introductory Reflections on Divine Mediators and the Origins of the Worship of Jesus." In *The Jewish Roots of Christological Monotheism: Papers from the St. Andrew's Conference on the Historiala Origins of the Worship of Jesus*, edited by Carey C. Newman, et al., 3–18. Leiden: E. J. Brill, 1999.
Decret, François. *Early Christianity in North Africa*. Translated by Edward L. Smither. Eugene, OR: Cascade, 2009.
Delgado, José Martínez. "Maimonides in the Context of Andalusian Hebrew Lexicography." *Aleph: Historical Studies in Science and Judaism* 8 (2008) 14–40.

Demura, Miyako. "Origen and the Exegetical Tradition of the Sarah-Hagar Motif in Alexandria." In *Studia Patristica* 56, edited by Markus Vincent, 73–81. Walpole, MA: Peeters, 2013.

Devine, Mark. *Bonhoeffer Speaks Today: Following Jesus at All Costs.* Nashville: Broadman & Holman, 2005.

Diamond, James A. *Maimonides and the Shaping of the Jewish Canon.* New York: Cambridge University Press, 2014.

———. "Maimonides, Spinoza and Buber Read the Hebrew Bible: The Hermeneutical Keys of Divine 'Fire' and 'Spirit' (Ruach)." *Journal of Religion* 91.3 (2011) 320–43.

———. "Maimonides and the Convert: A Juridical and Philosophical Embrace of the Outsider." *Medieval Philosophy and Theology* vol. 11, no. 2 (September 2003) 125–46.

Dobbs-Weinstein, Idit. "Matter as Creature and Matter as the Source of Evil: Maimonides and Aquinas." In *Neoplatonism and Jewish Thought*, edited by Lenn E. Goodman, 217–35. Albany, NY: State University of New York Press, 1992.

Dodd, Brian J. *The Problem with Paul.* Downers Grove, IL: InterVarsity, 1996.

Dodds, Jerrilynn D. "Mudejar Tradition and the Synagogues of Medieval Spain: Cultural Identity and Cultural Hegemony." In *Convivencia: Jews, Muslims, and Christians in Medieval Spain*, edited by Vivian B. Mann, et al., 113–31. New York: George Braziller and the Jewish Museum, 1992.

Downey, Amy Karen. "An Apologetic Response on How to Share the Gospel of Messiah Jesus in Light of the Holocaust." International Society of Christian Apologetics. Fort Worth, Texas (April 24, 2010). https://www.isca-apologetics.org/sites/default/files/papers/TzedakahMinistries/AN%20APOLOGETIC%20RESPONSE%20ON%20HOW%20TO%20SHARE%20THE%20GOSPEL%20OF%20MESSIAH%20JESUS%20IN%20LIGHT%20OF%20THE%20HOLOCAUST.pdf.

———. "Maimonides' *Via Negativa*: The Unknowable Nature of God as a Response to the Christian Doctrine of the Incarnation." A research paper for *Philosophy of Religion* 413. Fort Worth: SWBTS, 2005.

Drory, Joseph. "The Early Decades of Abbūyid Rule." In *Perspectives on Maimonides: Philosophical and Historical Studies*, edited by Joel L. Kraemer, 295–302. Littman Library of Jewish Civilization. Oxford: Oxford University Press, 1991.

Dunn, Geoffrey D. *Tertullian.* The Early Church Fathers. Edited by Carol Harrison. London: Routledge, 2004.

———. *Tertullian's Aduersus Iudaeos: A Rhetorical Analysis.* North American Patristics Society: Patristic Monograph Series 19. Edited by Philip Rousseau. Washington, DC: Catholic University of America Press, 2008.

———. "Tertullian and Rebekah: A Re-Reading of an 'Anti-Jewish' Argument in Early Christian Literature." *Vigilae Christianae* 52.2 (1988) 119–45.

Dunn, James D. G. "Who Did Paul Think He Was? A Study of Jewish-Christian Identity." *New Testament Studies* 45.2 (1999) 174–93.

Eckstein, Yechiel. *What Christians Should Know about Jews and Judaism.* Waco, TX: Word, 1984.

Edwards, Mark J., ed. *Galatians, Ephesians, Philippians.* Ancient Christian Commentary on Scripture. Downers Grove, IL: InterVarsity, 1999.

Efron, Joshua. "The Sanhedrin as an Ideal and as Reality in the Period of the Second Temple." *Imanu'el* 2 (1973) 44–49.

Eglash, Ruth. "Israel to Create an Egalitarian Prayer Plaza at Western Wall." *Washington Post* 31 (2016). https://www.washingtonpost.com/world/israel-to-create-a-new-egalitarian-prayer-plaza-at-western-wall/2016/01/31/ac48e9e7-e8b2-4301-a81e-2d192efe9359_story.html.

Ehrenkreutz, Andrew S. "Saladin's Egypt and Maimonides." In *Perspectives on Maimonides: Philosophical and Historical Studies*, edited by Joel L. Kraemer, 303–307. Littman Library of Jewish Civilization. Oxford: Oxford University Press, 1991.

Ehrlich, Dror. "Hidden Apocalyptic Messianism in Late Medieval Jewish Thought." *Review of Rabbinic Judaism* 12.1 (2009) 75–88.

Englebretsen, George. "The Logic of Negative Theology." *The New Scholasticism* 47 (1973) 228–32.

Epstein, Ann Wharton. "Frescoes of the Mavriotissa Monastery near Kastoria: Evidence of Millenarianism and Anti-Semitism in the Wake of the First Crusade." *Gesta* 21.1 (1982) 21–29.

Epstein, Isidore. "The Distinctiveness of Maimonides' Halakhah." In *The Leo Jung Jubilee Volume; Essays in His Honor of the Occasion of His 70th Birthday*, edited by Menahem M. Kasher, et al., 65–75. New York: Jewish Center, 1962.

Eran, Amira. "Al-Ghazali and Maimonides on the World to Come and Spiritual Pleasures." *Jewish Studies Quarterly* 8.2 (2001) 137–66.

Eraqi-Klorman, Bat Zion. "The Yemeni Messiah in the Time of Maimonides: Prelude for Future Messiahs." In *From Iberia to Diaspora: Studies in Sephardic History and Culture*, edited by Yedida Kalfon Stillman, 129–38. Leiden: E. J. Brill, 1989.

Erismann, Christoph. "The Trinity, Universals, and Particular Substances: Philoponus and Roscelin." *Traditio* 63 (2008) 277–305.

Eusebius. *Eusebius' Ecclesiastical History: Complete and Unabridged: New Updated Edition*. Translated by C. F. Cruse. Peabody, MA: Hendrickson, 2000.

Fackenheim, Emil L. "The Possibility of the Universe in Al-Farabi, Ibn Sina and Maimonides." In *Essays in Medieval Jewish and Islamic Philosophy: Studies from the Publications from the American Academy for Jewish Research*, edited by Arthur Hyman, 303–34. New York: KTAV, 1977.

Feldman, Seymour. "The Binding of Isaac: A Test-Case of Divine Foreknowledge." In *Divine Omniscience and Omnipotence in Medieval Philosophy*, edited by Tamar Rudavsky, 105–33. Boston: D. Reidel, 1985.

Fenton, Paul B. "A Meeting with Maimonides." *Bulletin of the School of Oriental and African Studies* 45.1 (1982) 1–4.

Ferrari, Leo C. "Isaiah and the Early Augustine." In *Augustiniana: Me'langes*, edited by T. J. Van Bavel, 739–56. Leuven: University Press, 1990.

Ferré, Frederick. "Natural Theology and Positive Predication: Might Maimonides Be a Guide?" In *Prospects for Natural Theology*, edited by Eugene Thomas Long, 113–27. Studies in Philosophy and the History of Philosophy 25. Washington, DC: Catholic University of America Press, 1992.

Ferré, Frederick, and R. Ferré. "In Praise of Anthropomorphism." *International Journal for Philosophy of Religion* 16.3 (1984) 203–12.

Finkel, Asher. "Yavneh's Liturgy and Early Christianity." *Journal of Ecumenical Studies* 18.2 (1981) 231–50.

Fishbane, Michael. "Some Forms of Divine Appearance in Ancient Jewish Thought." In *From Ancient Israel to Modern Judaism: Essays in Honor of Marvin Fox* vol. 2, edited by Jacob Neusner et al., 261–70. Atlanta: Scholars, 1989.

Fleck, G. Peter. "Jesus in the Post-Holocaust Jewish-Christian Dialogue." *The Christian Century* 12 (1983) 904–6.

Flusser, David. "The Jewish-Christian Schism, Part One." *Immanuel* 16 (1983) 32–49.

Ford, J. Massingberd. "Was Montanism a Jewish-Christian Heresy?" *The Journal of Ecclesiastical History* 17.2 (October 1966) 145–58.

Forman, Abra. "Chief Rabbi: It Is a Mitzvah to Kill Terrorists." *Breaking Israel News* (March 13, 2016). http://www.breakingisraelnews.com/63469/chief-rabbi-it-is-a-mitzvah-to-kill-terrorists-jewish-world/.

Fox, Bernie. "Hashem's Names and Their Meanings." *Jewish Times* 12.1 (2012) 8–9.

Fraade, Steven D. "Ascetical Aspects of Ancient Judaism." In *Jewish Spirituality: From the Bible through the Middle Ages* vol. 1, edited by Arthur Green, 253–88. New York: Crossroad, 1986.

Frank, Daniel H. "The Elimination of Perplexity: Socrates and Maimonides as Guides of the Perplexed." In *Autonomy and Judaism: The Individual and the Community in Jewish Philosophical Thought*, edited by Daniel H. Frank, 121–42. SUNY Series in Jewish Philosophy. Albany, NY: State University of New York Press, 1992.

———. "Maimonides and Medieval Jewish Aristotelianism." In *The Cambridge Companion to Medieval Jewish Philosophy*, edited by Daniel H. Frank and Oliver Leaman, 136–56. Cambridge Companions to Philosophy. New York: Cambridge University Press, 2006.

Frassetto, Michael. "Heretics and Jews in the Writings of Ademar Chabannes and the Origins of Medieval Anti-Semitism." *Church History* 71.1 (2002) 1–15.

Fredriksen, Paula. "Augustine and Israel: *Interpretatio ad litteram*, Jews, and Judaism in Augustine's Theology of History." In *Studia Patristica* vol. 38, edited by M. F. Wiles and E. J. Yarnold, 119–35. Leuven: Peeters, 2001.

———. *Augustine and the Jews: A Christian Defense of Jews and Judaism*. New York: Doubleday, 2008.

———. "*Excaecati Occulta Justitia Dei*: Augustine on Jews and Judaism." *Journal of Early Christian Studies* 3.3 (1995) 299–324.

Frend, W. H. C. "Some North African Turning Points in Christian Apologetics." *Journal of Ecclesiastical History* 57.1 (2006) 1–15.

Freudenthal, Gad. "The Biological Limitations of Man's Intellectual Perfection According to Maimonides." In *The Trias of Maimonides: Jewish, Arabic, and Ancient Culture of Knowledge*, edited by George Tamer, 137–49. Studia Judaica 30. New York: Walter de Gruyter, 2005.

Friedberg, Albert D. "An Evaluation of Maimonides Enumeration of the 613 Commandments, with Special Emphasis on the Positive Commandments." PhD diss., University of Toronto, 2008.

Frimer, Dov I. "Israel, the Noahide Laws, and Maimonides: Jewish-Gentile Legal Relations in Maimonidean Thought." In *Jewish Law Association Studies II: The Jerusalem Conference* vol. 2, edited by B. S. Jackson, 89–102. Atlanta: Scholars, 1986.

Fritz, Maureena. "A Midrash: The Self-Limitation of God." *Journal of Ecumenical Studies* 22.4 (1985) 703–14.

Froehlich, Karlfried, ed. and trans. *Biblical Interpretation in the Early Church*. Sources of Early Christian Thought Series. Philadelphia: Fortress, 1984.

Fromm, Erich. *You Shall Be as Gods: A Radical Interpretation of the Old Testament and Its Tradition*. New York: Holt, Rinehart & Winston, 1966.

Frydman-Kohl, Baruch. "Covenant, Conversion and Chosenness: Maimonides and Halevi on 'Who is a Jew?'" *Judaism: A Quarterly Journal* 41.1 (1992) 64–79.

Funkenstein, Amos. "Maimonides: Political Theory and Realistic Messianism." In *Die Mächte des Guten und Bösen: Vorstellungen im XII und XIII Jahrhundert über ihr Wirken in der Heilsgeschichte*, edited by Albert Zimmerman, 81–103. New York: DeGruyter, 1977.

Gager, John G. *The Origins of Anti-Semitism: Attitudes Toward Judaism in Pagan and Christian Antiquity*. New York: Oxford University Press, 1985.

Gamberini, Paolo. "Incarnation at the Crossroad: The Doctrine of the Pre-Existence of Jesus in Dialogue with Judaism and Islam." *Irish Theological Quarterly* 73 (2008) 99–112.

Gampel, Benjamin R. "Jews, Christians, and Muslims in Medieval Iberia: *Convivencia* through the Eyes of Sephardic Jews." In *Convivencia: Jews, Muslims, and Christians in Medieval Spain*, edited by Vivian B. Mann, et al., 11–37. New York: George Braziller and the Jewish Museum, 1992.

Garrett, James Leo, Jr. *Systematic Theology: Biblical, Historical, and Evangelical*, vol. 2. Grand Rapids, MI: William B. Eerdmans, 1995.

Genack, Menachem. "Rambam's Mishneh Torah: The Significance of Its Title." *Traditions* 38.2 (2004) 78–85.

Geraci, Silvia. "Jacques Derrida and Abraham's Heritage." *Bijdragen, International Journal in Philosophy and Theology* 72.3 (2011) 246–64.

Gero, Stephen. "The Stern Master and His Wayward Disciple: A 'Jesus' Story in the Talmud and in Christian Hagiography." *Journal for the Study of Judaism in the Persian, Hellenistic and Roman Period* 25.2 (1994) 287–311.

Gershenzon, Shoshanna G. "A Study of *Teshuvot Le-Meharef* by Abner of Burgos." PhD diss., New York: Jewish Theological Seminary of America, 1984.

Gillman, Neil. *Doing Jewish Theology: God, Torah & Israel in Modern Judaism*. Woodstock, VT: Jewish Lights, 2008.

Gittelsohn, Roland. "No Retreat from Reason!" In *Reform Judaism: A Historical Perspective: Essays from the Yearbook of the Central Conference of American Rabbis*, edited by Joseph Leon Blau, 186–203. New York: KTAV, 1973.

Gluck, Andrew L. "Maimonides' Arguments for Creation Ex Nihilo in the Guide of the Perplexed." *Medieval Philosophy and Theology* 7.2 (1998) 221–54.

Goitein, S. D. "Review: Maimonides as Chief Justice: The Newly Edited Arabic Origins of Maimonides' Responsa." *The Jewish Quarterly Review* 49.3 (1959) 191–204.

Goldman, Norman Saul. "Maimonides on the Pathology of Evil: Moses Maimonides and Pastoral Psychology." *Journal of Pastoral Counseling* 11 (1976–1977) 8–13.

Goldman, Solomon. "Halachic Foundations of Maimonides' Thirteen Principles." In *Essays Presented to Chief Rabbi Israel Brodie on the Occasion of His 70th Birthday*, edited by Hirsh J. Zimmels, 111–18. Jews' College Publications 3. London: Soncino, 1966–1967.

———. *The Jew and the Universe*. New York: Harper & Brothers, 1936.

Goodman, Lenn Evan. "Maimonides and the Philosophers of Islam: The Problem of Theophany." In *Judaism and Islam: Boundaries, Communication and Interaction:*

Essays in Honor of William M. Brinner, edited by B. H. Hary, et al., 279–301. Leiden: Brill, 2000.

Goodman, Lenn Evan, trans. *Rambam: Readings in the Philosophy of Moses Maimonides*. New York: Viking, 1976.

Goshen-Gottstein, Alon. "Judaism and Incarnational Theologies: Mapping out the Parameters of Dialogue." *Journal of Ecumenical Studies* 39.3–4 (2002) 219–33.

Grabbe, Lester L. "Sanhedrin, Sanhedriyyot, or Mere Invention?" *Journal for the Study of Judaism in the Persian, Hellenistic and Roman Period* 39 (2008) 1–19.

Graves, Michael. "'Judaizing' Christian Interpretation of the Prophets as Seen by Saint Jerome." *Vigiliae Christianae* 61.2 (2007) 142–56.

Gray, John. "The Diaspora of Israel and Judah in Obadiah v. 20." *Zeitschrift für die alttestamentliche Wissenschaft* 65 (1953) 53–59.

Grayzel, Solomon. "The Talmud and the Medieval Papacy." In *Essays in Honor of Solomon B. Freehof*, edited by Frederick C. Schwartz and Walter Jacob, 220–45. Pittsburgh: n.p., 1964.

Green, Kenneth Hart, ed. *Leo Strauss on Maimonides: The Complete Writings*. Chicago: University of Chicago Press, 2013.

Gregory of Nyssa. *On "Not Three Gods."* In *Nicene and Post-Nicene Fathers*, vol. 1, edited by Philip Schaff. Edinburgh: T. & T. Clark, n.d. http://www.ccel.org/ccel/schaff/npnf205.viii.v.html.

Gruenwald, Ithamar. "Manichaeism and Judaism in Light of the Cologne Mani Codex." *Zeitschrift für Papyrologie und Epigraphik* 50 (1983) 29–45.

Guttman, Julius. *Philosophies of Judaism: The History of Jewish Philosophy from Biblical Times to Franz Rosenzweig*. New York: Shocken, 1964.

Guttmann, Alexander. "Foundations of Rabbinic Judaism." *Hebrew Union College Annual* 23.1 (1950–1951) 453–73.

Haberman, Jacob. *Maimonides and Aquinas: A Contemporary Appraisal*. New York: KTAV, 1979.

Halbertal, Moshe. *Maimonides: Life and Thought*. Translated by Joel Linsider. Princeton, NJ: Princeton University Press, 2014.

———. "What Is the Mishneh Torah? On Codification and Ambivalence." In *Maimonides after 800 Years: Essays on Maimonides and His Influence*, edited by Jay M. Harris, 81–111. Cambridge, MA: Harvard University Press, 2007.

Halivni, David Weiss. "The Reception Accorded to Rabbi Judah's Mishnah." In *Jewish and Christian Self-Definition, Volume Two: Aspects of Judaism, in the Greco-Roman Period*, edited by E. P. Sanders, 204–12. London: SCM, 1981.

Hall, Christopher A. *Reading Scripture with the Church Fathers*. Downers Grove, IL: InterVarsity, 1998.

Halpern, Rick. *Choose Life: A Counter Missionary Study Guide*. Atlanta: Torah Atlanta, 2002.

Hamori, Esther J. "Divine Embodiments in the Hebrew Bible and Some Implications for Jewish and Christian Incarnational Theologies." In *Library of Hebrew Bible/Old Testament Studies: Bodies, Embodiment, and Theology of the Hebrew Bible*, edited by S. Tamar Kamionkowski and Wonil Kim, 161–83. London: T & T Clark International, 2010.

Hanafi, Hassan. "Maimonides' Critique of the Mutakallimūn in *The Guide of the Perplexed*." In *The Trias of Maimonides: Jewish, Arabic, and Ancient Culture of Knowledge*, edited by Georges Tarner, 267–87. Studia Judaica 30. New York: Walter de Gruyter, 2005.

Handley, Mark. "'This Stone Shall Be a Witness' (Joshua 24.27) Jews, Christians, and Inscriptions in Early Mediaeval Gaul." *Christian-Jewish Relations through the Centuries*, edited by Stanley E. Porter and Brook W. R. Pearson, 239–54. Sheffield, UK: Sheffield Academic, 2000.

Hann, Robert R. "Judaism and Jewish Christianity in Antioch: Charisma and Conflict in the First Century." *The Journal of Religious History* 14.4 (1987) 341–60.

———. "Supersessionism, Engraftment, and Jewish-Christian Dialogue: Reflections on the Presbyterian Statement on Jewish-Christian Relations." *Journal of Ecumenical Studies* 27.2 (1990) 327–42.

———. "The Undivided Way: The Early Jewish Christians as a Model for Ecumenical Encounter?" *Journal of Ecumenical Studies* 14.2 (1977) 233–48.

Harkins, Franklin T. "Nuancing Augustine's Hermeneutical Jew: Allegory and Actual Jews in the Bishop's Sermons." *Journal for the Study of Judaism in the Persian, Hellenistic and Roman Period* 36.1 (2005) 41–64.

Hartman, David. "Discussions." In *Epistles of Maimonides: Crisis and Leadership: The Epistle of Martyrdom, The Epistle to Yemen, and The Essay on Resurrection*, edited and translated by Abraham Halkin, 246–81. Philadelphia: Jewish Publication Society of America, 1985.

———. "Sinai and Exodus: Two Grounds for Hope in the Jewish Tradition." *Religious Studies* 14.3 (978) 373–87.

Harvey, Steven. "Maimonides in the Sultan's Palace." In *Perspectives on Maimonides: Philosophical and Historical Studies*, edited by Joel L. Kraemer, 47–75. Littman Library of Jewish Civilization. Oxford: Oxford University Press, 1991.

Harvey, Warren Zev. "Maimonides and Aquinas on Interpreting the Bible." *Proceedings of the American Academy for Jewish Research* 55 (1988) 59–77.

———. "Maimonides' Monotheism: Between the Bible and Aristotle." Center for Interdisciplinary Study of Monotheistic Religions 7, 56–67. Japan: Doshisha University, 2013.

———. "Maimonides and Spinoza on the Knowledge of Good and Evil." In *Binah: Studies in Jewish Thought* vol. 2, dited by Joseph Dan, 131–46. New York: Praeger, 1989.

———. "The Obligation of Talmud on Women according to Maimonides." *Tradition* 19.2 (1981) 122–30.

———. "A Third Approach to Maimonides' Cosmogony-Prophetology Puzzle." *Harvard Theological Review* 74.3 (1981) 287–301.

Hayes, Christine Elizabeth. "Displaced Self-Perceptions: The Deployment of *Minim* and Romans in B. Sanhedrin 90b–91a." In *Religious and Ethnic Communities in Later Roman Palestine*, edited by Hayim Lapin, 249–89. Bethesda, MD: University Press of Maryland, 1989.

Hebblethwaite, Peter. "St. Augustine's Interpretation of Matthew 5, 17." *Studia Patristica* 16.2 (1985) 511–16.

Held, Shai. "The Promise and Peril of Jewish Barthianism: The Theology of Michael Wyschogrod." *Modern Judaism* 25.3 (2005) 316–26.

Heldt, Petra. "Constructing Christian Communal Identity in Early Patristic Writers." In *One Lord, One Faith, One Baptism: Studies in Christian Ecclesiality and Ecumenism in Honor of J. Robert Wright*, edited by Marsha L. Dutton, et al., 29–41. Grand Rapids, MI: Eerdmans, 2006.

Helleman, Wendy Elgersma. "'Abraham Had Two Sons': Augustine and the Allegory of Sarah and Hagar (Galatians 4:21–31)." *Calvin Theological Journal* 48 (2013) 35–64.

Hellig, Jocelyn. *The Holocaust and Antisemitism: A Short History*. Oxford: Oneworld, 2003.

Hendel, Russell Jay. "Maimonides' Attitude towards Sacrifices." *Tradition: A Journal of Orthodox Thought* 13–14 (1973) 163–79.

Henrix, Hans Hermann. "The Son of God Became Human as a Jew: Implications of the Jewishness of Jesus for Christology." In *Christ Jesus and the Jewish People Today: New Explorations of Theological Interrelationships*, edited by Philip A. Cunningham, 114–43. Grand Rapids, MI: Eerdmans, 2011.

Hirschberg, Harris H. "Once Again—the Minim." *Journal of Biblical Literature* 67.4 (1948) 305–18.

Hillaby, Joe. "The Beth Miqdah Me'at: The Synagogues of Medieval England." *Journal of Ecclesiastical History* 44.2 (1993) 182–99.

Hoffman, Edward. *The Wisdom of Maimonides: The Life and Writings of the Jewish Sage*. Boston: Trumpeter, 2008.

Holtz, Barry W. *Finding Our Way: Jewish Texts and the Lives We Lead Today*. New York: Shocken, 1990.

Horner, Timothy J. *Listening to Trypho: Justin's "Dialogue with Trypho" Reconsidered*. Contributions to Biblical Exegesis and Theology 28. Leuven, Belgium: Peeters, 2001.

Hurtado, Larry W. "Pre-70 CE Jewish Opposition to Christ Devotion." *The Journal of Theological Studies* 50.1 (1999) 35–58.

Husik, Isaac. "An Anonymous Medieval Christian Critic of Maimonides." *The Jewish Quarterly Review* 2.2 (1911) 159–90.

Hyman, Arthur. "Maimonides on Religious Language." In *Perspectives on Maimonides: Philosophical and Historical Studies*, edited by Joel L. Kraemer, 175–91. Littman Library of Jewish Civilization. Oxford: Oxford University Press, 1991.

Idel, Moshe. "Maimonides and Kabbalah." In *Studies in Maimonides*, edited by Isadore Twersky, 31–81. Cambridge, MA: Harvard University Press, 1990.

Inowlocki, Sabrina. "Tertullian's Law of Paradise (Adversus Judaeos 2) Reflections on a Shared Motif in Jewish and Christian Literature." In *Paradise in Antiquity: Jewish and Christian Views* (103–19), edited by Markus N. A. Bockmuehl and Guy G. Stroumsa. Cambridge, UK: Cambridge University Press, 2010.

Isaacs, Ronald H. *Miracles: A Jewish Perspective*. Northvale, NJ: Jason Aronson, 1997.

Isaacs, Ronald H., and Kerry M. Olitzky, eds. *Critical Documents of Jewish History: A Sourcebook*. Northvale, NJ: Jason Aronson, 1995.

Itzkowitz, Joel B. "Jews, Indians, Phylacteries: Jerome on Matthew 23.5." *Journal of Early Christian Studies* 15.4 (2007) 563–72.

Ivry, Alfred L. "The *Guide* and Maimonides' Philosophical Sources. In *The Cambridge Companion to Maimonides*, edited by Kenneth Seeskin. New York: Cambridge University Press, 2005.

———. "Ismā'īlī Theology and Maimonides' Philosophy." In *The Jews of Medieval Islam: Community, Society, and Identity: Proceedings of an International Conference Held by the Institute of Jewish Studies, University College London, 1992*, edited by Daniel Frank, 271–99. Leiden: Brill, 1995.

———. "Strategies of Interpretation in Maimonides' 'Guide of the Perplexed.'" *Jewish History* 6 (1992) 113–30.

Jacobi, Margaret. "'In Its Time I Will Hasten It': Messianic Speculation in the Babylonian Talmud, Sanhedrin 96b–99a." *European Judaism* 40.1 (2007) 115–19.

Jacobs, Jonathan. "Forgiveness and Perfection: Maimonides, Aquinas and Medieval Departures from Aristotle." In *Ancient Forgiveness*, edited by Charles Griswold and David Konstan, 216–35. New York: Cambridge University Press, 2011.

Jennings, Margaret. "The Cathedral of Bourges: A Witness to Judeo-Christian Dialogue in Medieval Berry." *Studies in Jewish-Christian Relations* 6 (2011) 1–10.

Jerome. *Apology against Rufinus*. In *Nicene and Post-Nicene Fathers, Second Series* vol. 3, edited by Philip Schaff and Henry Wace. Translated by W.H. Fremantle. Buffalo, NY: Christian Literature, 1892. http://www.newadvent.org/fathers/27102.htm.

———. "Letter LXXV." In *Nicene and Post-Nicene Fathers*, vol. 1, edited by Philip Schaff. Edinburgh: T. & T. Clark, n.d. http://www.ccel.org/ccel/schaff/npnf101.vii.1.LXXV.html.

———. "Preface to the *Book of Hebrew Questions*." In *Jerome*, edited by Stefan Rebenich, 93–96. The Early Church Fathers. London: Routledge, 2002.

———. "Preface to the Vulgate Version of the Pentateuch." edited by Stefan Rebenich. The Early Church Fathers. London: Routledge, 2002.

Jervell, Jacob. "The Mighty Minority." *Studia Theologica* 34 (1980) 13–38.

Jocz, Jacob. "The Invisibility of God and the Incarnation." *The Canadian Journal of Theology* 4.3 (1958) 179–86.

———. *The Jewish People and Jesus Christ after Auschwitz: A Study in the Controversy Between Church and Synagogue*. Grand Rapids: Baker, 1981.

John Chrysostom. "On the Jews (Adversus Judaeos)." http://www.catholicapologetics.info/apologetics/judaism/jchrsos.htm.

Jordan, Mark D. "The Names of God and the Being of Names." In *The Existence and Nature of God*, edited by Alfred J. Freddoso, 161–90. Notre Dame, IN: University of Notre Dame Press, 1983.

Jordan, William Chester. "Jews, Regalian Rights, and the Constitution in Medieval France." *Association for Jewish Studies Review* 23.1 (1998) 1–16.

Justin Martyr. *Dialogue of Justin, Philosopher and Martyr, with Trypho a Jew*. Whitefish, MT: Kessinger 2010.

———. *The First Apology*. In *Ante-Nicene Fathers* vol. 1, edited by Alexander Roberts, et al. Translated by Marcus Dods and George Reith. Buffalo, NY: Christian Literature, 1885. http://www.newadvent.org/fathers/0126.htm.

Kannengiesser, Charles. *Handbook of Patristic Exegesis: The Bible in Ancient Christianity*, vol. 1. In *The Bible in Ancient Christianity*, edited by Jeffrey Bingham. Leiden: Brill, 2006.

Kaplan, Lawrence. "The Love of God in Maimonides and Rav Kook." *Judaism: A Quarterly Journal* 43.3 (1994) 227–39.

———. "Maimonides on the Miraculous Element in Prophecy." *Harvard Theological Review* 70 (1977) 233–56.

Kars, Aydogan. "Two Modes of Unsaying in the Early Thirteenth Century Islamic Lands: Theorizing Apophasis through Maimonides and Ibn 'Arabi." *International Journal for Philosophy of Religion* 74.3 (2013) 261–78.

Kasher, Hannah. "Self-Cognizing Intellect and Negative Attributes in Maimonides' Theology." *Harvard Theological Review* 87.4 (1994) 461–72.

Katz, Steven T. "Issues in the Separation of Judaism and Christianity after 70 CE: A Reconsideration." *Journal of Biblical Literature* 103.1 (1984) 43–76.

———. "Utterance and Ineffability in Jewish Neoplatonism." In *Neoplatonism and Jewish Thought*, edited by Lenn E. Goodman, 279–98. Albany, NY: State University of New York Press, 1992.

Katzoff, Binyamin. "'God of our Fathers': Rabbinic Liturgy and Jewish-Christian Engagement." *The Jewish Quarterly Review* 99.3 (2009) 303–22.

Kee, Howard Clark. "Central Authority in Second-Temple Judaism and Subsequently: From Synedrion to Sanhedrin." *Annual of Rabbinic Judaism* 2 (1999) 51–63.

Kelhoffer, James A. "The Apostle Paul and Justin Martyr on the Miraculous: A Comparison of Appeals to Authority." *Greek, Roman and Byzantine Studies* 42.2 (2001) 163–84.

Kellner, Menachem. "Could Maimonides Get into Rambam's Heaven?" *The Journal of Jewish Thought and Philosophy* 8 (1999) 231–42.

———. "How Ought a Jew View Christian Beliefs about Redemption?" In *Christianity in Jewish Terms*, edited by Tikva Frymer-Kensky et al., 262–75.

———. *Maimonides' Confrontation with Mysticism*. Portland, OR: Littman Library of Jewish Civilization, 2006.

———. "Maimonides' Disputed Legacy." In *Traditions of Maimonideanism*, edited by Carlos Fraenkel, 245–76. IJS Studies in Judaica 7. Leiden: Brill, 2009.

———. *Maimonides on Human Perfection*. Brown Judaic Studies 202. Atlanta: Scholars, 1990.

———. "Maimonides on the Science of the *Mishneh Torah*: Provisional or Permanent? *AJS Review* 18.2 (1993) 169–94

———. "On Reading Rambam in Brooklyn and in Haifa." *Hakirah: The Flatbush Journal of Jewish Law and Thought* 11 (2011) 225–33.

Kelly, J. N. D. *Jerome: His Life, Writings, and Controversies*. New York: Harper & Row, 1975.

Kimelman, Reuven. "*Birkat Ha-Minim* and the Lack of Evidence for an Anti-Christian Jewish Prayer in Late Antiquity." In *Jewish and Christian Self-Definition, Volume Two: Aspects of Judaism, in the Greco-Roman Period*, edited by E. P. Sanders, 226–44. London: SCM, 1981.

Kinzer, Mark S. *Postmissionary Messianic Judaism: Redefining Christian Engagement with the Jewish People*. Grand Rapids, MI: Brazos, 2005.

Kirsch, Adam. "True Confessions: A New Book Probes Augustine's Vexing 'Defense' of Judaism." *Tablet Magazine* (2008). http://www.tabletmag.com/arts–and–culture/books/1018/true-confessions/.

Kitchin, William P. H. "The Literary Influence of St. Jerome." *The Catholic Historical Review* 7.2 (1921) 165–72.

Klein, Carol. *The Credo of Maimonides: A Synthesis*. New York: Philosophical Library, 1958.

Klein-Braslavy, Sara. "Maimonides' Exoteric and Esoteric Biblical Interpretations in the *Guide of the Perplexed*." In *Study and Knowledge of Jewish Thought*, edited by Howard Kreisel, 137–64. Beer-Sheva, Israel: Ben-Gurion University of the Negev Press, 2006.

Klepper, Deeana. "Historicizing Allegory: The Jew as Hagar in Medieval Christian Text and Image." *Church History* 84.2 (2015) 308–44.

Kloner, Amos, and Boaz Zissu. "The 'Caves of Simeon the Just' and 'The Minor Sanhedrin.' Two Burial Complexes from the Second Temple Period in Jerusalem." In *What Athens Has to Do with Jerusalem: Essays on Classical, Jewish, and Early Christian Art and Archaeology in Honor of Gideon Foerster*, edited by Leonard Victor Rutgers, 125–49. Leuven: Peeters, 2002.

Korn, Eugene. "Covenantal Possibilities in a Post-Polemical Age: A Jewish View." *Studies in Jewish-Christian Relations* 6 (2011) 1–13.

———. "Gentiles, the World to Come, and Judaism: The Odyssey of a Rabbinic Text." *Modern Judaism* 14.3 (1994) 265–87.

Kraemer, Joel L. "How (Not) to Read *The Guide of the Perplexed*." *Jerusalem Studies in Arabic and Islam* 32 (2006) 350–409.

———. *Maimonides: The Life and World of One of Civilization's Greatest Minds*. New York: Doubleday, 2008.

———. "Moses Maimonides: An Intellectual Portrait." In *The Cambridge Companion to Maimonides*, edited by Kenneth Seeskin. New York: Cambridge University Press, 2005.

———. "On Maimonides' Messianic Posture." In *Studies in Medieval Jewish History and Literature* vol. 2, edited by Isadore Twersky, 109–42. Cambridge, MA: Harvard University Press, 1984.

Krakowski, Eliyahu. "What Must a Jew Believe: Dogma and Inadvertent Heresy, Revisited." *Hakirah: The Flatbush Journal of Jewish Law and Thought* 20 (2015) 91–98.

Kreisel, Howard. "*Imitatio Dei* in Maimonides' *Guide of the Perplexed*." *AJS Review* 19.2 (1994) 169–211.

———. "Miracles in Medieval Jewish Philosophy." *The Jewish Quarterly Review, New Series* 75.2 (1984) 99–133.

Kroemer, James. "Vanquish the Haughty and Spare the Subjected: A Study of Bernard the Clairvaux's Position on Muslim and Jews." *Medieval Encounters* 18 (2012) 55–92.

Kushner, Harold. *Who Needs God*. New York: Summit, 1989.

Lang, Uwe Michael. "Nicetas Choniates, a Neglected Witness to the Greek Text of John Philoponus' Arbiter." *Journal of Theological Studies* 48.2 (1997) 540–48.

———. "Notes on John Philoponus and the Tritheist Controversy in the Sixth Century." *Oriens Christianus* 85 (2001) 23–40.

———. "Patristic Argument and the Use of Philosophy in the Tritheist Controversy in the Sixth Century." In *The Mystery of the Holy Trinity in the Fathers of the Church: The Proceedings of the Fourth International Patristic Conference, Maynooth, 1999*, edited by Vincent Twomey and Lewis Ayres, 79–99. Portland, OR: Four Courts, 2007.

Lapide, Pinchas. *The Resurrection of Jesus: A Jewish Perspective*. Eugene, OR: Wipf & Stock, 2002.

Lasker, Daniel. "The Jewish Critique of Christianity under Islam in the Middle Ages." *Proceedings of the American Academy for Jewish Research* 57 (1990—1991) 121–53.

Lavinger, Jacob. "Was Maimonides 'Rais al-Yahud' in Egypt?" In *Studies in Maimonides*, edited by Isadore Twersky, 83–93. Cambridge, MA: Harvard University Press, 1991.

Lawlor, Leonard. "Jacques Derrida." *The Stanford Encyclopedia of Philosophy*, edited by Edward N. Zalta. http://plato.stanford.edu/archives/spr2014/entries/derrida/.

Leaman, Oliver. "Maimonides and the Development of Jewish Thought in an Islamic Structure." In *The Trias of Maimonides: Jewish, Arabic, and Ancient Culture of Knowledge*, edited by George Tamer, 187–97. Studia Judaica 30. New York: Walter de Gruyter, 2005.

———. "Maimonides, Imagination and the Objectivity of Prophecy." *Religion* 18 (1988).

Lebreton, Jules. "St. Justin. Martyr." In *The Catholic Encyclopedia*, vol. 8. New York: Robert Appleton, 1910. http://www.newadvent.org/cathen/08580c.htm.

Lehmann, James H. "Maimonides, Mendelssohn and the Me'asfim: Philosophy and the Biographical Imagination in the Early Haskalah." *Leo Baeck Institute Yearbook* 20.1 (1975) 87–108.

Lerner, Ralph. "Maimonides' 'Treatise on Resurrection.'" *History of Religions* 232 (1983) 140–55.

Levenson, Jon D. "The Eighth Principle of Judaism and the Literary Simultaneity of Scripture." *The Journal of Religion* vol. 68, no. 2 (April 1988) 205–25.

———. *Resurrection and the Restoration of Israel: The Ultimate Victory of the God of Life*. New Haven, CT: Yale University Press, 2006.

Levey, Samson H. "The Best Kept Secret of the Rabbinic Tradition." *Judaism* 21.4 (1972) 454–69.

Levine, Michelle. "Maimonides' Philosophical Exegesis of the Nobles' Vision (Exodus 24) A Guide for the Pursuit of Knowledge." *The Torah u-Madda Journal* 11 (2002–2003) 61–106.

Levine, Samuel. *You Take Jesus, I'll Take God: How to Refute Christian Missionaries*. Los Angeles: Hamorah, 1980.

Levy, Ze'ev. "Ultimate Reality and Meaning in Maimonides' Concept of God and Creation." *Ultimate Reality and Meaning* 14.3 (1991) 165–74.

Lewis, Bernard. "Maimonides, Lionheart, and Saladin." *Eretz-Israel* 7 (1964) 70–75.

Leyerle, Blake. "Blood is Seed." *Journal of Religion* 81.1 (2001) 26–48.

Libson, Gideon. "Parallels between Maimonides and Islamic Law." In *Thought of Moses Maimonides*, edited by Ira Robinson et al., 209–48. Lewiston, NY: Edwin Mellen, 1990.

Liebes, Yehudah. "Who Makes the Horn of Jesus to Flourish?" *Immanuel* 21 (1987) 56–67.

Litfin, Bryan M. *Getting to Know the Church Fathers: An Evangelical Introduction*. Grand Rapids, MI: Brazos, 2007.

Lobel, Diane. "'Silence Is Praise to You': Maimonides on Negative Theology, Looseness of Expression, and Religious Experience." *American Catholic Philosophic Quarterly* 76.1 (2002) 25–49.

Lorberbaum, Yair. "Imago Dei in Judaism: Early Rabbinic Literature, Philosophy, and the Kabbalah: The Teaching about God, the Human Person, and the Beginning in Talmudic and Kabbalistic Judaism." In *Concept of God, the Origin of the World, and the Image of the Human in the World Religions*, 57–74. Dordrecht: Kluwer Academic, 2001.

Lössl, Josef. "A Shift in Patristic Exegesis: Hebrew Clarity and Historical Verity in Augustine, Jerome, Julian of Aeclanum and Theodore of Mopsuestia." *Augustinian Studies* 32.2 (2001) 157–75.

Lowney, Chris. *A Vanished World: Medieval Spain's Golden Age of Enlightenment*. New York: Free, 2005.

Luz, Ehud. *Wrestling with an Angel: Power, Morality, and Jewish Identity*. Translated by Michael Swirsky. New Haven, CT: Yale University Press, 2003.

MacCoull, Leslie S B. "John Philoponus and the Composite Nature of Christ." *Ostkirchliche Studien* 44 (1995) 197–204.

———. "A New Look at the Career of John Philoponus." *Journal of Early Christian Studies* 3.1 (1995) 47–60.

MacLennan, Robert. "Four Christian Writers on Jews and Judaism in the Second Century." In *From Ancient Israel to Modern Judaism: Intellect in Quest of Understanding: Essays in Honor of Marvin Fox* vol. 2, edited by Jacob Nuesner et al., 187–202. Atlanta: Scholars, 1989.

Magid, Shaul. "Ethics Disentangled from the Law Incarnation, the Universal, and Hasidic Ethics." *Kabbalah: Journal for the Study of Jewish Mystical Texts* 15 (2006) 31–75.

Maimonides, Moses. *Epistles of Maimonides: Crisis and Leadership: The Epistle of Martyrdom, The Epistle to Yemen, and The Essay on Resurrection*. Edited and translated by Abraham Halkin. Philadelphia: Jewish Publication Society of America, 1985.

———. *Ethical Writings of Maimonides*. Edited by Raymond L. Weiss and Charles L. Butterworth. New York: Dover, 1975.

———. *The Guide for the Perplexed*. Translated by M. Friedländer. New York: Barnes & Noble, 2004.

———. "The Laws of Martyrdom: When Can a Jew Give Up His Life." Translated by Shlomo Katz. *Commentary* (July 1948) 77–78.

———. "Letter to the Community of Marseilles: Letter on Astrology." *Jewish Times: Mesora* (2013) 21–24.

———. *Maimonides' Introduction to the Talmud: A Translation of the Rambam's Introduction to His Commentary on the Mishna*. Translated by Zvi Lampel. Brooklyn: Judaica, 1998.

———. *A Maimonides Reader (including portions of the Mishneh Torah, The Guide of the Perplexed, Eight Chapters, b, Helek: Sanhedrin, Chapter Ten, Book of Commandments, Epistle to Yemen, Letter on Astrology, and Occasional Letters)*. Edited by Isadore Twersky. Library of Jewish Studies Series. New York: Behrman, 1972.

———. *Moses Maimonides' Treatise on Resurrection*. Translated by Fred Rosner. Northvale, NJ: Jason Aronson, 1997.

———. *Pirkei Avot with the Rambam's Commentary including Shemoneh Perakim: The Rambam's Classic Work of Ethics and Maimonides' Introduction to Perek Chelek Which Contains His 13 Principles of Faith*. Translated by Eliyahu Touger. Brooklyn: Moznaim, 1994.

———. *Rambam—Selected Letters of Maimonides: Letter to Yemen and Discourse on Martyrdom*. Translated by Avraham Yaakov Finkel. Scranton, PA: Yeshivath Beth Moshe, 1994.

———. *The Ways of Repentance: Moses Maimonides on Teshuvah*. Translated and commentary by Henry Abramson. Lexington, KY: Smashwords, 2012.

Makuja, Darius Oliha. "Gregory the Great, Roman Law and the Jews: Seeking 'True' Conversions." *Sacris Eruditi* 48 (2009) 35–74.

Malina, Bruce J. "Jewish Christianity or Christian Judaism: Toward a Hypothetical Defintion." *Journal for the Study of Judaism in the Persian, Hellenistic and Roman Period* 7.1 (1976) 46–57.
Manekin, Charles H. "Belief, Certainty and Divine Attributes in the Guide." In *Maimonidean Studies* vol. 1, edited by Arthur Hyman. New York: Michael Scharf Publication Trust of Yeshiva University Press, 1990.
Marcus, Joel. "A Jewish-Christian 'Amidah?" *Early Christianity* 3.2 (2012) 215–25.
Margoliouth, D. S. "The Legend of the Apostasy of Maimonides." *The Jewish Quarterly Review* 13.3 (1901) 539–41.
Marmur, Michael. "Heschel's Two Maimonides." *The Jewish Quarterly Review* 98.2 (2008) 230–54.
Martinson, Roland. "Spiritual but Not Religious: Reaching an Invisible Generation." *Currents in Theology and Mission* 29.5 (2002) 326–40.
Mayo, Philip L. "The Role of the Birkath Haminim in Early Jewish-Christian Relations: A Reexamination of the Evidence." *Bulletin for Biblical Research* 16.2 (2006) 325–44.
Mazuz, Haggai. "The Identity of the Apostate in the Epistle to Yemen." *AJS Review* 38.2 (2014) 363–74.
McGinn, Bernard. "*Sapientia Judaeorum*: The Role of Jewish Philosophers in Some Scholastic Thinkers." In *Continuity and Change: The Harvest of Late Medieval and Reformation History: Essays Presented to Heiko A. Oberman on His 70th Birthday*, edited by Robert J. Bast and Andrew Colin Gow, 206–28. Leiden: Brill, 2000.
McGrath, Alister. *Mere Apologetics: How to Help Seekers and Skeptics Find Faith*. Grand Rapids, MI: Baker, 2012.
———. *What Was God Doing on the Cross?* Grand Rapids, MI: Zondervan, 1992.
McMichael, Steven J. "The Resurrection of Jesus and Human Beings in Medieval Christian and Jewish Theology and Polemical Literature." *Studies in Jewish-Christian Relations* 4 (2009) 1–18.
Mégier, Elisabeth. "Jewish Converts in the Early Church and Latin Christian Exegetes of Isaiah, c.400–1150." *Journal of Ecclesiastical History* 59.1 (2008) 1–26.
Meiselman, Moshe. *Jewish Woman in Jewish Law*. New York: KTAV, 1978.
Melber, Jehuda. *Judaism: A Religion of Reason*. Middle Village, NY: Jonathan David, 2003.
Melnick, Olivier. *They Have Conspired Against You: Responding to the New Anti-Semitism*. Huntington Beach, CA: Purple Remnant, 2007.
Menache, Sophia. "Faith, Myth, and Politics: The Stereotype of the Jews and Their Expulsion from England and France." *The Jewish Quarterly Review* 75.4 (1985) 351–74.
———. "Tartars, Jews, Saracens, and the Jewish-Mongol 'Plot' of 1241." *History* 81.263 (1996) 319–42.
Menocal, Maria Rosa. *The Ornament of the World: How Muslims, Jews, and Christians Created a Culture of Tolerance in Medieval Spain*. Boston: First Back Bay, 2002.
Metaxas, Eric. *Bonhoeffer: Pastor, Martyr, Prophet, Spy*. Nashville: Thomas Nelson, 2010.
Meyerhoff, Max. "Jewish Physicians under the Reign of the Fatimid Caliphs in Egypt (969–1171 C.E.)." *Medical Leaves* (1939) 131–39.
Meyers, Eric M. "Early Judaism and Christianity in Light of Archaeology." *Biblical Archaeologist* 51.2 (1988) 69–79.

Milgrom, Jacob. "Magic, Monotheism, and the Sin of Moses." In *The Quest for the Kingdom of God: Studies in Honor of George E. Mendenhall*, edited by Herbert B. Huffmon et al., 251–65. Winona Lake, IN: Eisenbrauns, 1983.

Miller, Clyde Lee. "Maimonides and Aquinas on Naming God." *Journal of Jewish Studies* 28.1 (1977) 65–71.

Miller, Deena. "Jacob's Injury: Differential Diagnosis of Hip Pathology." download. yutorah.org/2014/1053/813251.pdf.

Miller, Stuart S. "The Minim of Sepphoris Reconsidered." *Harvard Theological Review* 86.4 (1993) 377–402.

Minkin, Jacob S. *The World of Moses Maimonides*. New York: Thomas Yoseloff, 1957.

Mork, Gordon R. "Christ's Passion on Stage: The Traditional Melodrama of Deicide." *Journal of Religion and Film* 8.1 (2004). http://www.unomaha.edu/jrf/2004Symposium/Mork.htm.

Mundill, Robin R. "Out of the Shadow and into the Light—the Impact and Implications of Recent Scholarship on the Jews of Medieval England 1066–1290." *History Compass* 9.8 (2011) 572–601.

Murphy, Cullen. *God's Jury: The Inquisition and the Making of the Modern World*. Boston: Houghton, Mifflin, Harcourt, 2012.

Nadler, Steven. "Baruch Spinoza." *The Stanford Encyclopedia of Philosophy*, edited by Edward N. Zalta. http://plato.stanford.edu/archives/fall2013/entries/spinoza/.

Netanyahu, B. *The Origins of the Inquisition in Fifteenth Century Spain*. New York: Random, 1995.

Netzer, Ehud. "The Last Days and Hours at Masada." *Biblical Archaeology Review* 17.6 (1991) 21–32. http://members.bib-arch.org/search.asp?PubID= BSBA&Volume= 17&Issue=6&ArticleID=13&UserID=0&.

Neusner, Jacob. "History Invented: The Conception of History in the Talmud of the Land of Israel." In *The Christian and Judaic Invention of History*, edited by Jacob Neusner, 181–208. Atlanta: Scholars, 1990.

———. "Is the God of Judaism Incarnate?" *Religious Studies* 24.2 (1988) 213–38.

———. "Judaism in a Time of Crisis: Four Responses to the Destruction of the Second Temple." *Judaism* 21.3 (1972) 313–27.

———. "Story-Telling and the Incarnation of God in Formative Judaism." In *The Incarnate Imagination: Essays in Theology, The Arts and Social Sciences in Honor of Andrew Greeley—A Festschrift*, edited by Ingrid H. Shafer, 197–228. Bowling Green, OH: Bowling Green State University Popular Press, 1988.

———. "Why Judaism Won the Fourth Century as the True First Century in the History of the Judaic and Christian West." In *Biblische und Judaistische Studien: Festschrift für Paolo Sacchi*, edited Angelo Vivian, 349–62. Frankfurt am Main: Peter Lang, 1990.

Newman, Hillel I. "Jerome's Judaizers." *Journal of Early Christian Studies* 9.4 (2001) 421–52.

New World Encyclopedia Contributors. "Erich Fromm." *New World Encyclopedia*. http://www.newworldencyclopedia.org/p/index.php?title=Erich_Fromm&oldid=976278.

Nieman, David. "Sefarad: The Name of Spain." *Journal of Near Eastern Studies* 22.2 (April 1963).

Nilson, Jon. "To Whom is Justin's *Dialogue with Trypho* Addressed?" *Theological Studies* 38.3 (1977) 538–46.

Nirenberg, David. *Anti-Judaism: The Western Tradition.* New York: W. W. Norton, 2013.

Novak, David. "The End of the Law: A Significant Difference between Judaism and Christianity." In *Transforming Relations: Essays on Jews and Christians throughout History in Honor of Michael A. Signer*, edited by Franklin T. Harkins and John H. Van Engen, 34–49. Notre Dame, IN: University of Notre Dame Press, 201

———. "Maimonides' Concept of the Messiah." *Journal of Religious Studies* 9.2 (1982) 42–50.

———. "The Treatment of Islam and Muslims in the Legal Writings of Maimonides." In *Studies in Islamic and Judaic Traditions: Papers Presented at the Institute for Islamic-Judaic Studies—Center for Judaic Studies, University of Denver*, edited by William M. Brinner and Stephen D. Ricks, 233–50. Brown Judaic Studies 110. Atlanta: Scholars, 1986.

Novenson, Matthew V. "Why Does R. Akiba Acclaim Bar Kokhba as Messiah?" *Journal for the Study of Judaism* 40 (2009) 551–72.

Nuland, Sherwin B. *Maimonides.* New York: Nextbook, 2005.

O'Meara, John J. *The Young Augustine: The Growth of St. Augustine's Mind Up to His Conversion.* New York: Alba House, 2001.

O'Neill, J. C. "The Mocking of Bar Kokhba and of Jesus." *Journal for the Study of Judaism in the Persian, Hellenistic and Roman Period* 31.1 (2000) 39–41.

Orfali Levi, Moisés. "Anthropomorphism in the Christian Reproach of the Jews in Spain (12th–15th Century)." *Immanuel* 19 (1984–1985) 60–73.

Osborn, Eric. *Tertullian, First Theologian of the West.* Cambridge, UK: Cambridge University Press, 1997.

Osborn, Robert, "The Christian Blasphemy." *Journal of the American Academy of Religion* 53.3 (1985) 339–63.

Papademetriou, George C. "Moses Maimonides' Doctrine of God." *Philosophia* 4 (1974) 306–29.

Parker, Pierson. "Early Christianity as a Religion of Healing." *Saint Luke's Journal of Theology* 19.2 (1976) 142–50.

Parkes, James William. "The Jewish Background of the Incarnation." *Modern Churchman* 4.1 (1960) 33–44.

Parvis, Sara, and Paul Foster. "Introduction: Justin Martyr and His Worlds." In *Justin Martyr and His Worlds*, edited by Sara Parvis and Paul Foster. Minneapolis: Fortress, 2007.

Peck, William Jay. "From Cain to the Death Camps: An Essay on Bonhoeffer and Judaism." *Union Seminary Quarterly Review* 28.2 (1973) 158–76.

Pessin, Sarah. "On Glimpsing the Face of God in Maimonides: Wonder, 'Hylomorphic Apophasis' and the Divine Prayer Shawl." *Tópicos* 42 (2012) 75–105.

Peters, Jeremy W. "Bloomberg Plans a $50 Million Challenge to the N.R.A." *New York Times* (April 2014). http://www.nytimes.com/2014/04/16/us/bloomberg-plans-a-50-million-challenge-to-the-nra.html?r=0.

Pew Research Center. "A Portrait of Jewish Americans: Findings from a Pew Research Center Survey of U.S. Jews." Washington, DC: Pew Research Center, 2013. http://www.pewforum.org/files/2013/10/jewish-american-full-report-for-web.pdf.

———. "U. S. Public Becoming Less Religious: Modest Drop in Overall Rates of Belief and Practice, but Religious Affiliated Americans Are as Observant as Before." Washington, DC: Pew Research Center, 2015. http://www.pewforum.org/files/2015/11/201.11.03_RLS_II_full_report.pdf.

Pines, Shlomo. "The Limitations of Human Knowledge according to Al-Farabi, ibn Bajja, and Maimonides." In *Maimonides: A Collection of Critical Essays*, edited by Joseph A. Buijs. Notre Dame, IN: University of Notre Dame Press, 1988.

———. "Maimonides." In *The Encyclopedia of Philosophy*, vol. 5. Editor-in-Chief Paul Edwards. New York: Macmillan & Free, 1967.

Pons, Mariona Vernet. "The Origin of the Name Sepharad: A New Interpretation." *Journal of Semitic Studies* 59.2 (2014) 297–313.

Poorthuis, Marcel. "Messianism between Reason and Delusion: Maimonides and the Messiah." In *Messianism through History*, edited by W. A. M. Beuken et al., 57–68. Maryknoll, NY: Orbis, 1993.

Potok, Chaim. *Davita's Harp*. New York: Alfred A. Knopf, 1985.

Prager, Dennis, and Joseph Telushkin. *Why the Jews: The Reason for Anti-Semitism*. New York: Touchstone, 1983.

Putnam, Hilary. "On Negative Theology." *Faith and Philosophy* 14.4 (1997) 407–22).

Quasten, Johannes. *Patrology*, vol. 1. Notre Dame, IN: Christian Classics, n.d.

Rashkover, Randi. "The Christian Doctrine of the Incarnation." In *Christianity in Jewish Terms*, edited by Tikva Frymer-Kensky et al., 254–61. Theology in a Postcritical Key. Boulder, CO: Westview, 2000.

Ravitzky, Aviezer. Ravitzky, Aviezer. "The Anthropological Theory of Miracles in Medieval Jewish Philosophy." In *Studies in Medieval Jewish Studies and Literature*, vol. 2. Edited by Isadore Twersky. Harvard Judaic Monographs 5. Cambridge, MA: Harvard University Press, 1984), 231–72.

———. "The Secrets of the *Guide of the Perplexed*: Between the Thirteenth and Twentieth Centuries." In *Studies in Maimonides*, edited by Isadore Twersky, 159–207. Cambridge, MA: Harvard University Press, 1990.

———. "'To the Utmost of Human Capacity': Maimonides on the Days of the Messiah." In *Perspectives on Maimonides: Philosophical and Historical Studies*, edited by Joel L. Kraemer, 221–56. Littman Library of Jewish Civilization. Oxford: Oxford University Press, 1991.

Rawidowicz, Simon. *Studies in Jewish Thought*. Philadelphia: Jewish Publication Society of America, 1974.

Ray, Jonathan. "The Reconquista and the Jews: 1212 from the Perspective of Jewish History." *Journal of Medieval History* 40.2 (2014) 159–75.

Rebenich, Stefan. *Jerome*. The Early Church Fathers. London: Routledge, 2002.

———. "The 'Vir Trilinguis' and the 'Hebrew Veritas.'" *Vigilae Christianae* 47.1 (1993) 50–77.

Reeves, John C. "The 'Elchasaite' Sanhedrin of the Cologne Mani Codex in Light of Second Temple Sectarian Sources." *Journal of Jewish Studies* 42.1 (1991) 68–91.

Reif, Stefan C. "Maimonides on the Prayers." In *Traditions of Maimonideanism*, edited by Carlos Fraenkel, 73–100. IJS Studies in Judaica 7. Leiden: Brill, 2009.

Reines, Alvin J. "Maimonides' Concepts of Providence and Theodicy." *Hebrew Union College Annual* 43 (1972) 169–206.

———. "The Polydox Confederation." *Religious Humanism* 19.2 (1985) 84–88.

Richardson, Peter. *Israel in the Apostolic Church*. Society for New Testament Studies Monograph Series 10. Cambridge, UK: Cambridge University Press, 1969.

Riddle, Donald Wayne. "The So-Called Jewish Christians." *Anglican Theological Review* 12.1 (1929) 15–33.

Rist, Rebecca. "Through Jewish Eyes: Polemical Literature and the Medieval Papacy." *History* 98.333 (2013) 639–62.
Robinson, George. *Essential Judaism: A Complete Guide to Beliefs, Customs, and Rituals.* New York: Pocket, 2000.
Robinson, Richard A., ed. *God, Torah, Messiah: The Messianic Jewish Theology of Dr. Louis Goldberg.* San Francisco: Purple Pomegranate, 2009.
Rokéah, Zefira Entin. "The State, the Church, and the Jews in Medieval England." In *Antisemitism through the Ages.* Edited by Shmuel Almog and translated by N. Reisner. Oxford: Pergamon, 1988.
Roos, Lena. "Paul Christian—A Jewish Dominican Preaching for the Jews." *Studia Theologica* 57 (2003) 49–60.
Rose, Paul Lawrence. "When Was the Talmud Burnt in Paris? a Critical Examination of the Christian and Jewish Sources and a New Dating: June 1241." *The Journal of Jewish Studies* 62.2 (2011) 324–39.
Rosenbaum, Stanley Ned. "Dietrich Bonhoeffer: A Jewish View." *Journal of Ecumenical Studies* 18.2 (1981) 301–7.
Rosensaft, Menachem Z, ed. *God, Faith & Identity from the Ashes: Reflections of Children and Grandchildren of Holocaust Survivors.* Woodstock, VT: Jewish Lights, 2015.
Rosner, Fred. *The Existence of God and Unity of God: Three Treatises Attributed to Moses Maimonides.* Northvale, NJ: Jason Aronson, 1990.
Roth, Cecil. "Maimonides and England." In *Moses Maimonides, 1135–1204: Anglo-Jewish Papers in Connection with the Eighth Centenary of His Birth*, edited by I. Epstein. London: Soncino, 1935.
Roth, Norman. "Bishops and Jews in the Middle Ages." *Catholic Historical Review* 80.1 (1994). *Religion and Philosophy Collection*, EBSCOhos.
———. "The Jews in Spain at the Time of Maimonides." In *Moses Maimonides and His Time*, edited by Eric L. Ormsby, 1–20. Washington, DC: Catholic University Press of America, 1989.
Rubenstein, Jay. *Armies of Heaven: The First Crusade and the Quest for the Apocalypse.* New York: Basic, 2011.
Rudavsky, T.M. *Blackwell Great Minds: Maimonides.* Hoboken, NJ: Wiley-Blackwell, 2009.
Russ-Fishbane, Elisha. "The Maimonidean Legacy in the East: A Study of Father and Son." *The Jewish Quarterly Review* 102.2 (2012) 190–223.
Sachar, Abram Leon. *A History of the Jews.* New York: Alfred A. Knopf, 1965.
Saint-Laurent, George. "Avicenna, Maimonides, Aquinas and the Existence of God." In *Festschrift in Honor of Morton C. Fierman*, edited by Joseph Kalir, 165–91. Fullerton, CA: California State University Fullerton, 1982.
Samuelson, Norbert. "Medieval Jewish Philosophy." In *Back to the Sources: Reading the Classic Jewish Texts*, edited by Barry W. Holtz, 261–304. New York: Summit, 1984.
Saperstein, Marc. *Jewish Preaching: 1200–1800—An Anthology.* Yale Judaica Series 27. New Haven, CT: Yale University Press, 1989.
Sarachek, Joseph. *The Doctrine of the Messiah in Medieval Jewish Literature.* New York: Jewish Theological Seminary in America, 1932.
Schaff, Philip. *History of the Christian Church: The Middle Ages from Gregory VII, 1049, to Boniface VIII, 1294*, vol. 5. Grand Rapids, MI: William B. Eerdmans, 1907.
Scharfstein, Sol. *Torah and Commentary: The Five Book of Moses: Translation Rabbinic and Contemporary Commentary.* Jersey City, NJ: KTAV, 2008)

Schiffman, Lawrence H. "At the Crossroads: Tannaitic Perspectives on the Jewish-Christian Schism." In *Jewish and Christian Self-Definition, Volume Two: Aspects of Judaism, in the Greco-Roman Period*, edited by E. P. Sanders, 115–56. London: SCM, 1981.

———. "How Jewish Christians Became Christians: Three Views of the Jewish-Christian Schism." http://www.myjewishlearning.com/history/Ancient_and_Medieval_History/ 539_BCE–632_CE/Palestine_Under_Roman_Rule/Jewish–Christian_Schism.shtml.

Schoon, Simon. "Christians and Jews after the Shoah and the Mission to the Jews." In *The Image of the Judaeo-Christians in Ancient Jewish and Christian Literature*, edited by Peter J. Tomson and Doris Lambers-Petry, 299–314. Wissenschaftliche Untersuchungen zum Neuen Testament Series 158. Tübingen: Mohr-Siebeck, 2003.

Schwartz, Joshua, and Peter Tomson. "When Rabbi Eliezer Was Arrested for Heresy." *Jewish Studies—An Internet Journal* 10 (2012) 145–81.

Schwarz, Michael. "Some Remarks Concerning Maimonides' Discussion of God's Knowledge of Particulars." In *Torah and Wisdom: Studies in Jewish Philosophy: Kabbalah, and Halacha: Essays in Honor of Arthur Hyman*, edited by Ruth Link-Salinger Hyman, 189–97. New York: Shengold, 1992.

Schwarzschild, Steven. "The Messianic Doctrine in Contemporary Jewish Thought." In *Great Jewish Ideas*, edited by Abraham Ezra Millgram, 237–58. Washington, DC: B'nai B'rith Department of Adult Jewish Education, 1964.

———. "Speech and Silence before God." *Judaism: A Quarterly Journal* 10.3 (1961) 195–204.

Scott, J. Julius, Jr. "The Effects of the Fall of Jerusalem on Christianity." *Proceedings* 3 (1983) 149–60.

Seeskin, Kenneth. "Sanctity and Silence: The Religious Significance of Maimonides' Negative Theology." *American Catholic Philosophic Quarterly* 76.1 (2002) 7–24.

Shakespeare, Steven. "Thinking about *Fire*: Derrida and Judaism." *Literature and Theology* 12.3 (1998) 242–55.

Shamir, Yehuda. "Allusions to Muhammad in Maimonides' Theory of Prophecy in His 'Guide of the Perplexed.'" *The Jewish Quarterly Review* 64.3 (1974) 212–24.

Shapiro, Marc B. "Maimonides' Thirteen Principles: The Last Word in Jewish Theology?" *The Torah U-Madda Journal* 4 (1993) 187–242.

———. *Studies in Maimonides and His Interpreters*. Scranton, PA: University of Scranton Press, 2008.

Shapiro, David S. "Possible Deus Homo?" *Judaism: A Quarterly Journal* 32.3 (1983) 358–65.

Shatz, David. "The Biblical and Rabbinic Background to Medieval Jewish Philosophy." In *The Cambridge Companion to Medieval Jewish Philosophy*, edited by Daniel H. Frank and Oliver Leaman, 16–37. Cambridge Companions to Philosophy. New York: Cambridge University Press, 2006.

Shepkaru, Shmuel. "The Preaching of the First Crusade and the Persecutions of the Jews." *Medieval Encounters* 18 (2012) 93–135.

Sherman, C. Bezalel. "The American Jewish Community." In *Great Jewish Ideas*, edited by Abraham Ezra Millgram, 45–57. Washington, DC: B'nai B'rith Department of Adult Jewish Education, 1964.

Shiffman, Yair. "The Differences Between the Translations of Maimonides' *Guide of the Perplexed* by Falaquera, Ibn Tibbon and Al-Harizï, and Their Textual and Philosophical Implications." *Journal of Semitic Studies* 44.1 (1999) 47–61.

Shivtiel, Avihai. "The 'Contribution' of Maimonides to the Cairo Genizah." *'Ilu, Revista de Ciencias de las Religionas* (2004) 95–106.

Shmidman, Michael A. "On Maimonides' 'Conversion' to Kabbalah." In *Studies in Medieval Jewish History and Literature* vol. 2, edited by Isadore Twersky, 375–86. Cambridge, MA: Harvard University Press, 1984.

Sigal, Philip. "Aspects of the Fall of Jerusalem." *Proceedings* 3 (1983) 161–75.

———. "Further Reflections on the 'Begotten' Messiah." *Hebrew Annual Review* 7 (1983) 221–33.

Silver, Daniel Jeremy. "The Resurrection Debate." In *Moses Maimonides' Treatise on Resurrection.* Translated and Annotated by Fred Rosner. Northvale, NJ: Jason Aronson, 1997.

Sim, David C. "How Many Jews Became Christians in the First Century? The Failure of the Christian Mission to the Jews." *Hervormde Teologiese Studies* 61 (2005) 417–40.

Simon, Marcel. *Verus Israel: A Study of the Relations between Christians and Jews in the Roman Empire, AD 135–425.* Translated by H. McKeating. Portland, OR: Littman Library of Jewish Civilization, 1986.

Sivan, Gabriel A. "Hymns of the Isles." *Judaism: A Quarterly Journal* 39.3 (1990) 326–37.

Skarsaune, Oskar. "The Ebionites." In *Jewish Believers in Jesus: The Early Centuries*, edited by Oskar Skarsaune and Reidar Hvalvik, 419–62. Peabody, MA: Hendrickson, 2007.

Smelik, Klaas A. D. "John Chrysostom's Homilies against the Jews." *Nederlands Theologisch Tijdschrift* 39.3 (1985) 194–200.

Soifer, Maya. "'You Say that the Messiah Has Come...': The Ceuta Disputation (1179) and Its Place in the Christian Anti-Jewish Polemics of the High Middle Ages." *Journal of Medieval History* 31 (2005) 287–307.

Solomon, Mark. "The Praise of Silence." *European Judaism* 46.2 (2013) 91–98.

Soloveitchik, Haym. "Mishneh Torah: Polemic and Art." In *Maimonides after 800 Years: Essays on Maimonides and His Influence*, edited by Jay M. Harris, 327–43. Cambridge, MA: Harvard University Press, 2007.

Soloveichik, Meir Y. "God's First Love: The Theology of Michael Wyschogrod." *First Things* 197 (2009) 43–48.

Sommer, Benjamin D. *The Bodies of God and the World of Ancient Israel.* New York: Cambridge University Press, 2009.

Sonne, Isaiah. "A Scrutiny of the Charges of Forgery against Maimonides' 'Letter on the Resurrection.'" In *Eschatology in Maimonidean Thought: Messianism, Resurrection, and the World to Come*, edited by Jacob Israel Dienstag, 48–64. New York: KTAV, 1983.

Sonsino, Rifat. *The Many Faces of God: A Reader of Modern Jewish Theologians.* New York: URJ, 2004.

Sonsino, Rifat, and Daniel B. Syme. *Finding God: Ten Jewish Responses.* New York: Union of American Hebrew Congregations, 1986.

Soulen, R. Kendall. *The God of Israel and Christian Theology.* Minneapolis: Fortress, 1996.

Spero, Shubert. "Is the God of Maimonides Truly Unknowable?" *Judaism: A Quarterly Journal* 22.1 (1973) 66–78.

———. "Maimonides and Our Love for God." *Judaism: A Quarterly Journal* 32.3 (1983) 321–30.

———. "Maimonides and the Sense of History." *Tradition* 24.2 (1989) 128–37.

Stacey, Robert C. "Crusades, Martyrdoms, and the Jews of Norman England, 1096–1190." In *Juden and Christen zur Zeit der Kreuzzüge*, edited by Alfred Haverkamp, 233–51. Sigmaringen: Jan Thorbecke, 1999.

———. "Royal Taxation and the Social Structure of Medieval Anglo-Jewry: The Tallages of 1239–1242." *Hebrew Union College Annual* 56 (1985) 175–249.

Statman, Daniel. "Negative Theology and the Meaning of the Commandments in Modern Orthodoxy." *Tradition* 39.1 (2005) 58–71.

Stefaniw, Blossom. "Reading Revelation: Allegorical Exegesis in Late Antique Alexandria." *Revue de l'histoire des religions* 224. 2 (2007) 231–51.

Stegner, William Richard. "Breaking Away: The Conflict with Formative Judaism." *Biblical Research* 40 (1995) 7–36.

Stemberger, Günter. "Elements of Biblical Interpretation in Medieval Jewish-Christian Disputation." In *Hebrew Bible/Old Testament: The History of Its Interpretation: From the Beginnings to the Middle Ages (until 1300)* vol. 1, edited by Christianus Brekelmans et al., 578–90. Göttingen: Vandenhoeck & Ruprecht, 2000.

———. "Rabbinic Reactions to the Christianization of Roman Palestine: A Survey of Recent Research." In *Encounters of the Children of Abraham from Ancient to Modern Times*, edited by Antti Laato and Petta Lindqvist, 141–63. Leiden: Brill, 2010.

Stitskin, Leon. "Maimonides Letter on Apostacy: The Advent of the Messiah and Shivat Zion (Return to Zion)." *Tradition: A Journal of Orthodox Jewish Thought* 14.2 (1973) 103–12.

———. "Maimonides on Refuting False Notions: A Letter to the Jews of Montpellier." *Tradition: A Journal of Orthodox Jewish Thought* 11.4 (1971) 99–104.

Stowers, Stanley K. "Text as Interpretation: Paul and Ancient Readings of Paul." *Judaic and Christian Interpretations of Texts; Contents and Context* (1987) 17–27.

Stroumsa, Gedaliahu G. "Form(s) of God: Some Notes on Metatron and Christ." *Harvard Theological Review* 76.3 (1983) 269–88.

Stroumsa, Sarah. "Elisha ben Abuyah and Muslim Heretics in Maimonides' Writings." *Maimonidean Studies* 3 (1992–1993) 173–93.

Stylianopoulos, Theodore. "New Testament Issues in Jewish-Christian Relations." *Journal of Ecumenical Studies* 13.4 (1976) 586–95.

Tait, Jennifer Woodruff. "Fire, Water, and a Risen Savior." *Christian History* (8 April 2009). http://www.christianitytoday.com/ch/bytopic/holidays/firewaterandrisensavior.html.

Talmage, F. E. "The Stumbling Block." In *Disputation and Dialogue: Readings in the Jewish-Christian Encounter*, edited by F. E. Talmage. New York: KTAV, 1975.

Ta-shma, Israel M. "Judeo-Christian Commerce on Christian Holy Days in Medieval Germany and Provence." *Immanuel* 12 (1981) 110–22.

Teicher, J. Louis. "Christian Theology and the Jewish Opposition to Maimonides." *The Journal of Theological Studies* 43 (1942) 68–76.

———. "The Mediaeval Mind." *The Journal of Jewish Studies* 6.1 (1955) 1–13.

Telushkin, Joseph. *Jewish Literacy: The Most Important Things to Know about the Jewish Religion, Its People, and Its History.* New York: William Morrow, 1991.

Tertullian. *Against Marcion.* Translated by Peter Holmes. In *Ante-Nicene Fathers* vol. 3, edited by Alexander Roberts, et al. Buffalo, NY: Christian Literature, 1885. http://www.newadvent.org/fathers/03125.htm.

———. *An Answer to the Jews.* Whitefish, MT: Kessinger, n.d.

———. *Apology.* http://www.earlychristianwritings.com/text/tertullian01.html.

———. *On Baptism.* http://www.earlychristianwritings.com/text/tertullian21.

Thurén, Lauri. "John Chrysostom as a Rhetorical Critic: The Hermeneutics of an Early Father." *Biblical Interpretation* 9.2 (2001) 180–218.

Tirosh-Samuelson, Hava. "Maimonides' View of Happiness: Philosophy, Myth, and the Transcendence of History." In *Jewish History and Jewish Memory: Essays in Honor of Yosef Hayim Yerushalmi*, edited by Elisheva Carlebach, et al. Hanover, NH: Brandeis University Press, 1998.

Tomson, Peter. "The Wars against Rome: The Rise of Rabbinic Judaism and of Apostolic Gentile Christianity, and the Judaeo-Christians: Elements for a Synthesis." In *The Image of the Judaeo-Christians in Ancient Jewish and Christian Literature*, edited by Peter J. Tomson and Doris Lambers-Petry, 1–31. Wissenschaftliche Untersuchungen zum Neuen Testament Series 158. Tübingen: Mohr-Siebeck, 2003.

Tov, Emanuel. "A Qumran Origin for the Masada Non-Biblical Texts?" *Dead Sea Discoveries* 7.1 (2000) 57–73.

Trautner-Kromann, Hanne. "Jewish Polemics against Christianity in Medieval France and Spain: Can the Intensity of Argumentation Be Measured?" In *Rashi 1040–1090: Hommage à Ephraïm E Urbach: IVe Congrès Européen des Études Juives*, edited by Gabrielle Sed-Rajna, 639–44. Paris: Cerf, 1993.

Trigano, Schmuel. "The Conventionalization of Social Bonds and the Strategies of Jewish Society in the Thirteenth Century." In *New Horizons in Sephardic Studies*, edited by Yedida K. Stillman and George K. Zucker, 45–66. Albany, NY: State University of New York Press, 1993.

Turner, Denys. "Apophaticism, Idolatry, and the Claims of Reason. In *Silence and the Word: Negative Theology and Incarnation*, edited by Oliver Davies and Denys Turner, 11–34. New York: Cambridge University Press, 2002.

Turner, Joseph Aaron. "Philosophical and Midrashic Thinking on the Fateful Events of Jewish History," In *The Impact of the Holocaust on Jewish Theology*, edited by Steven T. Katz, 61–81. New York: New York University Press, 2005.

Twersky, Isadore. *Introduction to the Code of Maimonides (Mishneh Toreh).* Yale Judaica Series 22. New Haven, CT: Yale University Press, 1980.

Urbach, Ephraim E. "Self-Isolation or Self-Affirmation in Judaism in the First Three Centuries: Theory and Practice." In *Jewish and Christian Self-Definition, Volume Two: Aspects of Judaism, in the Greco-Roman Period*, edited by E. P. Sanders, 269–98. London: SCM, 1981.

van der Heide, Albert. "'Their Prophets and Fathers Misled Them': Moses Maimonides on Christianity and Islam." In *The Three Rings: Textual Studies in the Historical Trialogue of Judaism, Christianity and Islam*, edited by Barbara Roggema et al., 35–46. Dudley, MA: Peeters, 2005.

van Oort, Johannes. "Augustine, His Sermons, and Their Significance." *HTS Teologiese Studies/Theological Studies* 65.1. http://hts.org.za/index.php/HTS/article/view/300/702.

———. "Manichaean Christians in Augustine's Life and Work." *Church History and Religious Culture* 90.4 (2010).

Varner, William. "In the Wake of Trypho: Jewish-Christian dialogues in the Third to the Sixth Centuries." *Evangelical Quarterly* 80.3 (2008) 219–36.

Verbin, N. "Can God Forgive Our Trespasses?" *International Journal for Philosophy of Religion* 74.2 (2013) 181–99.

Verseput, D. J. "Paul's Gentile Mission and the Jewish Christian Community: A Study of the Narrative in Galatians 1 and 2." *New Testament Studies* 39 (1993) 36–58.

Visotzky, Burton L. "Prolegomenon to the Study of Jewish-Christianities in Rabbinic Literature." *AJS Review* 1.1 (1989) 47–70.

Wacholder, Ben Zion. "Attitudes Towards Proselytizing in the Classical Halakah." In *Readings on Conversion to Judaism*, edited by Lawrence J. Epstein, 15–32. Northvale, NJ: Jason Aronson, 1995.

Weingarten, Susan. "'In Thy Blood Live!' Haroset and the Blood Libels." *Revue Des Études Juives* 172 (2013) 83–100.

Weissberger, Barbara. "Motherhood and Ritual Murder in Medieval Spain and England." *Journal of Medieval and Early Modern Studies* 39.1 (2009) 7–30.

Wendel, Susan. "Interpreting the Descent of the Spirit: A Comparison of Justin's *Dialogue with Trypho* and Luke-Acts." In *Justin Martyr and His Worlds*, edited by Sara Parvis and Paul Foster. Minneapolis: Fortress, 2007.

Werline, Rodney. "The Transformation of Pauline Arguments in Justin Martyr's *Dialogue with Trypho*." *Harvard Theological Review* 92.1 (1999) 79–93.

Wickham, Lionel R. "John Philoponus and Gregory of Nyssa's Teaching on Resurrection—A Brief Note." In *Studien zu Gregor von Nyssa und der Christlichen Spätantike*, edited by Hubertus R. Drobner and Christoph Klock, 205–10. Leiden: Brill, 1990.

Williams, A. Lukyn. *Adversus Judaeos: A Bird's-Eye View of Christian Apologiae until the Renaissance*. Cambridge, UK: Cambridge University Press, 1935.

Williams, Megan Hale. "No More Clever Titles: Observations on Some Recent Studies of Jewish-Christian Relations in the Roman World." *The Jewish Quarterly Review* 99.1 (2009) 37–55.

Williams, Rowan. "The Deflections of Desire: Negative Theology in Trinitarian Disclosure." In *Silence and the Word: Negative Theology and Incarnation*, edited by Oliver Davies and Denys Turner, 115–35. New York: Cambridge University Press, 2002.

Williams, Thomas. "Biblical Interpretation." In *The Cambridge Companion to Augustine*, edited by Eleonore Stump and Norman Kretzmann, 59–70. Cambridge, UK: Cambridge University Press, 2001.

Williamson, Clark M. "'Adversus Judaeos' Tradition in Christian Theology." *Encounter* 39.3 (1978) 273–96.

———. "Anti-Judaism in Process Christologies." *Process Studies* 10 (1980) 73–92.

Willis, Robert E. "Bonhoeffer and Barth on Jewish Suffering: Reflections on the Relationship Between Theology and Moral Sensibility." *Journal of Ecumenical Studies* 24.4 (1987) 598–615.

Wilson, Marvin R. *Our Father Abraham: Jewish Roots of the Christian Faith.* Grand Rapids, MI: Eerdmans, 1989.

Wilson, Stephen G. *Related Strangers: Jews and Christians 70–170 CE.* Minneapolis: Fortress, 1995.

Wohlmuth, Josef. "Twentieth-Century Jewish Thought as a Challenge to Christian Theology." In *Naming and Thinking God in Europe Today: Theology in Global Dialogue,* edited Norbert Hintersteiner, 389–409. Translated by Michael Parker. Amsterdam: Rodopi, 2007.

Wolf, Kenneth Baxter. "*Convivencia* in Medieval Spain: A Brief History of an Idea." *Religion Compass* 3.1 (2009) 72–85.

Wolfson, Elliot R. "Beneath the Wings of the Great Eagle: Maimonides and Thirteenth-Century Kabbalah." In *Moses Maimonides (1138–1204) His Religious, Scientific and Philosophical Wirkungschichte in Different Cultural Contexts,* edited by Görge K. Hasselhoff and Otfried Fraisse, 209–37. Ergon: Würzburg, 2007.

———. "Judaism and Incarnation: the Imaginal Body of God." In *Christianity in Jewish Terms,* edited by Tikva Frymer-Kensky et al., 239–54. Theology in a Postcritical Key. Boulder, CO: Westview, 2000.

Wolfson, Harry Austryn. "Maimonides on the Unity and Incorporeality of God." *The Jewish Quarterly Review* 56.2 (October 1965): 112–36.

———. "St. Thomas on Divine Attributes." In *Studies in Maimonides and St. Thomas Aquinas,* edited by Jacob Dienstrag. Bibliotheca Maimonidica 1. New York: KTAV, 1975.

Wyschogrod, Michael. "Incarnation." *Pro Ecclesia* 2.2 (1983) 208–15.

———. "A Jewish Perspective on the Incarnation." *Modern Theology* 12.2 (1996) 195–209.

Yuter, Alan J. "Menachem Kellner on Maimonides and the Mystics: The Search for a Usable Theological Past (Review Essay)." *Review of Rabbinic Judaism* 13.1 (2010) 126–33.

Yuval, Israel Jacob. "Christianity in Talmud and Midrash: Parallelomania or Parallelophobia?" In *Transforming Relations: Essays on Jews and Christians throughout History in Honor of Michael A Signer,* edited by Franklin T. Harkins and John H. Van Engen, 50–74. Notre Dame, IN: University of Notre Dame Press, 2010.

www.ingramcontent.com/pod-product-compliance
Lightning Source LLC
Chambersburg PA
CBHW062021220426
43662CB00010B/1427